Zero to Eighty
On Road
To Paradise

John Louis Westbrook

Zero to Eighty
On Road
To Paradise

John Louis Westbrook

PUBLISHED BY:
BRENTWOOD CHRISTIAN PRESS
4000 BEALLWOOD AVENUE
COLUMBUS, GEORGIA 31904

Table of Contents

3

Part I

Generalities

This section of the book deals with general items to acquaint the reader with the author, the dedication and personal information as to the beginning of this life and living conditions at that time.

About The Author

John Louis Westbrook was born October 23, 1926 in Wilcox County, Georgia to Homer Clyde and Cleo Alice Westbrook. The family lived there four years and moved to neighboring Crisp County. He was educated early in Cordele and Crisp County schools. The family moved back to Wilcox County when he finished high school.

In 1943 he entered Martha Berry College, Rome, Ga. at the age of sixteen and completed two years before entering military service at age eighteen, during World War II. Most of his military tenure was served in the Asiatic-Pacific Campaign and was stationed in Honolulu, Hawaii at Fort Shafter. Including the Reserves, he served five years in the U.S. Army.

After the war he finished two years at the University of Georgia, receiving an ABJ degree in Journalism. During this time he worked as a reporter and editor on The Red and Black, the campus newspaper.

He married Nancy White, of Atlanta, Ga., formerly of Chattooga County, in November, 1950 at Decatur, Ga. They later had two daughters, Elaine and Carol.

Working in the newspaper business for a couple of years as a news editor and state capitol reporter, he completed two additional years of college and received his LLB degree in law, at Woodrow Wilson College of Law.

He changed vocations to the insurance industry for seven years. From there he established his own business with his wife, as a manufacturers' representative. Opening a large lamp showroom in the Atlanta Merchandise Mart, the business was extended over the Southeastern part of the United States. The business was very successful and continued until retirement in 1986 at the age of 59.

For many years he served on the Advisory Board of Governors for the Gift Show at the Atlanta Merchandise Mart. He was elected president of the Georgia Home Furnishings Representatives Association and served in other capacities.

Dedication

This book is dedicated to my wonderful wife, Nancy White Westbrook, who has shown much patience and endurance with me as I have spent endless days and nights in my little cubby hole on the computer.

There are many things that go neglected when as a writer you dedicate yourself to one purpose, that of finishing the work you have started. She has understood this from the beginning and made it easier.

Our marriage has been a success in more ways than one. We have loved each other from the beginning and never wavered in our trust. That trust has lasted over fifty-four years and counting!

During the early years, as I was working a full-time job in the daytime and going to law school at night, she went to the library and read and wrote briefs on many cases for me. She should have been given the law degree instead of me.

Then, as we entered our self-employment as manufacturers' representatives for lamp factories, she worked the showroom at The Atlanta Merchandise Mart, along with raising our two daughters.

I am also grateful for the help that our daughters, Elaine and Carol, gave as they were growing into their teens. They spent so much time at our showroom working until one person threatened to turn me in for abusing the child labor laws!

On our Fiftieth Anniversary the daughters gave us a dinner party and a lot of nice things were said. Then there were other things told about my upbringing that I had tried to forget and didn't especially want to be revealed!

Regardless, writing this book has been an education for me and I thank everyone who, knowingly and unknowingly, contributed to the stories within these pages!

On the following page I have penned a poem about our married years. I won't vouch for following the rules for poetry, but I will for its sincerity!

We Married For Love and We Married For Life

By John Louis Westbrook

The word "Paradise" stands out in my mind.
I had paused briefly from the college grind.
It was in the summer of nineteen forty eight,
The day was Saturday and it was getting late.

We met that night in Paradise,
She had lots of curves and pretty eyes.
We married later---on Armistice Day,
Signed a peace treaty and began a new way.

Three years later our daughter Elaine was born.
I think it happened early in the morn.
Two years hence in the fall of fifty five,
Our daughter Carol decided to arrive.

The two little ones kept us on our toes,
They taxed our stamina, the Good Lord knows!
Soon it was time for them to go to school.
That was the beginning of the motor pool.

Piano lessons and girl scouts as well,
There was no end to the cookies to sell!
Then came books, college and boys,
But they graduated despite the noise!

Soon both married and the kids numbered six.
Four girls and two boys were a pretty good mix.
Now we have arrived at our fifty-year mark,
Our minds are racing, but our bodies are in "park!"

We may be senior citizens and live off of pills,
We've slowed some, but we've had our thrills!
The joys of the journey outweigh the strife,
We married for love, we married for life!

The days are shorter as our years fly by,
Our bodies are weaker, we admit with a sigh.
But we'll face them together as man and wife,
For you see---we married for love, and married for life!

Growing up Poor in the South and Knowing it!

"Idleness is the devil's workshop," the young man recalled his mother saying many times, as he arrived on the shores of a new land called America. If he had been busy at a job, and not standing on a London boat dock watching the ships come in, he would still be at home with his family, he mused.

As he had watched the ships come and go his mind had wandered, but all the while others were watching him with dollar signs (or pounds maybe) in their minds! At the right moment, they had seized him and thrown him in the hold of a nearby ship.

The attackers were slave traders and the man had been grouped with others to be shipped to the new country for money-making reasons.

His name was Westbrook, possibly one of my ancestors, and he had found himself in a predicament, not of his doing. The long sea journey had lasted for weeks and he had been required to work on the ship to help pay for his upkeep.

Now he faced other problems, since he had been indentured to a plantation owner for seven years to pay for his passage to America! He was having to pay for a trip he never wanted in the first place, but he had no choice. Being somewhere around the early 1700's, this seemed to be a common occurrence.

He decided there was no other way to pay for his voyage, and having no other recourse, set out to satisfy the debt with the only method available to him. He worked on the plantation for seven years, until he regained his freedom. He then married and began a family of his own.

Later, genealogy writers researched the arrival of three brothers named Westbrook from Scotland about the same time, who had possibilities of being my ancestors. They had settled in Virginia.

Most of my ancestors turned to farming for their living, since this required fewer skills and about the only thing available at this period in the history of America. Not many had the finances to go into business for themselves, so they worked for others.

Large plantation owners offered security, food, some salaries and hopes for a future, making farm work desirable for some, and a necessity for others. When the choices are few you go with what you have.

After my ancestors arrived in America in the early 1700's, they multiplied and scattered all over the new country. Most of my immediate family settled in north Georgia on farms, some with grants from the government. This seemed to be a common form of ownership of land in that era.

My great grandfather, who ended up in Cumming, Ga. came up with the idea that the farming land was better in northern Alabama, and got a bunch of his relatives together and moved to Fyffe, on Sand Mountain. This was several hundred miles and the only transportation was by covered wagons pulled by mules, or by human feet!

Some of the wagons were uncovered and as the miles grew longer, I'm sure parts of the journey was made on foot because of the monotony. The trip took over a week and the travelers were weary. The animals and equipment were showing wear and tear!

My dad was in the group and at this time was a small child. In Alabama others were added and his family grew to eight children. Later, my grandmother died and my grandfather married again. This wife gave him eight more kids, with one being adopted. He ended up with sixteen children, and despite this, lived into his nineties!

Some of them, including my dad, grew old enough to leave home and fend for themselves. He returned to Georgia and settled in Wilcox County. He and my mother married in 1917 and he had just bought a brand new Model T Ford. On their honeymoon my dad asked Mom if she would like to drive. She gleefully answered, "yes!"

He moved over and let her get under the steering wheel. She became excited with anticipation and poured the gas to the new vehicle! The car went straight to the ditch and considerable damage was done to the auto! That was the first time she had ever driven and turned out to be the last! She never drove a car again for the rest of her life!

The marriage weathered the storm, however, and the couple had five children. They took the kids and belongings and moved twenty-five miles away, near Cordele. I was five years of age at this time and my recollections of childhood began at this time.

The house we moved to was air-conditioned. It had holes in the floor, walls and roof. This permitted the air to flow freely in summer, winter and fall! That was the best we could do in 1931, since The Great Depression had set in as if to stay.

We couldn't have done worse if we had tried! This house was not even shelter from the elements, since it allowed them inside with us! It was built alongside a railroad but even the hobos wouldn't use it.

But we fixed it up a little and it was near livable! There were some nice neighbors around the area, but we were pretty much all in the same "boat." Times were just hard and everybody was poor. There were no jobs, and if so, there was no money to pay wages.

The name of the community was Penia and I guess it must have been a suburb of Seville, or if you wanted to stretch it a little, it might include Cordele, which was seven miles away. I'm not sure that either one would claim it!

Nevertheless, we resided there about eight months, long enough for me to enter the primer grade in school at the age of five. The school house was of the one-room variety, with a porch. Inside, each class would have a small corner and in the middle of the room was a big metal wood stove for heat.

We had two outhouses for comfort and necessity, one for girls and one for boys. There was the standard school bell outside fixed on a pole and some of the larger kids were allowed to ring it at the appropriate times.

Occasionally we would travel downtown to play baseball in a cow pasture. As I remember, the school and the cow pasture was the town! The adults and larger kids would make up the two

14

teams and playing the game was just about the total entertainment available.

It was not a good trip for me because the property owner had a retarded daughter who was about fourteen and she delighted in chasing me all over the place. Being much larger, she scared the daylights out of me! She hardly ever caught me, but when she did she loved to pull my hair!

One day my dad drove the old model T Ford and parked it on the grass. During the ball game I returned to the car to get something and noticed the girl standing next to the driver's seat. I could see smoke coming from under the dash! I made a run to get my dad and he discovered the girl had pulled several wires loose and was wrapping them together! We almost had a big fire, but he got it under control!

Our shotgun house was located at the intersection of a railroad and a state highway. The road had an overpass, allowing the trains to pass underneath. The railroad had a curve in it at this point and the trains would slow and sometimes stop.

Some of the local people who didn't have a ride to Cordele would wait on the overpass until a train came by and drop on one of the cars for a free ride into town! I'm glad we had an old car because I would never have tried that!

Soon we were able to move away from there, however, and I was happy to leave Penia!

Pre-depression years early in the century must have been just about as miserable as the ones that closely followed. My parents told me that we were as poor as "Job's turkey" and so were just about everybody else around us!

I didn't realize that he had a turkey, but if he did, it must have been a pitiful representative of the poultry family! The times were not kind to many people in 1926, the year that I was born.

Calvin Coolidge was president and when I was born in the fall of the year the family already consisted of two brothers and one sister. Later another sister was added. Keeping us all fed was a huge problem for my parents!

Three years later Herbert Hoover was elected president of the United States and the Great Depression set in for real! Economic conditions for the country were a real mess! Many banks closed for good, people lost their jobs, lost their income and savings, and some people lost their lives!

My father was a tenant farmer so many of these problems did not impact him directly, especially losing his savings, because he had none! We did grow vegetables and corn so we had something to eat. Sometimes we exchanged these for other things we needed for existence.

Farmers built a two-wheel cart with rigid wood guides for a mule to fit between and pull it. This served as a wagon to carry farm loads and was referred to as a "Hoover" cart. The near homeless built shacks to live in and when they were grouped together they were called "Hoovervilles."

Franklin Delano Roosevelt was elected president in 1933, when I was seven years old. In my estimation and many others, he was probably the greatest leader the country has ever had! Many new national programs, such as the (CCC) Civilian Conservation Corps and the (WPA) Works Progress Administration, were created.

The banking industry and the stock markets were stabilized and the country prospered during Roosevelt's sixteen years as president!

All of this is to give the reader an insight as to the multitude of problems facing anyone born and living in this era. But, as my dad would often say, "you better be thankful because it could have been worse!" Very true!

My parents were pretty special people. Not only did they grow up at an especially difficult time, but they managed to raise five children, who turned out to be good citizens and successful business people.

My dad only had a third grade education, but he learned the three "R's" pretty good! These were "reading, 'riting, and 'rithmetic!" Shortly after he married he owned and operated a fish market and later a service station and country store. However, farming was his main endeavor.

Mom was the steadying hand toward insisting that the kids get an education. She finished the seventh grade and recognized that was only a start towards learning. She had taken piano lessons as a child and was very accomplished at playing that and our old organ. In fact, she was the pianist for the small country church we attended.

Over the years my dad created a few axioms and old sayings that he related to his children. Some of these were probably passed down from his forbears. They are listed below:

1. The day is made for working. The night is made for sleeping!

2. While milking a cow, be sure to tie her tail to her left leg so she won't swat you up side the head when you least expect it!

3. Don't look a gift horse in the mouth, especially if he has big teeth and bites!

4. Always be wary of a person with a tattoo or mustache, or both, especially if it is a female!

5. Cooking a specialty dish like "possum" is easy. Cut up a dressed possum into bite-sized chunks and place "taters" all around it. Put it in the oven and cook until well done. Take it out of the oven, throw the possum away, and eat the "taters!"

6. Hang a horseshoe over the front door for "good luck."

7. Don't break a mirror or you will have bad luck for seven years!

8. If a rabbit or black cat crosses your path you will certainly have bad luck, unless you tear your slip or turn your hat around three times!

9. Pi R Square is a myth. Everybody knows when grandma cooks a pie, it is round!

10. A young lad went off to college for his freshman year. His money gave out and he sent a telegram to his dad. "No Mon. No Fun, Yo Son," it said. His dad replied, "So Sad, Too Bad, Yo Dad!"

11. The same son came home for a visit later and told his dad that he was studying a foreign language. His dad asked him if he could say "good morning" in algebra? He replied that he had not studied that yet!
12. If the sun sets behind a cloud, it will likely rain the next day!
13. If you hang a dead snake on a fence, it will rain within three days!

It's All About A Name

This saga began seventy eight years ago in Wilcox County, Georgia, where I was born but lived there only four years. It was night, I know, because the country doctor in attendance could not immediately determine my gender and I'm sure the problem must have been the dim kerosene lamps only used at night.

My mother asked, "what is it"?, as she bravely endured the lingering pain of just having given birth to a child. My dad said, "I'm not sure, let me ask the doctor."

The doctor replied, "I think that it is a boy. Yes, I'm positive that you have a new son." My dad said, "that solves a big problem of choosing his name....we will name him Son." I had no way of knowing that my parents had disagreed so much on choosing names for the three siblings that preceded me, that it was going to be such a chore.

Thus I became "Son" and later thought this wasn't so bad, considering the names that were given to my two brothers and sister. For instance, the first brother was given the middle name of "Adese". When he entered the military service during World War 11 often the sergeant at the end of a march would yell, "at ease", and my brother would holler, "present", thinking the roll was being called.

Then the other brother's middle name was Howard. My dad always called him "Hired". My sister hit the jackpot since she was given four names, which probably was the reason there were none left for me. I was grateful that they did not call me "sister".

So I became Son, even though my birth certificate listed me as "baby boy", and this was sufficient around the small farm where we lived. This worked very well especially when I was called at meal time.

All went well until I became five years old and entered the first grade of school where we encountered a problem. Having just moved to a neighboring county and being registered at a large new school, the teacher was trying to identify all of the kids.

She asked me, "little boy what is your name?" I said, Son." Then the teacher told me that she was sure that was a nickname and that I had another name. I was told to go home and ask my parents about this.

When I finished the three mile walk back home from school, I approached my mother and asked her what my name was. She said, "Son." I told her what had happened at school that day and that the teacher knew I had other names. My mama said that was the only name I had.

Since I did not seem to have a real name, I told my mother that the teacher said I had to have one and I would name myself. So, I had two uncles that I liked and one was named John and the other Louis. I decided on John Louis and I told my mama my decision and she said that was all right with her.

When I went to school the next day the teacher began calling the roll. She came to me and asked if I had found out my name. I proudly told her, "yes maam, my name is John Louis." She said knowingly, "I knew you had other names."

The years went by and I thought that I finally had outlived the moniker that had been hung on me at birth, until an old friend called. I hadn't heard from him in several years. He said to my wife, who had answered the phone, "I want to speak to "Son."

I lifted up the extension and after exchanging pleasantries he told me, "Son our Sunday School members wanted to invite you to our dinner meeting this weekend." I asked where and when it would be?

I was told the time and he said it would be at Sonny's Barbecue." That brought back memories I had tried so hard to get away from and I fumbled around and found a reasonable excuse to turn him down on the invitation.

Getting over that, a few years later I received a flyer in the mail from a political candidate who I wouldn't vote for "dog-catcher", and it was addressed to "J. Louise." This was a terrible insult, now they were changing my gender!

A few days later I found out where the candidate got the name. The county voter lists had been worked over and someone had made the error. When I entered the polling place, where I knew most of the workers, one lady called out in a loud voice, "here comes Louise!" Insult upon insult!

So I asked the lady to give me two ballots, one for Louis and one for Louise. She refused and I had to vote as "Louise" until the list could be corrected.

Despite all the problems with names, nicknames and other things I have been called throughout my years, I have survived and done well. My daddy always told me to never forget who I was. Trouble with that was trying to figure out which one I needed to remember!

My dad got a job on a nearby farm, doing any of the chores that were necessary and my two older brothers worked there also. Dad was paid one dollar for a day's work and my brothers fifty cents each. That was two dollars a day for three people! They weren't exactly getting rich, but they were surviving while they were looking for a farm to sharecrop.

I will never forget one incident that happened while living there. My parents were sleeping in their bed one night, when they heard a rustling sound in the old metal springs, holding up the mattress.

They investigated the problem, and to their surprise, found a rat snake had invaded the springs! Mama and the kids headed for a safe place while dad disposed of the reptile. He was three feet long and wrapped around the coils. Nobody got much sleep that night!

Finally we moved about ten miles away to a nice one hundred acre farm. The house was a considerable upgrade from the previous one and the owner of the farm depended on a tenant who would work the land as a sharecropper.

We loved the place, and the entire family worked the crops and did well for the owner and ourselves. The work was hard and time-consuming, since we kept busy from sunup to sundown planting and picking cotton, tending to corn rows, and generally trying to keep up with the weeds.

Mom insisted that the children go to school, and we were more than happy to do so! We got out of farm work during school hours, but before and after, when there was daylight we worked. We loved going to school!

I think this is when all of the siblings developed higher ambitions, because we knew there were other ways to make a living, and easier. All five of us went on to college and higher learning. Two completed two or more college degrees. All have been successful in life, and most had their own businesses.

Living on a farm is conducive to developing a great sense.of humor! That's a good thing to have for anybody, but you especially need one as a sharecropper to keep your mind off the impending problems! With a touch of humor the days are sometimes made shorter.

As an illustration, one day two of my mischievous cousins came to see us and they proposed to teach us a new game. Name of the game was "grab." Some other kids were visiting that day and we were all eager to learn the new game!

Gathering in a corner of the broom-swept yard, we were told to contribute an item, such as marbles, knife, etc., and throw them into a pile. Each gave something for the "grab." The object was to cover all of the items that had been gathered up in a neat pile with a large straw hat, and when the hat was lifted, and "grab" hollered, each player would grab at the items and whatever you came up with would be yours to keep!

With the completion of explaining the mechanics of this exciting game, everything was piled up and covered with a large ragged straw hat. The eager participants were told to turn away from the hat and close their eyes for a minute. Upon the word "ready", all the kids gathered around the hat again and waited for the order to "grab"!

The magic word was given and the big hat was lifted and everyone reached for the pile of possessions at the same time! Each intending to grab a much-wanted item!

All hands made it to the pile at the same time, but there was a surprise under the hat! The mean cousins had taken the personal objects out of the pile and substituted a fresh pile of cow dung!

Since all had dug in with enthusiasm, the result was messy! We chased the culprits around the barnyard but they ran faster! I'm not sure if we ever got even with them!

I didn't learn a lesson that day, because later as grownups, a brother and myself entered into an agreement with these same cousins to purchase seventy-five acres of mountain land.

After buying the land, the cousins decided we needed a trailer on the property and a tractor to cut grass. Pretty soon we needed to construct a thirteen-acre lake. After many other improvements and equally sharing the price, the cousins decided we didn't need the trailer and tractor and sold them to friends for practically nothing.

We couldn't agree on anything after that, except on the sale of the property. We lost money on the entire deal, but we were finally out of the partnership. That was the last time I had any dealings with the two cousins.

I felt a little sorry for them, however, because they had multiple problems throughout their lives, despite being financially successful.

Another time one of my uncles arrived from my dad's old home in Alabama, bringing his wife and three children. They needed a place to stay until they could find a permanent home and some type of work. So they moved in with us! This brought the total living in this old two-bedroom house to twelve, and they brought all of their worldly belongings with them!

Being a somewhat mischievous child myself, I learned that my aunt was deathly afraid of chickens, and this gave me an idea.

We had many white leghorn chickens running about the yard surrounding the house, and my aunt was trying to avoid all of them.

Somehow, this amused me and I wondered if I could give her a friendly scare without getting myself into trouble. The more I thought about it the more I was tempted! Soon, I couldn't stand it anymore! It was getting dark and the aunt was sitting on the porch by herself.

I couldn't catch one of the chickens, so I decided on the next best thing. I got a good-sized piece of white cloth and formed it in the shape of a chicken and it was dark enough that it would pass for a chicken. I ran up on the porch, cradling what looked like a mean specimen of poultry to my aunt, and yelling at the same time, "watch out!"

She almost lost her false teeth scrambling off the porch and running around the outside of our house! Just when I was having a lot of fun chasing her, my dad came to the door and saw what was happening! Not many seconds passed until I was real sorry that I had made a bad decision. He always kept a peach tree limb handy for such occasions! I also found out that a cotton stalk would make a good substitute, if the same need for correction arose in the fields!

It wasn't but a month or so that the relatives found a place to move to and I'll bet they were happy to do so! Their farm was kind of neat since it had a large sand pit on it and it was a perfect place to play. The farm owner sold sand to various builders around the area and there were always Ford trucks moving it.

When I was about six years old my dad decided to make a trip back to his old home in Alabama. All of the kids hopped into the old Model T and we began our journey from south Georgia. There were no expressways and not many paved roads, so it was quite a trip of about 325 miles.

As we drove through the city of Atlanta all of the kids stretched our necks trying to see all of these amazing sights! We saw buildings three or four stories high, cars of all descriptions, many people on paved sidewalks and what I thought were train tracks running down the center of the streets!

Suddenly I looked behind our car and saw what I thought was a train bearing down on us and I yelled for my daddy to get out of the way! I was only six but I knew that trains would run over you! He assured me that it was a streetcar and we were safe.

On the other side of the big city all of us were suffering from stiff and sore necks, since we had been exercising them considerably, trying to take in all of these unbelievable sights. I had never seen so many people in one place at the same time!

There were a lot of cars and most of them much nicer than our Model T. The streets were paved and electric lights everywhere! Occasionally you would see a wagon or buggy pulled by horses or mules.

We traveled north to the old Peggy Ann Bus Stop, where the road to Rome branched off from U. S. 41. Above Rome we traveled through the "narrows," and since I had never seen a mountain before, this was exciting! The "narrows" is a gap between mountains. Little did I know that my future wife was a toddler at this time and lived just a few miles away at Taylor's Ridge!

As we came to Alabama we had to go over Lookout Mountain, and our eyes did open wide. This looked like the highest in the world! On the other side we came to Ft. Payne, and soon found that we had to climb Sand Mountain in the old car.

Halfway up the mountain the car began to suffer from the long trip and the motor heated so that we had to stop and rest awhile. Quite a bit of water had boiled out of the radiator, so we scoured the area for a stream to refill it. Luckily we found one.

The auto was ready to go again after a cooling drink and we resumed our journey. The dirt road was too steep for the Model T and it just sat in the middle of the road and shivered, going nowhere! My dad was not about to give up this close to our destination, so he turned the car around and began to drive backwards up the mountain!

It worked and the car climbed the remaining mile to the top of Sand Mountain going backwards! It had been a long and grueling day, since we had started before sunup, and there was about twenty more miles to go.

Finally we made it and all of the relatives were happy to see us! They seemed to be people like us and very friendly. Soon I was having the time of my life, with so many new playmates.

Several adults played guitars and fiddles as they sang and the kids danced. One of my sisters and I began to do what we called dancing and the adults began to throw pennies at our feet. The more pennies they threw, the faster we danced. Soon the pennies gave out and so did we!

My grandfather passed around a jug of his peach brandy that he had made prior to our arrival, but I wasn't allowed to partake. I had to settle for a cool drink of water from his deep well. I was fascinated with his well, since it was on the back porch.

Soon the visit was over but the return trip to our home was not as exciting.

The little Baptist church where my family attended had services once a month, with a traveling preacher bringing the message. Each Sunday he would preach at a different church, and normally, most would hold down a full time job during the week. During revival, services would be held an entire week. Sunday school would convene every other week.

Located in the same little pine grove was also a Primitive Baptist church. We referred to it as a "Hard Shell" Baptist, for some reason that I never knew. Occasionally, we would go there when no services were being held at our regular church.

One Sunday we attended when they were having "foot-washing" and we had never seen this before. At least I never had. So the preacher and deacons began to prepare a pan with water and included a towel to dry the feet after washing.

After the preacher washed each deacon's feet, it came time for the head deacon to wash the minister's feet. He began to remove his socks and the deacons looked on in horror! His feet were black as the ace of spades!

This was a great embarrassment to the preacher and he immediately suspected the reason why his feet were so black. He had two preteen rowdy sons and he got the idea that they were playing an unfunny joke on him.

When the preacher returned home he confronted the kids with the situation and demanded an explanation. They admitted taking his Sunday socks, turning them inside out, and scrubbing them around the inside of a stove pipe until filled with soot! They probably never did this again because the minister undoubtedly taught them a lasting lesson!

Our family loved "all day singing and dinner on the grounds," and one Sunday we visited a neighboring church as they were having one. The adults were singing and creating a lot of noise, so the kids becoming bored went into an adjacent room to play.

As kids might do, they began to throw balls and other objects around the room. I decided it was getting too rough and I headed toward the door. Before I reached it someone threw a wooden croquet ball in my direction and it caught me in the forehead. I dropped to my knees and blood began to pour from the spot where I was hit!

Some adults cleaned me up and put a bandage on it and I walked three miles home, hurting all the way. That incident probably was the cause of my "addled brain" syndrome prevalent since!

Churches were at the center of most activities in the county and we attended all that we could. Our church held baptismal services at a large pond, called River-lake. It was a good-sized body of water, where we often went swimming and it was deep in spots.

This particular Sunday, there were about ten new members to be baptized and among them was one large lady who probably would push the scales in the vicinity of three hundred pounds!

The preacher who was doing the dunking was a small man but he bravely handled his duties until it was time for the large lady to go under. He asked for help from one of the deacons at this time, because he was getting weak-kneed. As the two stepped back to immerse the lady, they fell into a hole and released the woman at the same time!

She went floating away and it took several men to retrieve her! By this time she had immersed herself a number of times and the preacher considered her duly baptized!

Later, when I was twelve or thirteen I was baptized in the same lake, but I was prepared in case the preacher dropped me, because I had learned to swim when I was six. My cousins threw me in a pond and I "dog-paddled" until my brother helped me out of the water.

That same brother wasn't always this good to me. Sometimes I pestered him enough that he wanted to get even with me. This happened one night when he was invited to a dance at a neighbor's house and I wanted to tag along. My dad insisted that he take me.

Country dances at this time during the 30's were pretty harmless and more like a big party, with no drinking, fights, etc. People would play guitars, fiddles and jazz bows. Everyone would square dance and some would "round" dance.

With my brother objecting to my tagging along, he started the Model T and we began our trip about a mile away. Halfway there the dirt road passed through a swampy area and my brother stopped the car. I asked why he was stopping?

He didn't tell me but I found out right away! He grabbed and pulled me out of the car, and being six years older didn't have a hard time dragging me down the road away from the car.

Turning me loose, he ran as fast as he could to the car, jumped in and sped off! Arriving at the neighbor's house a few minutes later, he parked and walked to the front door, intending to have a fun night.

The first person he saw was me, grinning like a possum and standing in the doorway! He couldn't believe it because he knew he had left me standing in the dark half a mile down the road!

I was ten years old and he had not yet learned that I could run like the wind, having chased rabbits and other animals around the farm. When he started to run, so did I, and as he drove away I jumped onto the "Y" on the back of the car and hung on tightly! This would normally hold a spare tire but we didn't have one.

When he found out that I had outsmarted him he was rather amused and was fairly civil the remainder of the evening. He even let me ride back home after the dance.

27

That old Model T caused us a lot of misery though, along with serving as the only transportation we had, except the wagon pulled by two mules. One day my dad was driving the old car up the road to our house and on either side of the road were the fields of cotton and corn. There was no ditch. Suddenly, the car seemed to have a mind of its own and veered off into the cotton patch finally stopping in the field after destroying a lot of cotton plants! We found out later that the steering mechanism dropped off and there was no way to steer it!

The old Ford was also pretty dangerous to crank since it would backfire often and cause the crank handle to fly backwards. Many arms were broken this way, because it was impossible to jump back out of harms way quick enough. My brother broke his right arm this way! It was often necessary to put a jack under one back wheel in order to crank it. This would prevent some of the backfire and keep the car from running you over when it did crank.

After a few years the family moved a short distance to the farm where we attended the dance mentioned before. It was a better house and was located on the main dirt road, closer to the schools and the small town two miles away.

The county became the first one in the country to build and own its electric power dam. They began to run electric wires all over the county and they had a program to provide a free yard light if you had your house wired and ascribed to their services.

Up until this time the only light we ever had was kerosene lamps and it became difficult to see your school homework by the dim light they gave. In fact you couldn't see much of anything at night.

But when the man came and ran a line into our house and in each of the four rooms he hung a single wire with a bulb, we were really excited! I remember the first night we had lights, it was like some kind of miracle! We walked round and round the little farm house looking at the way it was lit up! The kids wanted to leave the bulbs burning all night, we were so fascinated, but we were reminded that we had a monthly bill to pay.

Money was hard to come by during this period of the depression and most people who lived in the rural areas were poor, but most didn't know it. We raised vegetables to eat and animals for meat and didn't need much else.

When Christmas came the kids could depend on a couple of items in their shoebox under the bed without having to guess what it was. That morning each had an apple and orange and sometimes a candy cane. That didn't reduce the excitement, however, as we checked the shoebox several times the night before as we awakened before morning!

Going back to school after the holidays was somewhat depressing because some of the kids from well-to-do families would be showing or telling about what they received as gifts. When we were asked what Santa Claus brought us we tried to avoid the subject, since we never got anything hardly! But we understood, because there was never much money available. That probably helped build our resolve to get a good education and try to do better.

Occasionally we picked blackberries in the spring and sold them to a winery in the nearby town. The kids picked up a little change this way. In the fall of the year I would boil peanuts and walk three miles to town to sell for ten cents a bag. Of course they were cold by the time I got there but they always sold well!

When my dad carried a wagon load of cotton to the local gin it would usually take all day, and to keep us working while he was gone, would pay us a quarter for each hundred pounds of cotton that was picked. It would take steady picking to yield one hundred pounds.

But a quarter would get you in the local theater to see a good "horse opera," or western movie with horses and cattle rustlers. My favorite characters were Ken Maynard and Gene Autry!

One day I went to see a movie and two local buddies accompanied me. They got in free since the ticket taker was their uncle, but he made me pay! The younger of the two was about seven years old and he had gotten a chew of tobacco somewhere. I wasn't aware he even knew how to chew it!

We filed into the movie house and watched a thriller! As we exited the building I looked at the boy and was astounded at the condition of his white shirt! The shirt was black and brown with tobacco juice! He said there was not a place to spit his juice so inside his shirt seemed to serve his need! That was the last time I ever went to a movie with him!

Recently several hurricanes hit the state of Florida and there was much destruction of homes and buildings and some loss of lives! It was devastating to the residents and their relatives who were also affected even though they were not present at the time.

One resident, whose home was damaged but was still livable, stated "you never know the luxury of power until you don't have it at all," referring to electricity.

Well, I guess we didn't know much about this kind of luxury growing up in the south, because electrical power was not available to anyone hardly! I was probably thirteen or fourteen years of age when we got electricity for the first time. Then it was only used for light because we had nothing to plug in.

There were no refrigerators, washing machines, toasters, television, computers or the like. But we marveled at the light that was available from the single bulbs with a flip of a switch!

Water for drinking or other uses was taken from a shallow well near the house. It was drawn to the surface by a rope or chain and some people had a windlass to roll the rope on.

We had no indoor plumbing, thus creating the need for outdoor privies, some even were of the two to three-hole varieties. I guess the families with the most children needed the larger ones!

After a hard day's work in the fields we were in need of a bath and it was quite a chore to draw water from the well and pour it into a tub and then bathe in cold water! So I came up with the idea of building a platform for a five-gallon lard bucket and filling the can with water in the morning and let it warm during the day as the sunshine hit it. A makeshift shower head was placed at the bottom, consisting of a snuff can with holes punched in it, and a valve to turn it on.

A shower curtain was made from burlap bags and we had created probably the world's first solar-heated outdoor shower facility! It was a shame we never got a patent or I'm sure we would have been rich and famous by this time!

All cooking was done on a wood stove in the kitchen and keeping it filled with wood was a never-ending task Washing of clothes was done outside in a large pot, heated by wood burning. After the clothes had boiled sufficiently, they were taken to a tub of water to be rubbed back and forth until clean and the soap washed away. Then the clothes were beaten with a battle to remove water and further clean them, hung on a clothesline or fence for the sun to dry them.

The clothes and sheets would smell real good and clean after having dried in the hot sunshine all day. There was very little pollution in the air at this time. That all came later with the industrial revolution.

Life was not complicated at all. We didn't know what we were missing, since so many of the luxuries available now had not even been invented then. Telephones were almost non- existent and very few people had radios. If so, it was usually one operated by a battery and not very dependable.

I remember going to a relative's house one night in order to listen to a boxing match between Max Schmelling and Joe Louis, I think. The static was so loud you couldn't understand which was winning, but it was exciting anyway!

Hog killing time was a joyful occasion at our house because it brought with it plenty of fresh ham, sausage, liver, bacon, and just plain good eating! It was always cold and considerable work to prepare the meat after the hog was killed. The animal was immersed in a barrel of boiling water to loosen the hair on its body in order to remove this from the skin. Then hung from a pole to remove all unwanted parts before cutting it for consumption later. The hams and shoulders were salted and cured in a smokehouse.

My dad made syrup for many people in the county, since we had a cane grinder and the various boilers and pans to cook the juice. A mule would go round and round the cane mill and someone would feed the cane into the grinder to squeeze the juice out. This was caught in a large barrel and carried to the cookers. Wood fired the boilers and it would take most of a day to complete one vat full. Dad was paid in syrup for his work so we always had plenty of that in the house. In fact, many times our school lunches would contain biscuits with holes punched in them and syrup poured into the holes!

During the summer we canned many vegetables and fruits to store up for winter. The county had a place where residents could take their produce and can them in a place that was built to facilitate the process.

We had fun doing all of these things as a family and it was time-consuming and hard work at times. But as I look back, it was all worth it, because it kept us busy and out of mischief and enabled us to understand why it was necessary to work. This was a good way to build character!

Mama was not only the educational advisor for the family, she also worked in the fields, cooked the meals, handled the housework, did the washing, milked the cows and worked at a myriad of other chores! Sometimes she got a little help from my two sisters, when they were not in the fields.

It was an unending job she held but she managed well! Most times anyway!

I'm reminded of one event, however, that she encountered a small problem! She had invited our local preacher to eat Sunday dinner with the family, as was often the norm. Mom had spent hours getting the meal ready and the preacher finally arrived.

Generally, the adults ate first and the kids waited their turn, unlike what occurs today, when the children have to be fed first!

So it was that day, with the adults eating the fried chicken, fresh vegetables, and finally the dessert. Everything seemed to proceed smoothly and the preacher was impressed with how good the food was.

He was served a large piece of cake and bit down in it with gusto! Mom was watching and noticed that the minister had a quizzical look on his face. She inquired about the taste of the cake and proceeded to try it herself.

She immediately found her answer. In making the cake, she had used corn meal instead of flour! The cake was nothing more than chocolate-covered cornbread! Needless to say, her embarrassment was great! This didn't deter the preacher from returning to eat many times again, however!

We had several relatives living in the same area and when we were not farming we visited. One uncle had a flock of chickens with two or three roosters. One rooster didn't like anybody and it seemed that he took as his job to be protective of his territory. He would attack anyone in the yard, pecking and spurring visitors! He was fast and I always had trouble out- running him.

Another relative was driving to town one day and as he was coming into the business section he was confronted by a mule in the road! The old Model T had a loud horn and the relative tried to scare the mule off the road!

The animal was scared all right! In fact it was so scared, that it leaped across the hood of his car and lodged there! Several minutes the mule flailed away at the auto and finally slid off to the ground. The mule survived without much harm, but the car was badly damaged!

We lived on a two horse farm (actually two mule farm) and raised such crops as corn, cotton, peanuts and watermelons. I don't really know why they called them horse farms, because mules were more dependable as a work animal, and everybody had mules.

I began following a plow, pulled by a mule, early in life at the age of six. That was as soon as I could see over the handles, and worked alongside my dad and two brothers in the fields.

Many people today don't understand how to talk to a mule and to get him to do the things you want him to. But I learned early that if you want a mule to go to the right, you tell him "gee," and if you want him to go left, you holler "haw."

If you want the mule to stop, you yell "whoa." If he is to start, you say "get up," and make a clicking sound between your teeth.

33

Anything beyond that, you're talking to yourself! I never saw one that understood any other words.

I believe they understand a lot of unsaid things, though, since they will automatically stop if the plow strikes a stump. Also, most of them understand that you want a ride back to the house, if you climb on their back.

One day my older brother, Grady, hitched the mules to the wagon to haul something. As he hopped aboard the wagon the mules became frightened! They took off down the country dirt road as fast as they could, running away, as we called it!

My brother was holding on as best he could, but the mules were pulling the wagon from one side of the road to the other! "Whoa" never worked until he was about a mile down the road and the animals had given out of steam! He never could control them since the reins had fallen under the wagon, out of his reach.

He said that was one wild ride, since he was in danger of being thrown out, or the wagon being overturned! My dad finally chased them down in the Model T.

There was a constant fight with the boll weevil on the farm. They had not yet developed a remedy for the insect, and they would destroy the cotton bolls. The farmer was very dependent on the weather during the year. Too much rain would destroy the crops and a drought would keep them from thriving.

To further confuse the situation, during World War II the government began to tell the farmers the amount of acreage they could devote to each crop. This was done through "allotments."

If you planted cotton in your field that exceeded your acreage allotment, you were required to plow the surplus under and destroy it. This never made sense to me.

But along with this came "rationing." Every family was given ration tickets for the amount of food they could buy. We were allowed to buy only a certain amount of flour, meal, sugar, coffee, etc. But living on a farm had some advantages since we could take corn to a mill and have it ground into meal. So we always had cornbread. At least this was filling!

Many people got into trouble with the government in the "black market" by finding a way around regulations. They would illegally acquire ration tickets and sell them to anyone who would buy and pay a profit. This was considered a serious offense and many people were sent to jail, if caught. Sugar rations were more coveted than others. We raised sugar cane and often substituted syrup for much-needed sugar.

I didn't realize it but when lunch time came during my grammar school and I pulled out my fried cornbread and fatback, that many times I was the envy of a lot of the city kids. In fact some wanted to exchange lunches with me! I was glad to accommodate them, but I felt like I was cheating a little. The "town bought" store bread they had for sandwiches appealed more to me.

The county had surplus food that would be given out in the cities at certain times. This would include, grits, rice, meal, flour and other staples. But my parents were too proud to participate in this. Welfare was a "no no" in our family. I think they would rather have gone hungry than to accept charity.

We had a tough time getting things that we would have liked to have had, but food was not one of them. There was always corn in the field and potatoes in the garden. We had tomatoes, squash, onions, cabbage and many gallons of syrup. Since we had a cane mill and syrup pan, we were never out of syrup.

In the Spring we always had blackberries and blueberries growing wild in the area. In the summer we had citrons that grew alongside the roads, looking like green watermelons. They made good pickles. Maypops and dewberries would grow wild and were edible. Some people would eat wild persimmons but I didn't, since they tended to "turn my mouth inside out." That is another way to express how sour and tart they are to me!

All of this must have been good for me, however, since I have been inclined to be slim most of my life. In my latter years I have reversed that trend and I have put on weight in places I didn't realize existed. It must be the "eat all you can" diet that I'm on nowadays!

The other day a group of us seniors gathered at a restaurant to eat and I was standing outside waiting for the others. One of the ladies saw me standing there and commented, "you look like you have already eaten!" I knew she was joking, but I begin to try to pull my stomach in to hide some extra weight that I was carrying!

You hear the expression from some older people nowadays, "those were the good old days!" This evidently referred to the living conditions following World War II, since it was a simple life in a way.

It's true that about the only crime you would hear of would be someone stealing a chicken or two, or a watermelon out of a neighbor's patch! Nobody hardly ever ran off with someone else's wife, and most of the deaths were natural.

If an underage girl got pregnant and was not married, she was sent off to another city or state to visit a relative, until the child was born. Most were given up for adoption and it was unheard of to abort a pregnancy.

When a neighbor's house burned, the people around gathered and rebuilt whatever was burned. If a family came upon hard times and didn't have anything to eat, people chipped in and helped them.

When my family was struggling to make ends meet and some of my siblings were small, I remember a neighbor offering milk from his two milk cows. Every other day one of the kids would go to the neighbor's house and he would fill a gallon bucket with fresh milk! He did this without being asked, and was happy to do so!

Neighbors would come to visit and bring a sack of black-eyed peas, piece of fat back, or a pone of freshly-cooked cornbread. We would return the favor as we visited.

When there was canning to be done, neighborhood females would gather to help, and the same when quilting was necessary.

There were a lot of things good about the "good old days," but all was not a bed of roses. One elderly man related to me that his family was so poor that they could only buy a small piece of meat for a meal. In order to make it last, he would tie a string around the meat and everybody would take turns swallowing it! That way they could pass it around and each get a little nutrition!

I kind of believe that he was telling a tall tale! How about You?

My mother would cook fried cornbread in small cakes and when I got to grammar school with my lunch, the school janitor would ask to swap his sandwich for my lunch. We were both happy, because it was a rare occasion that I ever got "loaf" bread from a store. I would have swapped if the bread had nothing in it! He was evidently tired of his "town bought" bread. Sometimes, I had biscuits with a hole punched in them, filled with cane syrup! He loved that!

A recent television series was named "The Simple Life." This had a complete different meaning and theme than life as it was in the "olden days," as our two daughters called that era.

Living in the 30's everything you had was simple! Your house, the furniture inside, your car (if you were lucky enough to have one), your schedule of activities, all were pretty much uncomplicated. That is except "making ends meet" and this was constantly a problem!

In the spring of the year our time was filled with clearing the fields and planting the crops. The summer was busy with tending the crops and keeping the weeds out. The fall was harvest time and winter was time for wood cutting and tending to the farm chores.

In between these times, food that we could not raise on the farm, had to be purchased. Often we had little money to do this so we carried eggs, chickens or garden produce and swapped them for other things we needed.

When the weather prevented us from working the crops, the family had a few hours of leisure. My dad built several toys for the family to use and one of these was a "flying jenny." It consisted of a long board, which was fastened to a stump with a large iron bolt. It was situated evenly on the stump so that one person could push the board and it would spin very fast around and around! Handles were nailed to the board to give the rider on each end something to hold to.

We had a "seesaw" and it looked like the "flying jenny" except that it was stationary on a block and would only go up and down, Both items required one person on each end of the board to make them work and it would help if the persons were about equal in weight.

Each one of the kids had what we called our car! We took a gallon syrup bucket filled it with rocks and ran a piece of baling wire through it. As we ran pulling the bucket with rocks in it, it made a rattling noise and this was as close as we could come to the real thing!

We had "flips" and slingshots made with rubber slings, gotten from old auto inner tubes. The wooden handle was made from a "Y" branch from a tree. The homemade toy would propel a rock and could do some damage if aimed at a person!

I always wanted a bicycle but could never afford one! We found an old bicycle frame in a dump, where someone had discarded it. We carried it home and put some metal wheels on the frame and made our own. We had no way to move it except someone had to push while another rode it. There were no brakes on it and we all had many scrapes and scratches resulting from collisions."

They say "necessity is the mother of invention" and if we had anything to amuse ourselves with most of the time we had to invent it. My dad invented a cotton machine that would separate the seeds from the cotton. The cotton was then used to make mattresses for beds. He made quite a few mattresses for neighbors and his machine would have been a real money-maker had he gotten it patented! But he never tried to do this and only used it locally for friends and family.

When I was fifteen years of age and a senior in high school, my dad became sick and could not work on the farm most of the year. My two older brothers were in military service during World War II at this time and the farm work was left to myself and two sisters.

I missed half of the year in school having to plow and plant the crops. Somehow I passed my grades and graduated, though. In fact we made enough money that year to buy the old family farm in the adjoining county we moved from!

We began to move from sharecropping to tending our own farm and the family had reached a new milestone! The old beat-up truck we had at this time was loaded with our belongings and the moving chores began.

38

It fell my lot to drive the two mules and a wagon loaded with corn to the farm twenty five miles away. My dad must have had a lot of confidence in my accomplishing the task because he didn't give me very many instructions as to how to get there.

The first two miles was a dirt road and from there the road was asphalt. No trouble was encountered on the dirt road but when the road turned to pavement my problems began! The iron rims on the wooden wheels began to loosen and were in danger of running off completely!

I had brought some haywire along and it really came in handy. I wrapped the wheels with wire and the mules and I were on our way again! This lasted for a couple more miles and the process began again. This repeated itself several times until I had covered about twenty miles and it was getting dark. I had given out of wire and I could no longer repair the wheels!

The trip had taken all day and I was sitting on the side of the road with no way to get further! I was a little angry with my dad for getting me in this mess and entrusting such a formidable job to a fifteen-year-old!

About this time I heard an old truck drive up! I was never so happy to see my dad in my life! He checked the problem, brought out more wire and we finished the trip an hour or so later! The moving was complete and we began a new phase of our lives!

The first fifteen years of existing on this planet and spending them in the south shaped and molded what I was to become in the years that followed. My parents were poor and simple people, but had strong principles of integrity and knowledge that most people succeed in life by setting goals and working toward these.

Thus, we were taught to work hard and save for the future. Study and learn because knowledge was the road to freedom. Freedom was being set free from the bonds of containment. The world would hold no boundaries to our ambitions!

Then, we were taught also to live our lives in accordance with the commandments from The Almighty. To make sure that we were always on His side and never asking that He change to our side! Because He is the same and if we are separated, it is our fault!

Before finishing high school I knew what I wanted to do with the next phase of my life. I wanted desperately to continue my schooling at Martha Berry College in Rome, Ga., where an older brother had gotten his degree earlier. He had been called to military duty during World War Two at this time.

This was a college where you could work for the tuition and offered a perfect opportunity for me, not having other means to pay. Also, it is a school that is somewhat faith-based which appealed to me.

Upon finishing high school at the age of sixteen, I left home on a Greyhound bus, having five dollars in my pocket and a battered old suitcase containing a couple of blue work shirts and two pairs of overalls. This was the uniform for the students. Girls wore gingham dresses.

I found later that most of the young men who might have been going to college were off to the war, since it had begun two years previously. So there were only about two hundred boys at the school and the girls numbered twice as many.

Under ordinary circumstances this would have been an ideal situation but I found that the rules and regulations prevented very little contact between boys and girls at this school. For instance, the only so-called dating would be a couple of hours spent sitting around the Ford Triangle on Sunday afternoon. If a boy and girl happened to sit too close or held hands, the monitors would immediately put a stop to this shameful action!

A few years ago I returned to the campus for a reunion and was delighted that many of these old customs had gone away with the progression of the times! I supposed they served well at that time, however. The overalls and gingham dresses had disappeared and the boys and girls were mixing and mingling at will! Some even had cars, something never allowed in 1943, even if we could have afforded one.

Music has always played a large role in our family. My mother was a church pianist during the time that my dad was a deacon and Sunday School Superintendent. All of the kids would sing in church, school or wherever the occasion arose.

We were delighted as kids when the family acquired an old pump organ, the kind that had to be pumped with your feet as it was played. As mom would play hymns the entire family would gather around and sing! A wagon load of corn was exchanged for the instrument. That was the method used to buy many things in that day.

However, dad could not "carry a tune in a paper bag," but that didn't stop him from trying. There was an old song that he sang, which seemed to be tuneless, which he composed or it was passed down to him. The name was "Tumma Whim Dum!"

The song went something like this:

"Tumma whima dum, paddle on a Ree

He's about as big a sheep as you'd ever see."

"The first tooth in that old ram's head was a Frenchman's horn."

"The next one to it held forty barrels of corn."

(to be sung to any tune that would fit and as long as you could stand it)

He accompanied the song with a shuffling dance, similar to "buck-dancing" done in a circular fashion! This was a sight to see!

Other members of the family were constantly composing songs just to pass the time away and for amusement purposes. For instance one of the kids wrote a little ditty on Valentine's Day. It was appropriately named "Georgia Valentine." It went like this:

I went to see my "country" gal,
She met me at the door.
Shoes and socks in her hand,
And feet all over the floor!

I asked that gal to marry me,
She said she'd tell me later.
She punched my nose all over my face,
'Til it looked like an Irish potato!

I went to see my other girl,
I thought she was "hot stuff."
Until I kissed her on the lips,
And tasted Bruton snuff!

A valentine I had that day,
To give some lucky lass.
I tried to give it to them both,
But they decided to "pass"!

It was some kind of "whing ding" when the family gathered around the old organ and sang songs that were made up or other favorites such as "You Are My Sunshine", "Red River Valley", "Coming Around The Mountain" or church hymns!

My brother got a guitar from Sears Roebuck and he would accompany the singers. One of the kids would place a thin piece of paper over a comb and blow on it, making a "whanging" noise. Another grabbed a tin bucket and drummed along! This resulted in a lot of racket but was questionable as far as music goes!

I'm sure this was good training for me though, since one of my daughters graduated from the University of Georgia with a degree in music! It must have been passed down the line.

Artistic aptitudes ran rampant in our family! One distant relative grew tired of the family newsletters he received each Christmas, telling of the accomplishments they had made the previous year. He decided to compose a satirical response!

It went as follows: "Merry Christmas To Everybody!" A lot has happened during the past year, so let us begin: January: Cousin Jed was locked up for peeping at a neighbor. The neighbor, Billie Jo Fullbody, was attacked by a bunch of yellow jackets and she ran into her house, losing a lot of her clothing in the process. Jed saw the whole thing and wanted to see more!

February: Uncle Festus broke his leg and ended up in the hospital. He received a letter from Readers Digest, saying, "you have won 10 MILLION DOLLARS" and he commenced to dance a jig, and his arthritis would not cooperate! He never read the part that said, "if your name is drawn."

March, April, May, June: Grandpa Snort was plowing some new ground in the "back forty" and a lizard ran up his pants leg. After a few minutes of wild jumping and other gyrations he had to go to the house and rest a while with a near nervous breakdown!

Rest of the year: Aunt Bloom and Uncle Fudd moved to Alabama. Aunt Bloom left the new house a short time. Before she left she hid her purse in the dishwasher, and not knowing the "delayed wash" switch was on closed the door to the appliance. While she was gone she "laundered" all of her money!

That's all of the news this time. As for us two, we are expecting! We are expecting a lot of gifts!

P.S. I almost forgot to tell about Uncle Elmer! He got up early one morning, ate his breakfast real fast, and went to the back porch to brush his teeth. That's where the bucket of water was and they kept a tube of Colgate toothpaste nearby.

Uncle Elmer grabbed his brush and the tube of toothpaste and applied a generous portion. After finishing brushing his teeth, he rinsed his mouth out and he glanced at the tube he had just used. It looked a little different!

He didn't think anything more about it until a few days later! His mouth seemed to be shrinking, and a couple of teeth were loose! A few days passed and all of his teeth fell out!

Poor old Uncle Elmer went to see a dentist, to ask about getting some false teeth. The dentist looked at his gums and said, "they sure have shrunk, what kind of toothpaste have you been using?"

My uncle told him he thought it was Colgate and that he would check when he got home. When he arrived home he looked and saw the tube on the shelf. He began to read what was on the tube, and he made out "Preparation H!"

Uncle Elmer hurried back to the dentist and told him how he had picked up the wrong tube and brushed his teeth with Preparation H! The dentist told him that was his problem! He said, "you know what that is used for, and it will work the same way on your gums!" "You applied the salve to your gums, they shrunk up and your teeth fell out!"

So, Uncle Elmer has a brand new set of "chompers!"

Speaking of teeth, one of my friends told a story the other day about a country preacher having a problem with his speech delivery one Sunday.

It seems the minister was to speak at a revival meeting and a large crowd had gathered to hear him. His reputation as a dedicated man of the cloth had preceded him.

He was properly introduced and began to speak. The more he spoke, the louder he became. He was really getting into his sermon and he was gesturing and spitting out his words!

Suddenly, his false teeth, uppers and lowers, went flying out of his mouth and settled somewhere in the congregation!

The country preacher didn't miss a beat! He kept on giving his message and calmly walked down to where his teeth lay. He picked them up, shook them a little and replaced them in his mouth!

The sermon continued and the audience was mesmerized! He had handled a very embarrassing situation with not a titter from his listeners! The preacher must have used a good portion of wisdom in this instance, even though his wisdom teeth had temporarily left him!

A few years ago, I went to the dentist for my annual teeth-cleaning ritual and he mentioned that I still had all except one of my original teeth. That one had been pulled several years prior.

I inquired about having my wisdom teeth out, since it seemed to be in vogue lately. He looked at my teeth and said that I must have had them pulled because I didn't have any. As I assured him that they had never been pulled, he said that some people are born without them.

A sobering thought struck me, no wonder that I have wisdom lapses on occasion! I have never had wisdom teeth and that must be the cause of my wisdom impairment!

Work has always been a large part of my life and I never considered whether it was a job that I particularly liked. Instead, it was mostly chosen out of necessity, with thoughts of providing extra income.

On the farm I looked for ways to make some spending money when my presence wasn't required in the cotton patch. We picked blackberries and sold them in town for twenty-five cents a gallon. Have you ever tried to pick a gallon of blackberries? It takes two or three hours and you have to brave the thorns and possibly snakes in the bushes!

I picked up leftover peanuts after the threshing machine processed the nuts away from the hay portion. These were laying around on the ground where the machine was used. They were sold in town for a few cents a pound. Sometimes I boiled the peanuts and sold them on the streets for ten cents a bag.

After the cotton was picked, we always had some leftovers in the field and these were gathered and sold.

While in high school we had to wait for the bus to carry us home and I used this time working for the school. I picked up trash over the school yard and was paid a little for this.

In college I worked two days a week to pay my tuition and had classes four days. The work was done on the school farm, the campus crew and the janitor crew. I also worked at an off campus job as a yard man and chauffeur for an official of the school.

When I was serving in the U. S. Army, my time was my own after five o'clock. I got a job at the local U.S.O. and made more money than the military service paid. I also was allowed to attend the Army University of Hawaii for one quarter. Some courses were offered that counted on my college credits later.

Returning from the service, I entered the University of Georgia to continue my education toward a journalism degree. During this time, I worked on the school newspaper, the Red and Black. I was a reporter for a while and the feature editor my last year. I loved football, so when they needed ushers in the stadium, I applied.

While going to law school in Atlanta, I held a full-time job as an insurance company staff manager in the daytime. My wife often did briefs for the many cases that I didn't have enough hours in the day to do! She should have been given half of my law degree!

Later, going in business for myself, there was no opportunity for off-time work. I was on the job all of the time. But it finally began to pay off, and I never regretted creating my own job! As a person told me one time, "I have never been afraid of work, I can lay down beside it and go to sleep."

My dad could do just about anything related to a farm and its upkeep. Many times he would go out to his blacksmith shop and forge new plow points and scrapes after the ones being used were broken. He could fix anything used on the farm.

As he grew older, and most of his kids had left home, he sold a portion of his land and built a new house and country store on his highway frontage. My wife and I vacationed down there as he was doing this and helped to build a wooden floor in the house.

Very soon, we realized this was not the best way to spend your vacation! We measured and sawed pine tongue and groove boards, and nailed them down until it was difficult just standing upright! What a relief it was when our "vacation" ended!

He operated the store and gas station until he was in his eighties and finally closed it. He had supported himself and wife for several years from the store, but decided to retire.

The store served as a meeting place for the community and he had many friends that stopped by, even if they didn't buy anything.

It wasn't always rosy, though, as he worked alone most of the time. One day two young boys from the next county came in and loudly told him that "this is a robbery, give us your money!" One had a gun and pointed it at him!

He did as he was told and opened his cash register. As they were eying the cash, my dad reached under the counter and got his 38 caliber police special revolver and the two ran from the store! Running out the door, he shot at them several times, but missed!

The county sheriff arrived almost immediately, after being called, and the two would-be robbers were picked up in nearby woods. The officer said the two thugs were almost scared out of their shoes, from dodging my dad's bullets!

Later, he told my dad that he was going to give him some shooting lessons, so he could do more than scare them next time!

Some time after that a customer came into the store and bought some blades for his safety razor. Two days passed and the customer came back in the store, with his face all scratched!

He angrily demanded, "why didn't you warn me that them blades were so sharp?" "I took the blades home and tried to shave and I cut my face several times!"

He was offered his money back, but this didn't satisfy him. He told my dad, "if you will come outside, I will beat the #@&# out of you!"

This didn't set so well with my dad, who was only five-feet-six and one hundred fifty pounds, but all muscle. So he complied with the man's request, disregarding the fact that my dad was seventy-five years old!

So they began to swap blows and finally, my dad knocked him down on the ground and jumped on top of him, and pounded the man a few more times. He was told that he would let him up if he would behave himself. The man agreed and the fracas was soon over!

I think he lost a customer, however!

About this time my mother passed away at seventy-eight years of age, and my dad lost all interest in the store. They had been married fifty seven years! He entered a nursing home a few years after and soon passed away at age eighty five.

The property was sold and the little country store was never reopened. Last time I was down there, renewing old memories, the place looked a bit run-down. The little fish pond, where my dad would "call" his fish and throw bread crumbs to them, was covered with green scum. I doubt if there were any fish in the pond.

But my parents, who lived a somewhat simple life, left a legacy of memories for their five children, who married and raised families of their own. Many things we learned from them were passed down to our children. All of their offspring were successful, and so far, have led godly and meaningful lives.

I'm reminded of a customer, who asked my dad one time, "have you lived here all of your life?" He told him, "no, I'm not dead yet!"

Part II.

Miracles

This section of the book deals with what I believe are genuine miracles! They either happened to me or to someone close to me, and can only be explained as a very unusual occurrence that needed help from the Almighty to have come about in the manner that is evident.

Miracles occur to all types of people and in many ways. Some will never be understood here on earth. But the following true occurrences were very personal to me and my faith has been increased because of them!

The Miracle In The Well

When I was a six-year-old lad our family lived on a farm in rural south Georgia. We did not have many of the modern conveniences that are available today. We had a shallow well for household water and sometimes the water would dry up and the supply would be depleted.

It was on such an occasion that my dad decided the well had to be cleaned on the bottom, to allow fresh water to flow in. Since I was a small child and would fit into the bucket I was chosen to be the one lowered into the well for the job.

So I began the trip down into the semi-darkness below, riding the bucket, as my dad lowered the chain about fifty feet below the surface. The muck and sludge on the bottom was up to my waist as I got out of the bucket!

It was my job to direct the bucket and tip it over, so it would fill up with the mud. Then the bucket was raised to the surface and emptied above.

All went well until the muddy water was drawn out and the last bucket was being emptied above. Suddenly, there was a "whooshing" sound and I was engulfed with water and mud almost to the top of my head, It looked as if the walls of the well were caving in around me, and I was extremely alarmed!

I looked up at the tiny opening of light at the top of the well, and my lifeline of bucket and chain seemed a mile away! I was small but I understood the situation was dangerous!

At six years of age I couldn't have known much about praying, but I must have made some kind of attempt at it. I needed help badly, and it was just me and a whole lot of sludge down there in that hole! All at once, the water stopped rising and my dad responded to my cries and lowered the bucket. I didn't hesitate to jump in and was raised to the surface. What a great feeling it was to have my feet on solid ground above!

Later, I learned the wooden curbing, that was about six feet high in the bottom of the well, had rotted and the pressure behind it had caused the release of water being held back. As it rushed out from the rotted curbing I believed the well was caving in! If so, that probably would have been the end of me!

My dad probably didn't use his best reasoning process that day when he decided to lower me into that well, but I guess he didn't realize the danger of the situation.

At any rate, I firmly believe that my life was spared by a miracle in the well that day, and not wanting to tempt fate a second time, I ceased all of my well-cleaning activities from that time on!

The Daring Duck That Came For Dinner

Thanksgiving of 1944 has lingered in my memory as one of the most satisfying events in my life. It not only was extremely satisfying to the stomachs of the family members who were present at our country home, but was a time of "spiritual awakening" as we witnessed a miracle of sorts.

We lived off the beaten path, so to speak, in south Georgia about three miles from the nearest town We were poor like most others around us.

Thanksgiving Day came and there probably was not an over abundance of food available in the house. There hardly ever was, except at hog killing time and then only meat. My mother must have been pondering as to what she would cook for dinner.

As we all sat on the porch, as country people were apt to do in that day, we spied some kind of animal coming our way down the road As it came closer we finally figured out that it was a duck. As it waddled along the road, it came to our turn- off and approached the porch area with a couple of quacks.

If I had been a swearing person at this time. I would have sworn that the duck's quacks sounded like he was saying, "I am your Thanksgiving dinner."

I began to approach the large fat duck and it slowly moved around the yard to our woodpile. There in a block of wood waited a sharp axe! The duck just stood there, hardly moving.

51

Believing that a Divine Being had somehow sensed that we had little to eat at this particular holiday, and that this duck had been sent for our nourishment, I caught it and we had a wonderful meal for Thanksgiving!

We gave thanks to our Lord for his miraculous gift and marveled at the events of the day! Later, we enquired around the neighborhood as to anyone who may have owned the duck, having intentions of paying for it. Nobody knew of anyone raising or having ducks in the community. Seemingly, this large, fat, healthy duck just appeared out of nowhere! But we knew this duck was on a mission!

The Lord Of The Ring

One cool day in February of 2004, my wife and I went for a short drive to tend to some domestic chores that had been building for a few days. The county where we live does not have garbage pickup, so we have to carry ours to a garbage collecting area and throw it into a large container.

We carried the garbage and made a few shopping stops, then on to the grocery store for some items. On the way back we stopped at a park and walked some, and returned home.

Sitting in the house later, I looked down at my left hand and noticed my wedding band was missing! Fifty three years it had always been there! Panic set in!

With the realization that it had slipped off my finger sometime during the day, possibly at one of our stops, I just knew that it was lost forever! Night was approaching and I had to put off retracing our steps until the next day.

The following day I prayed that we would be successful in finding the ring. From a monetary standpoint it was not so valuable, but it was irreplaceable as far as memories go.

My wife and I retraced our steps from the day before but had no luck finding the ring. The last stop was the grocery store and that didn't look very encouraging. Once there, something nudged me to a grapefruit bin where I had chosen a sack and put it on the shopping cart the day before.

I asked a clerk if it would be all right to look in the large box, and told her why. She approved and I began emptying all of the bags onto the floor. Being restocked overnight, there were quite a few in the box.

When all but two bags had been removed, I saw a shiny object lodged between them. It was hard to see what it was because it was on the very bottom of the box and the lighting was not to good. I picked it up and couldn't hardly believe my eyes! Yes! It was my gold wedding band! I shouted for joy and so did a couple of clerks! My wife came up at that time and she too was elated!

This truly had to be a miracle because it was literally a "needle-hunt-in-a-haystack" kind of search. We gave thanks for an answer to my prayer, in such a dramatic fashion! This day my request had surely been answered by "The Lord of the Ring!"

Hospital, Doctors and Amazing Calm Before Surgery

At the age of forty seven I was told by my doctor that it was inevitable that I was going to require surgery for a gallstone condition that had come upon me in 1973. This would be my first hospital stay and I was somewhat unnerved with the news.

My doctor was a former practitioner with the U. S. Military during World War II and I had great confidence in him and his prognosis. So we set the date to remove the gall bladder, since that was the only treatment available at that time.

It was necessary to be in the hospital the night before surgery, and I checked into the facility with trepidations. As I lay there in the bed, a minister came in and visited with a patient also in the room. This man was deathly ill and the preacher assured him that whatever happened to him the Lord would take care of him.

The conversation could be heard easily, since there was only a curtain between us, and I got to thinking about my situation. I had been a "lukewarm" Christian for several years even though I had been saved at age thirteen.

So, I prayed to God and told Him that I didn't deserve His help in a situation such as the one that was confronting me the next day. However, I made Him aware that I sure would appreciate any help He might give, since I was a little nervous about anyone cutting on my insides! I guess you might say, I was somewhat scared!

Suddenly, a warm glowing light appeared around my hospital bed, and I could feel the warmth and a calming peace encompassed me! Not a word was said, but I had a great reassurance immediately that everything was going to be all right!

After a peaceful night, the surgery went well the next day and the healing process set in. Although the hospital stay was ten days, they went without incident and I thanked the Lord for the demonstration that miracles do happen today.

The day I returned home from the hospital was very memorable for me. My wife and two daughters placed a large banner inside our home with the words "WELCOME HOME!" I was surprised and almost overcome with emotion and gratitude!

The Cranky Car That Refused To Crank!

It was a very hot summer day in July in north Georgia and dutifully carrying out a husband's role of performing "honey- do" tasks, I agreed to grocery shop for my wife. So I got in my trusty car and headed toward the nearest grocery store about a mile away.

Things were going well as the shopping cart was being loaded with essential staples, such as ice cream, cake and candies to munch on. I even threw in some pork chops, ribs and steaks. Soon the cart was loaded and I reached for my credit card as I neared the cashier.

After looking suspiciously at the card. the clerk finished his transaction and I headed out to my car. "Boy, was it a hot day, and

I had to get this stuff home quickly or the ice cream would melt and the meat would spoil," I said to myself.

I jumped into the vehicle after loading the groceries and stuck the key in the ignition. Turning the key produced no results so 1 tried again and again, The car would not crank. It was only four years old and had been very dependable, but not this time.

The ice cream began to soften, the meat was getting warm and I decided to call my wife to get her to rescue me before the groceries spoiled. Not having a cell phone, I went back in the store and tried to make the call, but the line was busy. I tried several times but the line was still busy! I later found out that my wife was on the computer and the internet and that cut off all in-coming telephone calls!

Meantime, I knew all those groceries were sitting out there in that hot car and would not last much longer. So, as I walked back to the car, not knowing what to do, I said a little prayer and asked the Lord for help. I was thinking that I shouldn't bother Him with such a small thing, but it seemed like a big problem to me at that time!

I reached the car and moved into the drivers seat, turned the key and the car started as if there had never been a problem with it! To my great delight, I found out that day, the Lord solves small problems as well as large ones! I thanked Him several times!

I got home with the groceries and everything was o.k. I later found that the vehicle was being recalled for a faulty switch, but that day I had a Master Mechanic fix it!

Miracle Of The Thug Attack

Several years ago I was driving my late model car along the expressway close to a large city. Not far ahead was my exit and I began to slow down after I put my right signal on. Suddenly, a car pulled in front of me at a high rate of speed and stopped dead in the center of the off ramp. The vehicle completely blocked my exit.

As I stopped, a young man jumped from his car and approached mine in a fit of rage. I lowered the car window a little and asked what the problem was? To my surprise he said to me, "you know very well what the problem is and if you will get out of your car I am going to beat the #*@_out of you!

Well, I didn't understand at all what the young man's problem was, but it was fast looking like I was going to find out! He snarled at me "you know what you did back up the highway---you ran out in front of me about four exits ago and almost caused me to have a wreck!"

I tried to explain to him that I had been on the highway for about fifteen minutes and had passed several entrances, quite a few more than four, and when I entered the road there were no other cars around. It must have been a similar car at another entrance, I tried to point out to him.

He was not appeased with my statements, however, and insisted on beating me up in the middle of the off ramp. By this time several cars had pulled behind us and the drivers were getting impatient! My patience had worn thin about this time and I was of the mind to accommodate him.

I began to open the car door and was in the process of getting out when there was a loud explosion under the hood of my car! Steam began to pour from the hood area!

The young man was startled and so was I, and neither of us realized what had happened. I lifted the hood of the car and smoke and steam flew in all directions. It was easy to see that the radiator hose had burst and was causing a loss of water fast!

With that threat pending I told the man I had all of the problems I needed and asked him to move his car out of the way. I added if he didn't, I was going to push his car out of the way!

He angrily moved his car and I drove to a gas station nearby. The service man put a new hose on the radiator and added water. I then went on my way, a little shaken, but okay.

Since then I have thought about the situation and am convinced that a higher power selected the exact time for the hose to burst, and prevented a much larger problem!

A Miraculous Cure For
A Mysterious Ailment

In the 1930's my older brother, four siblings and our dad and mother lived as sharecroppers in south Georgia. We were poor as was everybody else and medical care consisted of castor oil and bed rest....that is between trips to the outdoor privy!

My brother took sick and a trip to a local doctor's office did not provide much information or help in solving his problem.

For several days he got worse and we began to really get concerned. He had a high fever and wasn't responding to any treatments.

We had heard of an old "granny" woman who was black and lived nearby. She was rumored to have curing powers for the ailing and my mother asked if she would help my brother.

She said she would try and came to our house. She entered the room where the young boy was lying deathly ill. Everybody was asked to leave and we anxiously awaited the results we were hoping for.

We heard the woman's chanting voice and it sounded like she was saying, "I sic him, I sock him, I sock him in the eye." I told my momma, "she's going to kill him" and I was very afraid for my brother.

Soon, she emerged from the room looking as if she had been drained of all her energy. She said, "I think he will be all right now. I tried my best." With that she left and we went into the room she had just left. The brother had roused and seemed to be getting better.

Shortly after that he got better and better and soon was completely well! We did not understand what had happened but instead of "killing" him as I thought the old woman had somehow caused a mysterious cure!

A Homegoing Experience

My younger sister was in her early seventies and was in fairly good health. She went for a doctor's checkup to investigate a persistent pain in her abdomen, that seemed to be getting worse.

She was given some shocking information! The doctor told her she had acute leukemia and had only a few weeks to live! The cancer had invaded her lymph glands, liver and other organs.

Being a Christian most of her life, she did not necessarily fear death, but for it to come so quickly and unexpectedly, was startling news.

They removed her spleen, hoping for a miracle, but it wasn't to be. She was told that the disease had progressed too far to stop by any known method.

After getting her final affairs in order, she told her daughter that she wanted to go back to her home to die, and not in the hospital. So an ambulance carried her home, and she had been there almost three hours, when she told the daughter and son-in-law to look out the window.

They looked but saw nothing unusual. She said, "look at all of those people, they have come to get me!" The two looked outside the window again, but saw nothing except the house and yard next door.

My sister then told them she would like to be left alone for a while. She was tired and needed to rest. They complied with her wishes and left the room, thinking she needed to sleep a while.

A short time later they checked on her to see if she was resting comfortably. They found that she had entered into her eternal rest! She had actually seen some beings of some sort, who had come for her!

The daughter and son-in-law had witnessed a miracle. They could not see the miracle, but they knew that one had occurred!

The Tornado That Rocked A Southern Baptist Church

It was an ordinary Sunday at this country home in south Georgia. The skies were overcast and the weather was rather warm and humid. Our family was nearly ready to climb aboard the two-horse wagon and make the round trip to church, some five miles away. It would take nearly an hour to get there.

We made the trip earlier for the eleven-o'clock service and was returning for the evening preaching event. My father was the Sunday school superintendent and my mother was the pianist at this small country Baptist church.

When we arrived, with other members and visitors, the service commenced. In the distance you could hear rolling thunder and see flashes of lightning!

The preacher began to speak and the thunder became louder and the wind began to get stronger. The old kerosene lamps hanging from the ceiling began to swing as the wind pummeled the old wooden building!

The louder the noise from the storm, the louder the preacher would speak! Suddenly, the windows blew out behind the preacher and rain pelted him, but he continued to preach!

The congregation was petrified and tried to concentrate on the service but the wind was rocking the old building! The lightning was flashing rapidly and the thunder was booming! The mules outside tied to trees were moving about restlessly!

The storm subsided just as quickly as it began and the building, though badly damaged, was still standing but leaning somewhat. The pastor gave the invitation for new members and several persons came forward.

The next day the men of the church came to check on the condition of the building and found that it was so badly damaged that it was a miracle that it had not fallen over with all of the people inside!

The church members cut down tall pine trees, trimmed off the limbs and leaned them against the church to hold it up until repairs could be made.

Two miracles appeared to have happened that night of the tornado. One miracle saved the church building from total destruction, another one saved many people. Some were physically saved and some were spiritually saved, and some both!

The Guardian Angel On The Road

After a week of camping with one of my brothers and his wife in Florida, we were returning to Atlanta, Ga. by way of the 1-75 interstate. My wife was with me and it was on a Sunday. The road traffic was heavy and the drive was a tiresome one.

We looked like a convoy with two campers and the two vehicles pulling them. I'm sure the other travelers experienced some irritation with the slower traffic we created.

About fifty miles from our destination my brother pulled over to the side of the highway and we investigated a screeching noise coming from one of the wheels on his camper. We didn't know what the problem was nor did we have the means to attempt to fix it. So we decided to move further up the road and seek help.

Soon we came to the next exit and pulled off the road at a small store. Nothing else seemed to be open, since lots of businesses close on Sundays.

My brother and I, along with our wives, were looking at his camper's wheels and hoping to find a solution to the problem. A black customer there saw us examining the wheels and asked us what the problem was? I answered, "we have no kind of idea, the wheel is just making a terrible noise and we still have a long way to go."

He looked at it and told us that it looked as if the wheel bearings had messed up. He added that he was a mechanic and that he had a shop a short distance away and if we would follow him he would fix the wheel.

We could not believe our good fortune and we followed him to the shop. He had the right bearings and fixed the wheel in a short time. He was asked what the charge was and he refused any pay! He said that he could see that we needed help and he was very glad to be of assistance.

My brother finally convinced him to take enough money to cover the parts. We thanked him considerably and told him that he had gotten us out of a jam and that we were very grateful.

The four of us took to the road again and marveled at how a guardian angel must have been watching over us and caused the series of events that led to the solution to our problem.

This man just happened to be there in the right place for us and solved all of our needs at the right time. This gave me another opportunity to witness to someone about miracles that certainly do happen in this day and time!

The Lightning Strike

During the summer of 1944, while I was attending Berry College at Rome, Ga., the students were required to work two days each week, to pay for their tuition. We attended classes four days, worked two, and went to Sunday school and church every Sunday.

My work assignment this unusually hot summer day was to shovel coal in a railroad car, making sure the coal would tumble down to a chute at the bottom. There, it would be shoveled into dump trucks to be transported to various campus buildings for heating purposes.

Suddenly, a thunderstorm formed and the weather became an issue at this time. Lightning began to pop around the area and it appeared that I was in considerable danger of being struck!

While thinking of seeking cover of some kind, I heard a deafening clap of thunder! Before I could ponder the situation, I was knocked off my feet and wound up in the bottom of the coal car!

I was dazed and disoriented and covered in black coal dust. It was a few minutes before I could assess the situation.

After gathering my wits, I realized that a bolt of lightning had either struck the coal car, the rail, or something nearby. Evidently, the bolt had not hit me directly or I probably wouldn't be here today!

Even though I had taken a pretty good tumble to the bottom of that car, I was not harmed physically. A little soap and water would erase most of my problems.

Mentally, however, I was thinking that this occurrence was too close for comfort! I was thankful for the Providential help from above!

The Miracle of
The Guardian Angel in Arizona

In the summer of 1975 my family and I were traveling to San Bernardino, Calif. to carry our oldest daughter to train for tenure with the Campus Crusade for Christ. She had just completed four years at the University of Georgia and had received a degree in music. She had decided to make the Crusade her life work or pursuit.

We hooked up her new Toyota, which was a graduation gift, to our car and filled it with all of her earthly belongings. We took off from the city of Atlanta, Ga. heading west and looking like a convoy.

All went well until we entered the state of Arizona. We decided to stop at a wayside park and eat a sandwich. We pulled off the road and parked close to a nice picnic table. The sun was bearing down on us with a temperature of about 100 degrees, but the natives said that "it was a dry heat and you would not feel it as much."

We were extremely uncomfortable and gathered our belongings and piled into the car to resume the journey.

Forty five miles down the expressway my wife and I heard a moan and a voice from the rear seat saying, "I can't find my purse anywhere." "I must have left it on the picnic table at the park."

Well, needless to say, this got our attention! The purse contained all of her money, credit cards and personal items and addresses with phone numbers.

A freeway exit was just ahead and we reversed our course, hoping to get back and find the purse where it was left. As we rode, I got on the car CB and talked with any persons who may have stopped at the same park, hoping to learn some good news about someone possibly having found it. No one had and we spent an agonizing three-quarters of an hour retracing our miles.

Finally, we arrived and drove to the table we had occupied. No one was around and neither was the purse. There was nobody around to ask information. We were resigned to the fact that someone had taken it and we would never see it again.

Back on the highway I noticed the gas gauge indicated the fuel was low and the first exit we got off and turned into a gas station. There was a police car at the station and the suggestion was made to report our experience to the police that they might make a record of the loss.

I told the state patrolman our story and he listened intently. After describing the purse and contents to him, the patrolman reached in the back seat of his vehicle and came up with an object. He said, "Is this your purse?"

We were dumbfounded! It was! The officer said someone had found it and flagged him down on the highway and turned the purse over to him. What a Good Samaritan this was!

We expressed our most grateful thanks to the officer! We gave thanks to the Lord, for He is the only one that could have orchestrated this scenario! How else could we explain the "good Samaritan" who turned in the purse, or the choosing of that particular service station to refuel, where the officer was waiting with the purse to return it?

We had seen another miracle and it had been amazing!

By the way, at this writing some twenty two years after this incident, the same daughter with her husband and three children remain on the Campus Crusade For Christ staff, having served most of this time overseas in southeast Asia.

Camping, Fishing and the
Miracle of the Eye Glasses

My brother and I, along with our wives, were camping in Florida, when the two women and I decided to fish off a nearby dock. The campground owners said alligators had been seen around the lake and to be careful!

As soon as my lure hit the water a large fish grabbed it and the water around began to explode with action! My sister- in-law got so excited at the commotion she threw her hands up in the air. My wife just happened to be standing in front of her and was inadvertently shoved off the dock into the murky water!

Fortunately, she can swim, but with all of her fishing clothes wet and pulling her down she was having some difficulty getting back to the dock. The sister-in-law had a long fishing pole, which she immediately stuck over in her direction and my wife grabbed onto it.

When my wife grasped the end of the pole and began to pull, the one on the dock became over-balanced and fell in also. She had never learned to swim!

With two women in the water, threshing about and hollering, I was in a quandary! I knew that all of the commotion was getting the attention of alligators, if any were close by! I jumped into action and pulled my wife to safety on the dock and both of us attempted to get the sister-in-law back on the dock, but failed!

Finally, we had to "walk" her around the structure, through thick weeds and undergrowth back to the shore. This was frightening, not knowing what might be in the weeds! In the excitement she had lost her brand new prescription glasses in the water, which was fifteen feet deep.

It was dark, we were thankful to be alive and not eaten by alligators, and returned to the campers to sleep and recuperate.

The next day we borrowed a long rake from the campground owner and tried to find the glasses, which were probably somewhere on the bottom of the pond. My sister-in- law raked and raked but to no avail.

We were about to the point of giving up and something told me to try one more time. I said a silent prayer and asked for help from above as I dipped the rake again in the water. Raising the rake to the surface, I was astonished at what I saw! There was the pair of shiny new glasses in perfect condition, hanging on the rake!

We had just witnessed a modern day miracle! By the way, the fish got away. I'm convinced it was a world record trophy, though!

Easy Sale of Camper and Van

After about thirty years of camping all over the United States and parts of Canada, my wife and I decided that our advancing ages dictated that we should either slow down our traveling, or quit altogether. So we decided to sell the thirty- four foot camper and Ford 350 van we used to pull it.

This was not a happy decision, because we loved our camper and it represented many memories and enjoyable experiences. Also, we dreaded the very mechanics of getting the vehicles ready, advertising them and showing them for sale. It was going to be a lot of work.

We checked the camper to make sure that all equipment was working and in good condition, and in the process found the refrigerator was on the blink. In order to have it fixed it would be necessary to carry the camper twenty miles away to a dealer, who would service it.

After much trouble in moving the large camper that distance, we arrived at the dealership and parked it for repair. The owner said he would have it ready for us in a week.

A vehicle this large was going to be difficult to show and sell, we thought, and were having misgivings about the entire project.

While we were pondering the situation the phone rang. It was the service mechanic. He asked if we would sell the two vehicles and the amount we were asking.

I told him they were indeed for sale and the amount we would sell them for. He said that he would do some checking and get back to us.

There was no way to know how serious the mechanic was about the sale and we couldn't generate much excitement. However, we thought the situation called for a prayerful request of Divine help. If it was to be that the sale should be made, we made it known that we were willing and ready for this to occur!

Shortly after our prayer, the phone rang again. The mechanic told me the good news, that his father was visiting and saw the camper and van. They were exactly what he had been looking for and he was ready to buy them both! He asked that we come by his store and pick up a certified check!

My wife and I could hardly believe our ears! We should have, since we had just asked for Divine help! Somehow we had been surprised that it came so soon!

Nevertheless, we accepted the blessing and knew it had been another miracle!

The Destructive Tornado of 1936 in Cordele, Georgia

The sun had not yet come up and the two kerosene lamps gave off very little light, as the five children scrambled to ready themselves for the three-mile trek to grammar school in the city. The sky was illuminated intermittently by rapid lightning bursts and thunder was booming!

The country house we lived in was simple and old, and much in the need of repair. Suddenly, the wind began howling outside and the storm became noisy and dangerous!

The barn roof became caught up with the wind and was blown across the field nearby. The house roof raised several inches above the supporting structure and finally settled back in its original position!

Inside the house, the family was severely shaken and fright had set in! We expected the next wind burst to take the entire house with it, along with the seven inhabitants!

The storm suddenly waned and moved on by our house, leaving all in a state of shock!

Trying to get things back to normal, mom packed our lunches and the five of us walked slowly toward the school house. This was a six-mile trip, being three miles there and three miles back.

After some time, we finally made it to the school area. Not believing what we saw, there was no school! Nothing much except piles of brick and debris!

We found that the tornado had passed directly over the school and demolished it. I walked around to the area where my classroom had been. Hanging precariously from what was left of the second floor, I saw my desk.

The gravity of the situation sank in quickly. If I had been at my desk a little earlier, when the tornado struck, there was a good chance that I would not have survived! At the time the storm hit the school, we were pretty busy at home, or we might have been there and many school children might have been killed or injured.

Later, we were told that 23 people had been killed in that tornado and 500 injured. Two hundred and eighty nine buildings were damaged or destroyed causing a property loss of $3,000,000! The tornado had struck April 2, 1936 at 7:30 a.m.

Our family, along with many others, survived because of a miracle that day! We had been delayed just long enough, that we missed the destruction at the schoolhouse!

The Teton Adventure

In the 70's our family bought a 24-foot motor home and set off on a trip out west to explore the new frontier (at least it was new to us.)

In addition to my family, which consisted of me and my wife and two daughters, we were accompanied by a brother-in-law and his wife.

After a week or two of traveling we wound up in the Teton Mountains in northwestern Wyoming, and settled in a nice camping space at the Grand Teton National Park. The views were fantastic and we marveled at the sights we were witnessing for the first time.

About a quarter of a mile from the campground was a large lake, and we were told the trout and cutthroats were biting! Several of us grabbed fishing poles and away we went to the fishing hole.

Everything was going well, and we were having fun pulling in the fish, when across the lake appeared a blue haze, just above the lake level. The longer we fished the higher the haze grew above the water.

Soon the gentle breeze gave way to a brisk wind and the haze that had been off in the distance, was now upon us. Getting uneasy about the weather, we decided to return to the campers.

We had waited too long! The wind was really strong and increasing by the minute! The tall slender lodge pole pines around us began to fall to the ground! We were somewhat scared!

The more trees that fell, the faster we ran, and arrived at the campers in short order without a scratch. That night we had no power, because many trees had fallen on the power lines.

We later learned that a powerful tornado had zeroed in on that part of the Tetons and caused much damage.

It took two days to get back to civilization, because we had to wait for the forest rangers to clear the roads of fallen trees. But we were thankful that we had safely endured the scary run back to our campers, and hadn't been blown away or struck by a falling tree.

We knew our "Guardian Angel" was watching over us and kept us safe and healthy for more adventures!

Part III.

Almost Miracles, Near Misses and Plain Living

Just about all of us have experiences throughout our lives that imitate miracles, but are not hardly believable as such. Some could be placed in the category of close encounters. Others could be unexplained mysteries.

So this part of the book has been created from true occurrences that could be listed as near misses, mysterious happenings or just plain everyday living. Some deal with forces of nature. Some deal with peculiar people and folk lore. But are they believable? Let your imagination run wild!

The Copperhead at Roundtop

Several years ago my wife, our two daughters and I walked around a thirteen-acre lake that had just been bulldozed and built in North Georgia. It had partially filled with water and we were doing some exploring. It was part of a seventy-five acre farm that five partners, of which I was one, had acquired on Roundtop Mountain.

Something had caused me to include my 22 caliber rifle on the walking tour, since the terrain was rugged with many bushes around the trail.

Our attention was focused on the new lake as we walked, admiring the many wild plants and rhododendron. Suddenly, I saw a slight movement out of the corner of my eye at the edge of a bush. I was fixing to step very close to a large snake, that was later identified as a copperhead moccasin!

Without thinking, I raised the rifle and fired in an instant. The snake, which was coiled and ready to strike, fell dead with a bullet between his eyes! If I had deliberately aimed the gun and tried to hit the reptile, it never would have happened! A snake is a difficult target to hit, especially between his eyes.

The only way this feat could have been accomplished was with some great help from above, because it was possible that I would have shot myself in the foot instead of the snake.

Some environmentalists might want to argue that no wildlife should be destroyed, but I am convinced that it was either him or me in that situation. A person always has the right to defend himself or his family.

This copperhead almost scared me out of my wits!

The property had an old house on it, but it was in bad shape and almost beyond repair. So my brother, Milton, and I decided to build a three-room cabin from leftover building materials we had accumulated.

This being the first project both of us had attempted as house-builders, we decided not to spend too freely on this project. We cut down some trees to make the framework for the cabin and worked in a lot of two-by-fours and other lumber in the construction. Our thinking was that it didn't matter if it didn't last long!

Topping the cabin off with a sloped tin roof, we left an opening for a metal stove pipe to carry the smoke from a pot- bellied stove below. We sheet-rocked the walls and added a triple portion of insulation in the bedroom walls to lessen the snoring noises!

Before the cabin was completely finished, the four of us decided to give it a trial run one cold weekend. Only one room was livable and we placed a double bed in one corner with two bunk beds in another. We filled the little stove with wood and warmed the cabin with a cozy fire!

About one o'clock that night we were awakened to intense heat in the room! I raised up from the bed and looked at the stove. It was red hot and glowing all over! The heat was unbearable! Another few minutes and we would have been toast!

I flung the door open and let the freezing air into the room, over objections from the sister-in-law. She was more afraid of wild animals in the woods that might be nearby!

When the stove cooled, and the situation was brought under control, we settled down to salvage a little sleep before sunup. Needless to say, we were more careful in firing up the stove after that incident.

We had been told there were many wild animals, including bears, in the area but never came face-to-face with any.

One morning before daylight we were awakened by a pack of dogs chasing something! Looking out a window, we saw a large male deer bounding through the yard. Close behind were two or three hunters trying their best to get off a shot at the buck. It didn't seem to matter that the land the hunters were crossing belonged to someone else!

Since we were only up there occasionally, many times we would find the cabin had been broken into and ransacked. One scary-looking mountaineer showed up one day and informed my wife that he would fish in our lake anytime he pleased! "I've been in these woods all of my life and nobody's going to stop me now," he snarled.

71

She was there alone at the time and didn't want to challenge him! She shut the door and the unsavory character left.

A cold mountain stream ran through the property and provided us with all of the clean drinking water we needed. We installed a pump and brought water into the cabin until a thief relieved us of the appliance. After that we had to carry water by hand.

When we reported the theft, the local sheriff offered to check on the property now and then, if he was given a key to get in the gate. We had heard some unfavorable comments about law enforcement in the county and we decided not to comply with his request.

Shortly after that, we were notified that a moonshine still was found on the backside of the property, located beside the mountain stream. The Internal Revenue department got wind of the illegal still and raided it. We found evidence of several barrels and cans with holes in them, probably made by officers.

After checking with the other partners of the properly, we were assured that none of them had been involved in the illegal operation! The underbrush was pretty dense around the still and the operators probably thought it wouldn't be found.

Soon after that incident the mountain retreat was sold. It seemed to have more problems than pleasures and we moved on to "greener pastures."

Going Swimming at the Railroad Trestle

Swimming was a big occasion with our family during the summer, because we lived on a farm and the children were always happy to get out of the cotton patch, and other work that seemed to have no end. The nearest swimming hole was about a mile away at the railroad tracks, where a stream ran underneath a bridge.

My cousins didn't like for me to tag along since I hadn't learned to swim, and being only six years old, I was generally considered a pest. So, one day when my parents insisted that I be allowed to go, I followed my brothers and city cousins to the pond.

About halfway to the pond was an old abandoned house, with a mangy building behind it, where chickens had roosted at one time. One of the cousins came up with the bright idea to shut me in the chicken house to keep me from going swimming with them.

It must have appealed to my older brothers because they agreed to the plan. They grabbed me and forced me into the rickety old building where chickens had roosted on poles across it. Droppings were still evident on the ground beneath the poles. The door was wired shut and I was left alone. This was a scary place but I couldn't get out.

Finally, they came back after swimming for two hours and let me out of the place. Back home I told my parents and I think they meted out an appropriate punishment for them!

Learning to Swim and Being Bitten by a Moccasin Snake

Another such incident occurred shortly after the "chicken-house" imprisonment, exemplifying the inhumane treatment I received during my early childhood from my cousins and sometime from my older brothers.

We were going swimming that day and as usual, I was an unwelcome tag-along! After arriving at the pond, we grouped together on the railroad bridge over the pond. Some of the kids used this concrete structure as a diving launch.

Stripping off naked as we always did, we made ready to jump in. In fact, none of us had bathing trunks and they were almost unheard of at this time. Because of our exposure, we probably put on some good shows for passing train riders at times!

One mean cousin sneaked up behind me and gave me a shove into the pond! It was deeper than I was tall and I had not yet learned to swim!

Coming to the surface, I began to thresh around in the water and dog-paddle to stay afloat! The action must have attracted a small moccasin snake, which promptly bit me on the right ankle under the water!

One of my brothers sensed my dangerous predicament and jumped in to help me out of the pond. Knowing that I could not swim, he had no part in shoving me in. I think someone killed the snake.

The others didn't let my incident stop their fun and went on swimming and having a good time. Finally, they got enough of the activity and we all returned home.

My mother put a cloth with some sort of salve on it and tied it around my ankle. This was changed a few times for about a week and then removed for healing.

A large sore developed at the snake bite and stayed on my ankle the entire summer. Finally it healed, but a scar remains today. The snake probably would have died from biting me, had he not been killed by a stick!

The cousin never apologized for pushing me in the pond and I don't believe he ever received any punishment. I sometimes wonder how kids get to be grown people with the things some have to endure! Guess some don't!

Fifth Grade in Grammar School was Worst Challenge

When I reached eleven years of age I became old enough to think for myself somewhat and I began to question things I had learned and rethink the direction my life was taking. For instance, I wondered why it was necessary to work so hard on the farm, leaving little time for play and leisure. My dad soon straightened this question for me!

I was in the fifth grade in grammar school and had an unusually strict teacher. She did not put up with much nonsense in the class.

One day in the fall of the year Mrs. Perkins informed the class that we were going to take a field trip to the county fair, which was only about four blocks from the school. There we would tour the livestock exhibits and then return to our class.

Some of the farm boys in the class couldn't generate much interest in looking at cows and hogs, since we saw them every day on the farm. One of the boys talked me into playing a little prank on the pupils as the trip was made.

So, as the class filed along the sidewalk they came upon a large oak tree with a lot of limbs hanging over the area. This boy and myself had previously climbed the tree and as the class walked beneath we peppered them with small rocks from above. We were really having fun until Mrs. Perkins spotted us in the tree!

She ordered us to come down from the tree but we refused, suspecting that we would receive a full measure of punishment there on the spot. Teachers were not prevented from handing out a good paddling at this time and Mrs. Perkins was sturdy enough to do this!

They left us in the tree and proceeded on the class trip to the fair. Sometime later we returned to the school and found that the class had beaten us back. Mrs. Perkins stopped the class instruction and ordered us to an adjoining room. "Here it comes," I thought!

The teacher had the other boy to bend over a table and began to pound him on his backsides with a large yard stick ruler! The harder she pounded the more noise it made! She stopped and asked the boy to remove what object there was in his rear pocket. He refused and the teacher reached in and came out with a can of Prince Albert smoking tobacco!

This really made her angry and she began to unleash her corrective energy until he was hollering "bloody murder!" Or something of that nature!

Soon it was my time and I dutifully bent over the table expecting the worst! Suddenly, she struck several blows on the table and did not hit me one time! She looked really tired and told me to return to the class and not tell anyone what happened!

I'm not sure what happened that day, whether she was worn out and couldn't get around to me or by this time was feeling sorry for me! Whatever it was I was grateful that I was spared the misery that was inflicted on my buddy! I knew that the licks she gave the table were done to make the pupils in the other room think I was the recipient of the blows!

Lady Luck was smiling on me that day, and what I witnessed must have worked because I never misbehaved to this extent in any class since!

Later in the year, however, the teacher's love for the job must have been severely tested! When we arrived at the school she ordered all of the pupils to line up outside the classroom.

We were then told to file by her desk and look at the report cards in an open drawer. As the kids filed by the desk we could see many almost to the point of vomiting and holding their noses! I walked by and saw why! Someone had used the drawer for a bathroom and had really messed up the drawer, report cards and any other items inside!

As far as I know the culprit was never caught but I felt really sorry for the teacher! I couldn't imagine anyone mean enough to pull off this caper! Everyone in the class was made to clean up the mess!

Going To College Was Not Much Of A Change From Home

Many kids going off to college expect everything to be different from what they are used to, with much more freedom and constant entertaining activities. They are loosed from parental reins and are able to make their own decisions. Or so they think!

Sometimes it works out this way, but not at the private college I entered at age sixteen in north Georgia, and it's probably a good thing, because I was not ready for all the freedom of fending for myself.

I had been living on a farm all my life, and that was all that I essentially knew, cows, mules, chickens, growing cotton and plowing corn rows, etc. Everything was done by seasons. The plowing and preparing the fields in the spring, followed by the planting and tending to the plants in summertime. Then came the harvesting in fall. The winters called for sawing wood for heat and cooking and grinding corn for bread.

As I entered this college I was aware of what they offered and how it was provided. I knew that all of the students had to work two days, go to school four and attend church each Sunday. The two-day work program would help pay tuition, along with additional work each summer while school was out.

So it was, when I arrived at college in the summer of 1943. I was filled with expectations and excitement! I had my battered suitcase, containing my required uniforms, overalls and blue shirts. There were no kinds of rules regarding the underwear. But for the outerwear everyone wore the same thing according to their class status.

Arriving on the campus, I registered at the main office and was assigned a dormitory room which was already occupied by a person who was to be my roommate in the two person room. We became acquainted with each other and then looked over our work assignments.

He was going to work on the janitor crew, which consisted of keeping all of the buildings clean and ready for use. I was hoping for that job also, since I had a brother who preceded me on the campus and he had told me it wasn't bad.

I looked at my assignment and was somewhat disappointed to find that I had been chosen to work on the school farm, where they raised garden vegetables, field crops and had several herds of cattle to look after. That was a natural choice for the officials, I suppose, since I had a lifetime of experience.

Beginning work on the farm, I was anticipating doing a good job and pleasing my bosses. As the other boys and I arrived at the farm barn, we learned that we would be loading trailers with cow manure and distributing it over the field where crops were to be planted.

The boss asked me if I could drive a tractor and I replied that I could. Although I had been used to plowing and working with mules, I had learned from others enough about driving a tractor to get by.

He told me to shovel the trailer full of cow manure and drive to the other side of the field and distribute it by the "paraline", alongside other loads recently dumped there.

That seemed like a simple job, so l got busy on it and the boss went on to another part of the farm. I finished loading the trailer, hopped on the tractor and away I went to the other side of the field. I located a place where others had been dumping their loads and proceeded to empty the trailer there.

Going back to the barn I felt real good about what I had done. I knew the boss would be pleased with his new worker!

In a little while, I saw the boss coming in his old beat up truck. He was stirring up dust on the dirt road. He jumped from his truck and I could see that something was bothering him.

"Boy, I told you to distribute that load of manure over by the "paraline" and you emptied your load before you got there," he snorted! I said defensively, "I carried it over to the area where the other loads were dropped, just like you said"

"But, I told you to take it over to the "paraline" and you didn't," he said, in a voice that was getting more impatient by the minute. One of the boys nearby, overhearing the conversation and understanding what the problem was told me in a low voice, "he means to say "power line."

It hit me like a ton of bricks, the man had a hillbilly accent and when he told me the place to go was a "paraline", I had never heard that used for "power line", and I had made a big mistake!

In fact, I realized that I was making a bigger mistake standing there talking about it, because the boss was now thinking I was making fun of the way he was talking! I told him that I understood the situation much better then and apologized for my actions.

I thought that was the end of the episode but my boss wasn't going to let me get off so easy! The big boss called me into his office the next day and told me that the little boss had complained to him and he proceeded to "chew me out" and told me never to do that again!

Eventually it all worked out and I convinced them I could do the job. I continued to work on the farm for another year.

I got to thinking, that this going to college was not much different from being raised on a country farm. I didn't have much freedom. I wasn't allowed to make my own decisions. Among my duties at home I had to haul fertilizer and I got yelled at if I made a few mistakes!

This was one of the few colleges that I was privileged to attend however, because there was no money to pay for one. I could work out all of the tuition here and the school had a good reputation and turned out young men and women of character.

For two years I continued to work for my tuition and concentrate on my studies until the military draft caught up with me at age eighteen and I was whisked away to World War II duty.

By the way, I worked on the farm assignment one year and finally was given janitorial duty at the school! This was very pleasant and the lady boss was real nice!

My brother, who had recommended working on the janitorial crew there, finished his four years before he was drafted into the war. Instead of working summers he decided to get a job outside the school. He applied to a firm in Nashville, Tennessee that made religious books and he was chosen to sell Bibles to people in the rural areas of Kentucky.

He was given a brief case with his materials and transported to a town named Hopkinsville and told that he would have to stay with the people where he ended the day. Most of the time the people were nice enough to ask him to stay with them but sometimes he would have to pose the question himself. He didn't have a car so he was kind of at their mercy. The sales trip was entirely on foot.

He reported that he finished the week one time and was invited to spend the weekend at a rural house way back in the mountains. They invited him to church with them and told him that the preacher was not able to make the trip. Since he was a Bible salesman, they assumed that he was knowledgeable about the contents, and he was asked if he would preach!

He objected, since he was certainly not a preacher, but they insisted! So he agreed! He was in a quandary about what to say! So he prayed about the situation and commenced his sermon. It consisted mostly about his sales pitch he had learned to sell Bibles.

The "sermon" was so well received that he was invited back to "preach" again!

Many students worked as Bible salesmen each summer to pay their way through school and the tales they told were interesting! My brother had others but this was the most memorable.

His religion was suspect, however, since once in a while he would use it as an end to a means! For instance, he became an insurance adjuster later in life and it was on such an occasion that he was sent to settle a claim for a Baptist preacher.

The claim was regarding a small fire that was set by a bolt of lightning to his home. The damage was slight but important enough to the minister.

My brother and the preacher began to discuss the fire and the preacher told him that he had talked to the Lord just prior to his arrival and the Lord told him that the damage claim should amount to $5,000.

Thinking of settling the claim for a smaller amount, my brother hesitated and told him, "preacher, you know, I talked to the Lord about this too and He told me that the damage was $2,500!

They finally agreed on an amount that both figured would please the Lord!

College Pranks And Other Stupid Human Actions

It's oftentimes a mystery how kids, teenagers and other pre-adults survive the first nineteen years of growing up on this planet. Some of the actions and reactions of this group test the very limits of rationalization! Not all are guilty, mind you, but a large percentage are.

Recently I read of two girls in their early teens who were jailed and charged with the murder of one's grandparents. Another case involved a high school student who was reported to have run an ad on E-Bay advertising a plasma large screen television set for half the price it should have been, except in small letters he explained that he was selling a picture of the item. Several customers thought they were buying the appliance!

But, thank goodness, these are two very extreme cases and probably should not even be mentioned in this particular story except for the fact that some innocent pranks begin that way, but have a way of growing into criminal activity.

I have written elsewhere in this attempt at writing a book, where two cousins locked me in am abandoned chicken house for several hours. The same cousins shoved me into a swimming hole when I was five years old and I couldn't swim. Fortunately a brother pulled me out! These are pranks that worked themselves out without too many after effects. But many end up with tragic consequences.

When I entered college as a sixteen-year-old I thought everyone was there to study and learn. Little did I know that some were there to study the wrong things. For instance, the college I was attending was one that depended largely on donations from corporations and charitable foundations.

They had what the school called "Pilgrim Day" and the donors would come through the campus in a motorcade with the students lining the driveway on each side waving at them. We all wore overalls and blue shirts as uniforms and the girls wore green and pink dresses.

On such an occasion, the students lined the driveway and waited for the arrival of the "pilgrims." It was explained to some of us freshmen that we should look as poor and pitiful as possible in order that the donations to the school would be larger.

A group of seniors began to take charge of the operation as one spotted the donors' motorcade approaching and told the freshmen to take off their shoes and stand there barefoot so as to impress them. They gathered the shoes in a basket and put them aside.

When the motorcade was near I looked around to see if everyone was barefooted like myself. Only the freshmen were! The juniors and seniors were standing there laughing and pointing at our bare feet! We caught on to the embarrassing joke too late to do anything about it! So, as the rich people rode by I found a large clump of grass and stood in it, hoping my feet wouldn't be seen! It was never known if we looked pitiful enough to the pilgrims to evoke more money!

After two years there I entered the army during World War II and the pranks continued in service. One night during basic training I was a few minutes late for "lights out" in my barracks. I stumbled along in the dark to my bunk and lay down to sleep, hopefully! As I hit the bed it was obvious that someone had tampered with it, removing the mattress and all cover. Nothing remained but the thin metal springs!

Laughter broke out around the room and my embarrassment turned to anger! I challenged the person, whoever it was, to a round of fisticuffs if my bedding wasn't returned. A recruit nearby admitted to the theft but he wouldn't return the items. With that I attempted to get my "pound of flesh" but in the dark both of us kept hitting the eight-by-eight posts and we decided to finish our argument with boxing gloves the next day. He returned my bed, however.

The next day our contest went for about fourteen rounds until both of us were exhausted. The rounds, it seemed, were ten minutes or more long, however long the onlookers decided to make them. We finally quit, calling the match a draw. I'm not sure anything was accomplished except we both got all of the exercise we needed that day!

After serving two years in the Army I returned to college at a large state university. The pranks continued at this school.

I lived in a dormitory and we had a live-in lady who was the dorm monitor. One student who lived on the third floor of the building was extremely mischievous and thought that he would play a prank on the elderly lady. He stripped down to his under shorts and applied a large amount of catsup to his upper body. Then he attached a fake dagger to his chest in the heart area!

He lay on the floor in front of the lady's room and let out a yell you could hear a city block away! The woman ran out the door and spotted what she thought was a dead body! She promptly fainted and fell over beside the "dead man!"

Someone called a hospital and two emergency workers arrived with a stretcher within minutes. As the workers neared the "dead man" he suddenly jumped up and ran down the hallway, making his escape! The men then revived the woman but she was well shaken up!

A few weeks later a fraternity had its initiation for new members and the inductees were required to do many unusual things. One involved two young men who were taken some seven miles from the Fraternity house to an old abandoned home, where they had been promised that two beautiful girls would be waiting for their attentions!

The fraternity brothers promptly left the area after they let the two inductees out of the vehicle. The boys approached the house with all kinds of things going through their minds, when suddenly, a menacing figure appeared in the doorway with a shotgun! Shots rang out and the two students ran for their lives! They didn't know that the shotgun was loaded with blanks and that it was all a big joke!

The frightened boys ran and walked the seven miles back to the frat house with a tale that would make your hair stand on end, only to find that the experience was part of the initiation!

This type of story could go on and on with similar circumstances and endings but many do not. So, I return to my opening comment, "it's a wonder that kids grow up to be adults!" I guess some never do!

Times were a little tight on pocketbooks in the 1940's. All three males in our family were called up for military service, leaving only two girls and our parents to tend the farm. A lot of work was left undone, fences began to deteriorate and the house needed a coat of paint.

Bills began to mount and incomes were just about nonexistent. My parents were having a hard time keeping their "victory garden" growing during World War Two.

Each of the boys sent money home from their service pay, which was also meager!

So it was with eager anticipation when I received my discharge in San Antonio, Texas and made my way to south Georgia on a Greyhound bus! I knew that I had sent a good bit of my pay home each month and that it must be a sizable sum after a couple of years.

After greeting the family and settling down for a few days, I thought that it would be an appropriate time to bring up the subject to my dad. I asked, "how much money have I accumulated in my account?"

"Well, I have been meaning to talk to you about this," he answered. "Do you see that young heifer cow over there," he went on, "our old cow died and I had to buy another, so I had to use part of your money!"

I found out that I owned a cow, but in a way I didn't, since I never took possession of the farm animal. I had no use for the animal anyway, because I was going to the University of Georgia to finish my education in a few weeks. They probably would not allow me to keep a cow on the campus, nor did I want to!

But there was about two hundred dollars left in the account and one of my brothers had about the same amount. So we combined our leftovers and purchased an old car to take to the school.

It was ten or twelve years old and "on it's last leg," but it did run somewhat! It would come in handy to haul our belongings to the school, which was two hundred miles north.

My brother had to be at school a few days before me, so he left his clothes for me to bring along. A few days later I began the trip with a loaded car. For twenty miles the car chugged right along and I was beginning to feel good about our purchase.

Suddenly the car sputtered and quit! It rolled to a stop on the shoulder and I tried everything to get it going again! No luck! So I just sat there pondering the situation and wondering what to do.

After about fifteen minutes I tried to crank the vehicle and, to my surprise, it started! So I began the journey again, not believing my good luck!

Would you believe that it ran real good for another twenty miles and stopped again! By this time, I thought I had found the problem. The car seemed to get heated and had to cool down after twenty miles of traveling.

So I waited fifteen minutes, cranked the car, and continued the trip! This continued for the entire two hundred miles, but I finally made it! After I found that the car just became tired every so often, and allowed it to rest, the trip was a cinch! Just slow!

The auto didn't have a brake or stop light on the rear, so l rigged a line from the battery and placed a light on the back with a toggle switch. When it was necessary to be lighted we stopped and went to the rear of the auto and turned the switch.

Neither my brother or myself knew much about the mechanics of a car, so we had to depend on "rigging" remedies. The steering got screwed up somehow and it took about three turns of the wheel to get it around a comer!

One day my brother was driving it and he needed to round a corner! Another car happened to be in his way and he plowed into the driver's side of the other car! Thankfully, no one was hurt, but a lot of damage had been done to the man's car.

Being college students and not having any insurance or money, my brother gave the man our car for his damage! Later he told me he would reimburse me for my share and did. This was probably a blessing in disguise because we were spending all of our money on repairs to keep it going!

Just about every place we needed to go was within walking distance on the campus and we needed the exercise. This did cramp our style, however, when it came to dating! Even back in the forties college girls liked riding better than walking!

After finishing college with a journalism degree, I began to look for a job in Atlanta. I had to stay at the local YMCA, because money was short, as usual. I shared a room with two other young men who seemed to be in similar circumstances. About a week later one boy asked me if I had seen a suit he had in the closet previously. I told him no, and that I had noticed a couple of my items were missing also!

We began to be suspicious of the other boy and decided to follow him one morning. He walked down the street to the Greyhound Bus Station. Inside he walked over to a locker and opened it. Walking closer, we could make out familiar- looking clothing hanging in the locker!

It turned out to be our clothing! The boy had been taking our clothing and other objects from the YMCA!

A policeman standing nearby was summoned and promptly locked the young man up! Later, he agreed to enter the military rather than be sentenced to jail.

The Confused and
Inebriated Marine On Leave

During World War Two I was stationed at Fort Shafter near Honolulu, Hawaii. It was a territory then, not yet having become a state. Living on military pay was a "hard go" even with most of your expenses paid by the government.

So, I enquired about working part time in the nearby city after my duties were finished at the 15th Base Post Office each day. The commander gave permission to do this and I applied at the local USO.

The only jobs available at that time were for an elevator operator and manager of the Roof Top dance floor. I agreed to take either job and it ended up that I did both. This was very interesting work and I made more money at this than my military check each month.

I met many of the local girls at the dances held on the roof top and running the elevator proved to be interesting also. I'm reminded of an unusual passenger that I transported on the elevator one night.

The activities had finished on the dance floor for the night and everyone had left for home or wherever they were going next. I had a couple more hours to put in as elevator operator.

I stopped the elevator on the second floor of the seven story building. On this floor was the theater and many military men would watch a movie there. A marine entered the elevator and demanded to go to the roof top. He was told that the top floor had closed for the night and everything was dark up there.

He again demanded to go there, and since I could see that he was somewhat drunk, I agreed to humor him, especially after I assessed that he was much larger than me. We moved to the roof top, opened the door and showed him that everything was closed down.

He didn't want to get back on the elevator so I closed the door and left him in the dark. There was a security man on a lower floor and I summoned him to assist me with the marine.

We moved back to the floor where I had left the man in the dark. When the door opened he stood nearby where I left him and he was told that he must leave this floor. He entered the elevator without a word.

Halfway down to the street floor I saw some movement in the direction where the marine was standing. I looked up just in time to see a huge fist as it was about to engage my jaw! He hit me with a tremendous blow and I staggered a little and noticed out of the corner of my eye my security man trying to exit the elevator as it moved!

I managed to keep the marine at bay until we reached the first floor, opened the door and shoved him out. He staggered across the floor and attacked a sailor who was sitting and reading a newspaper!

That was not a real smart thing to do, because this sailor was huge. He scrambled out of the chair and flattened the marine!

About this time the military police appeared and hauled the marine away to the lockup. He probably slept off his inebriation in the brig and was released later to continue his partying on his shore leave time.

I learned a lesson or two that night, and put up with a lot of ribbing from my buddies later because the black eye the marine left with me was impossible to hide!

Paradise Awaited Me

In my last year of college at the University of Georgia, a group of students decided to make a weekend trip to Atlanta and get away from the stress of term exams. I thought it would be fun, so l tagged along.

It was Saturday night and we had heard of a nightclub called the Paradise Room in the old Henry Grady Hotel downtown on Peachtree street. It had a good reputation and a lot of single people frequented the spot on weekends.

I noticed a couple of cute girls sitting at a table and I went over to ask one for a dance. A band was playing a slow number like "Blueberry Hill" and I figured I could negotiate that without falling down.

To my surprise, the young lady agreed to dance and we proceeded to whirl about the floor! She was friendly and smiled and laughed a lot! I liked that, and after talking a while we both found a lot of things we had in common. For instance, she was raised on a farm in north Georgia and knew all about picking cotton, etc.

We became good friends and dated occasionally as I was finishing my last year of schooling. After graduating I moved to Atlanta and started to work for a newspaper as news editor.

During that year we became engaged and were married on Armistice Day of 1950. Two years later it was changed to Veteran's Day. Either way it was a day of celebration and that was a fitting memorial for our wedding. The entire country now celebrates our wedding anniversary with a lot of parades and fun programs!

We have had fifty-four of these celebrations and are looking forward to more! We met in Paradise and it has been that ever since! Sure, there have been a few bumps in the road but none we couldn't maneuver over or around.

A few years after our marriage we were blessed with two beautiful daughters and watching them grow up gave us a lot of joy! Many memories have been built as they went through their teens, finished college, and married later.

They each have three children, giving us six grandchildren to watch the growing process all over again. All of our children and grandchildren are Christians, a fact that we are extremely proud of!

One day when our children were small and Christmas was approaching we were wondering if we would have a white Christmas this time. It was getting cold and it was a possibility.

As a kid growing up in south Georgia, I don't remember ever having snow for Christmas. It was a rare occasion when snow fell that far south. But we always cut a pine tree from the woods behind our house and decorated it with homemade things.

We would take colored paper and cut it in pieces and glue it together in rings. Each ring was joined into a chain to place around the tree. We had no electricity for lights, so it just sat there, without much personality. There were no gifts because our parents had no money to buy any. A few oranges and apples were usually bought. That was Christmas as far as the commercial part was concerned.

But we did place a lot of emphasis on the religious aspect and gathered at the churches to sing carols and put on Christmas plays.

As I was thinking about the possibility of a white Christmas that year, an amusing aspect went through my mind. My wife had always had a white Christmas, every year that she had been in the world! That is until she was married.

You see, her maiden name was White, and regardless of the weather she always had a White Christmas! When she married, her name was changed and no longer had White Christmases, unless it snowed!

In fact, we must have had a "storybook" wedding, because Snow White, as in Snow White and The Seven Dwarfs, probably was a cousin of my wife! Also, Bing Crosby became famous with his song about "White Christmas!"

With that I'm leaving this subject, because I think I have stretched it a little "thin." Humor is one thing that has held our marriage together, but "too much of a good thing is bad!"

The Honeymoon Celebration Started With A Bang!

My brother loaned us his new car for our honeymoon and this was a godsend because my old Studebaker would never have made the journey! We had planned a trip to the Smoky Mountains and had reservations at a hotel in Gatlinburg, Tenn.

We settled in our room at the hotel and the weather outside was cold! It was November and near freezing.

We turned the electric heater as high as it would go, anticipating a cozy night. Later we awoke to a room full of almost unbearable heat! It must have been 125 degrees and it was a wonder the room had not caught fire!

We opened the door and turned off the heater. We almost froze then! Not a good way to begin a honeymoon! But newlyweds are supposed to snuggle and the weather was cooperating!

Later in the week, we drove by my wife's parents' home in north Georgia. We were having a good time getting acquainted with everyone, when I noticed a lot of people gathering at the house. Some were neighbors and some relatives.

I thought, "they must think I am an important person, and everyone came to meet the new husband."

I soon found why the crowd had gathered, and seemingly all at once! Everything got so quiet you could hear a pin drop.

All of a sudden there was a thunderous explosion! It was followed by more quiet. Then another explosion, louder than the first, erupted close by!

My wife and I stood there with our mouths hanging open! We didn't know whether to run or stand still! It seemed the entire county was being attacked by a mad bomber!

Then, all around us, the crowd permeated the air with laughter! They seemed to know something that we didn't!

It turned out that a couple of my wife's brothers had set off two sticks of dynamite and the neighbors wanted in on the fun! The boys worked for the state highway department and had access to the explosives. Everyone was in on the surprise except the bride and groom!

We had no warning that this was about to happen and it scared the living daylights out of us! The ground underneath us shook with the tremendous explosion!

When the initial shock wore off and we realized that we had been the butt of a huge practical joke, we decided to join in the fun! Never had I heard of anything like this. I had heard of "shotgun" weddings but never dynamite!

So our marriage started off with a "bang" and after that I guess we were conditioned for anything that was to happen later. There probably were some smaller explosions that occurred throughout our marriage but we managed to control them before they got out of hand!

Like the time I invited a customer, his wife and two children to spend a few days at our home. Somehow I had managed to not inform my wife until they had arrived! After, and during, the visit we did have a small explosion or two, but I lived through it!

Then there was the time we rented a small house in Panama City Beach, Florida for a week's vacation. Some of our relatives learned we were there and assumed it was all right to move in with us for the week! All that cooking and washing dishes for the mob wasn't our idea of an ideal vacation. We had a few spats but nobody lost their lives!

After we returned home we looked at and bought a new home. It was a nice three bedroom home but we didn't check out the neighbors too well. Early one morning we heard some loud singing permeating the hills around the area! It seemed to be originating at a house behind ours.

Later we met the neighbors and found that they were well-known gospel singers who sometime practiced on their back porch. So we had a free concert often but it occurred sometimes when we would have rather enjoyed quiet!

While I am on the subject of explosions, reminds me of the time my daughter and family were visiting and we were subjected to an incident, which was not too astounding in my estimation, but of greater importance to a few others.

My wife and daughter decided to travel to a relative's home in a nearby city and were going to spend the day. They left specific instructions to look after three kids until they returned that evening.

It seemed like a good time to cut down a pine tree that was too near the house. So my son-in-law and I cut the tree down and gathered the branches and debris in a pile on the gravel driveway.

The branches and leaves were green and I foresaw that they would be difficult to burn. So, not having anything else to pour on the debris like diesel oil, I poured a generous portion of gasoline in the pile.

My son-in-law said he would toss a match into the pile. I cautioned him to stand as far away as he could when he threw it.

He tossed the match and the result was deafening! I stood there at a safe distance with my mouth hanging open! The first words he could utter were, "do I have any eyebrows?" I looked and assured him they were there, but probably rearranged."

The kids came running out of the house and the older daughter told her dad, "I bet my mom will never let you keep us again, while she is away!"

A neighbor ran down the hill and asked if everyone was all right! He looked excited and must have been expecting to see a terrible disaster! Another neighbor came over and said the explosion had shaken a large picture off his wall! Later I noticed a picture over our fireplace mantel hanging crooked.

The neighborhood soon returned to normal, after finding that no one was hurt. That is until my wife and daughter returned later that evening! No further explanation will be given, but it is safe to say that they were not pleased!

A very important lesson was learned that day! Young people and old people, *never start a fire with gasoline!*

The Good Lord must have been with me one day as I was taking my wife for a short drive to get her out of the house, following a minor surgery. It was her first time away from the house, after being confined and she was still somewhat weak!

The fuel indicator in the car showed the gas was low, and I pulled into a service station to fill the tank. A Wells Fargo armored truck was sitting between two gas tanks and the others were busy with customers.

The vehicle was preventing anyone from using the two tanks, since there was not enough room to pull up. I waited and I waited! The truck just sat there! I turned my car around and backed toward one tank. Before I could get close to the hose, the driver in the armored truck pulled forward and prevented me from reaching it.

This made me somewhat angry, and I walked to the door of the vehicle and pecked on the glass window with my car keys. I intended to get the driver's attention and ask him to back away from the pump.

As I looked at the tinted window, I got a good look at some threatening object pointing directly at my head! It was a huge weapon and it was getting larger by the minute!

Moving away from the truck, I walked into the store to complain to the manager. There stood another guard, who was collecting the receipts for the day. I told him what happened and he nonchalantly informed me that he would be out of my way shortly.

The store owner said the driver had been robbed recently, and must have thought I was trying to set up some sort of robbery.

In the meantime, my wife was getting nervous, not knowing what was going on! She was already in a weakened condition and this couldn't be helping much. I returned to my car and drove to a competitor, where I filled my tank. I didn't need the aggravation that day!

After refueling, we drove back toward home and passed over a bridge with a small creek underneath it. On the other side of the bridge two low-flying ducks emerged from the creek, and just missed the car! At least I thought they did!

Arriving back home, I parked the car and went around to help my wife out the door. In front of the vehicle I was astounded at what

I saw! There, lodged in the grill was a big Mallard duck! Evidently the duck didn't make it safely by the car back at the bridge.

Later when I reported the damage to my auto insurance company, they were a little skeptical. So I sent them a picture, showing the poor creature embedded in the grill. As they say, "a picture is better than a thousand words!"

After all that had happened that day, we made a decision not to leave again. I almost got shot, killed a duck and I didn't want to tempt fate again!

My First Law Case And The Judge's Attention-Getting Decision!

It was in the early nineteen fifties and I was almost through with my studies for a degree in law. I was pretty confident that I knew the law and was eager to get tested. Little did I know that the first test was forthcoming so soon.

The new northeast expressway had just been built out of the large city where we lived, and most of the drivers were not used to driving on it yet. There were many accidents on the road since the traffic moved faster than the two-lane road we were used to. Also, some drivers would stop dead still on the road and cause pileups.

That was the case on a Monday morning as I headed downtown to my job. Everybody was in a rush to get somewhere that day. In the middle of the rush a lady driver ahead of me got startled at something and stopped dead still in the middle of the road!

I could not stop in time to avoid her car and plowed into the rear. About four others behind me did the same thing. Fortunately, nobody was injured and we exchanged insurance information, phone numbers, addresses etc. while we were awaiting the police.

The policeman gave all of us tickets and we were required to be in court the next week. I noticed that the policeman had listed the accident as having occurred on the wrong date. So, being the smart law student I thought I was, I said to myself, "self you have a great legal defense for this case, you can prove you were in church at the time stated on the ticket, the day prior being Sunday."

The judge called the woman who caused the accident to the stand and heard her story. He then told her to sit down. My time came and the judge asked me what was my plea, guilty or not guilty. I proudly told the judge my plea was "not guilty" because I could prove that I was not anywhere near the scene of the accident at the time that it was charged.

This declaration must have struck the judge the wrong way. He told me in a stern voice, "Son, just shut your mouth and sit down over there!" Well, you could have knocked me over with a feather! I had no idea that judges took this kind of attitude in a public court! So, I did as I was told, sat down and shut my mouth!

After all involved in the accident had entered their pleas, the judge told all of us that it was his intention to sentence all to two night sessions of drivers' school. He called me back to the stand and asked if I still wanted to plea "not guilty." I replied, "no sir, I want to change my plea to "guilty."

The judge seemed amused with the situation and told me that if I had pursued my original plea I probably would have been successful, but that he figured I could use the drivers education sessions.

I thanked the judge and left the court feeling that I had learned a valuable lesson. First, try not to irritate him with too much confidence and knowing information, especially from a law student's perspective. Also, even though you might be right, real court cases just don't proceed as they appear to on TV, or as you might have been taught in the law school room!

I never intended to be a lawyer, however, but the basic knowledge has been helpful throughout my life. This was the first time to appear as a defendant before a judge or jury, and it also was the last time.

The Stone Mountain Adventure

Fresh out of college, I was beginning a new job as news editor for a Decatur, Ga. weekly newspaper in 1950. The editor and owner, a prominent legislator in the Georgia House, assigned me to write an article about new developments planned for Stone Mountain Park.

The park was to surround the mountain, the largest exposed mass of granite in the world, and a motorized lift was being planned to carry people to the top.

Arrangements were made with a State Park Ranger to meet a photographer and myself at the foot of the mountain, a popular place for the locals to begin their climb on foot to the top. A makeshift road had been constructed to haul building materials up the mountain.

The ranger met us with his jeep, the only vehicle allowed on the rough steep incline. So the three of us climbed aboard the jeep for the scary ride.

The journey up was uneventful and the view from the top of the mountain was fantastic. You could see the city of Atlanta some twenty miles away and in all directions the sights were unbelievable!

We gathered our information and pictures for the story and learned of a building that was to be built on top with the necessary lightning rods to the ground, since the mountain suffered many strikes, being the tallest point around.

Then we began our descent down the mountain and came to the steepest part and the ranger spied an object that had dropped from the jeep on the way up. He stopped the vehicle and pulled the emergency brake on, got out of the jeep and picked up the object.

The photographer sat in the front and I in the back. Suddenly, the brake snapped off and we began a fast trip down the side of the mountain towards a sheer drop off! I scrambled out the back onto some granite rocks and the photographer was fighting to reapply the brakes. Shortly before the jeep would have tumbled off the side of the mountain, my companion got the vehicle stopped!

Stunned from the experience I sat on the rock for some time trying to get my senses back to somewhat normal. After all three of us calmed down and got our nerves functioning again the ranger undertook the job of driving us back to the foot of the mountain.

Back on level ground we were thankful to have survived the trip! We had learned some safety lessons, gathered the necessary information for the story and truly grateful that we had not become the news story ourselves!

A Message From The Dead

Two years out of journalism school, I was working for a network news organization in a large city and my beat was generally at the state capitol. However, the local office was understaffed and I was assigned to cover anything that came along.

I had to be in the office each day (or night) at four thirty in the morning in order to get the network news to the various subscribers for their six-thirty radio broadcasts.

The day began as usual with a confusing array of duties only no one other than myself showed up for work. The network central office in New York began to send messages that a well known baseball player had committed suicide in a local hotel room.

Well, as a semi-experienced reporter, I could handle a normal amount of work but this seemed to be overwhelming with the extra duty and no one in the office to help. So the pressing news reporting was delayed somewhat.

As soon as I could get to the story I called the police and several sources for information and was getting routine accounts until I talked to a bystander who had witnessed the hotel cleanup in the room.

It seems that the man had shot himself as he was sitting in the bathroom. When the shooting was over the man fell and lodged himself between the commode and the wall. After the detectives finished their work they instructed two workers to remove the corpse to be carried to the morgue.

As the workers reached down and each took an arm to dislodge the dead man from his position, they began to lift him away from the commode. When he was lifted into a sitting position, the corpse's mouth flew open and a gargling sound said "aah aah"!

The two men dropped the dead man and scrambled out of the room! Never had they been confronted with a situation like this! There was a simple explanation for this, I learned, for there was just enough air left in the dead man's stomach to cause this reaction as he was doubled up and being moved.

At any rate this caused a great commotion but there was no way that this could be included in my news story since I would have been labeled an insensitive clod!

But I finished the story and got my other tasks under control and the boss strolled in several hours late. He had been out boozing most of the night and needed time to sleep it off.

The New York office began to pressure my boss for somebody's head because the suicide story was delayed. So, my head was the only one available, except the boss's, and it was easy to figure which it would be.

I was fired and that probably was a good thing because I found another job that was considerably less stressful and paid over twice as much!

Sometime, I believe, you are rescued from a dead-end situation to move on to bigger and better opportunities! As I look back this was true in my case!

A Shocking Situation

Many years ago when our two daughters were toddlers, my wife left me in charge of their safe-keeping while she ran an errand. I dutifully watched over the children for some time, for they were my pride and joy.

Soon my mind was diverted by another matter and I needed to go into an adjacent room to get something. I left the room for just a moment, thinking that the children could not get into any trouble.

But, as soon as I moved into the next room, the lights went out in the house and a loud yell was heard! I rushed back into the room where I had left the two children playing and the younger child was sitting next to the wall with a pair of scissors in her hand.

She had a dazed expression on her face and was just sitting there! So I picked her up to see what the problem was and she started crying. I looked at the scissors she held in her hands and saw that about one inch on both blades had been burned off.

An electrical socket on the wall got my attention next and it dawned on me what had just happened. The toddler had taken the scissors and inserted them into a wall socket, not just any socket, this was a 220 line that had been used for a window air conditioner!

She could have been killed on the spot but she must have inserted both ends of the scissors at the same time and the circuit ran through the scissors only. She was unharmed as her Guardian Angel watched over her!

Needless to say, I gave thanks that my poor babysitting did not cause a catastrophe and all was well with the world! Well, it was somewhat o.k., at least until my wife got home!

By the way, the child never stuck anything in an electrical socket that didn't belong there after that experience.

The Grinning Raccoon Chasing Two Dogs Down A Street

It was close to midnight when I opened the back door of our home to place the garbage in the large can left there for that very purpose. This was a cold winter night and I was responding to a request from my wife.

As I opened the door a large raccoon began to move rapidly away from the area and I could see the reason immediately! Garbage was strewn all over the ground!

I remembered on several occasions the last few weeks it appeared that something had rummaged through the garbage and left a mess to clean up but I couldn't figure out what it was. So, this was the culprit!

Several neighbors had a similar problem and most of us blamed it on rogue dogs that seemed to rove in groups.

After this incident, I tried trapping, scaring and finally killing the pest in order to get rid of him, but the 'coon was always one step ahead of me! Nothing seemed to work!

That is until the suggestion was made to poison the critter. This sounded like it was about the only thing left, because this animal was very smart! But we did not have any poison.

So, we searched the medicine cabinet for something that might make the raccoon sick enough to go away. My wife came up with a bottle of very old hormone pills that had been outdated for some time.

The pills were mashed and spread over a couple slices of bread and placed in a prominent spot over the garbage inside the can. The lid was left partly open because we didn't want to make it very difficult to get into.

The next morning we checked out the garbage can, and sure enough, the bread was gone and we knew he had eaten the hormone pills! We had no inkling of what the result would be, if any. However, we did not have long to wait because we heard a terrible commotion on the street in front of our house!

Rushing to the front door, we saw two neighborhood dogs running for their lives! In hot pursuit close behind was the 'coon who seemed to have a large amorous grin on his face!

We never saw that animal again and often wondered what happened to him. If he is still living, he must have some tall tales to tell! If he died, he must have done so with a huge grin all over his face!

The Timely Death of a Fish, Snake and Fish Basket!

My wife likes to tell a fish story that involves a skirmish with a fish, a snake and a whole lot of scary movements! It all happened one hot steamy day in July on the shores of Lake Lanier in north Georgia.

She was spending a couple of days at our lake house with our two daughters, enjoying the atmosphere along with a little swimming and fishing. I was a traveling salesman and was away on a trip.

They had caught a small fish and placed it in a new enclosed basket when someone mentioned it being about lunch time. So the three left the dock for a sandwich at the house.

One of the daughters gulped her food down and returned to the dock to see the fish again. She immediately came flying back to the house exclaiming, "there's a snake in the fish basket!"

They all returned to the dock and was amazed at what they saw! There, halfway inside the fish basket was a large snake of undetermined species! Inside its mouth was the fish scrambling around and desperately trying to get out of the snake. The reptile could not back out the small opening it entered because the fish made the snake larger than the wire hole!

His tail was threshing about wildly outside the basket and the lake water was boiling with activity!

In the excitement that followed my wife jumped into action! She grabbed a garden rake nearby and attacked the snake! In the ensuing action, the snake, the fish and the brand new fish basket were all killed on the spot! Later, all were buried in the same hole that was dug close by!

The moral to this true story seemed to be to temper your greed with a little common sense or make sure there is a way out of a predicament before you enter it! This snake did neither!

Our house on the lake became a popular place for us, several neighbors and relatives to visit. It was hard to find time to go there, since it was fifty miles from home and our work. But holidays were very enjoyable!

We had a small motor boat and dock and they were both used for fishing, swimming and learning to water ski! The motor needed work, however, and it turned out to be a daunting task to ski behind the boat, when the boat motor wouldn't idle.

I remember one day when I was determined to get up out of the water on the skis! Since the boat wouldn't idle, my wife driving had to pass by me in the water as slow as possible, and I was holding the rope handle. As she came by I made an effort to follow on the skis!

There was a little problem, however, because the rope became entangled around my neck and the result was a near strangling! Not really! Just like to kid my wife about trying to do away with me and get my money! That wouldn't work either, since I didn't have any!

I finally became able to ski and found out that it was more fun than the learning process! However, the fun soon goes out of it too, when you are middle-aged. It became more work than fun!

Numerous times when we were on the lake in the boat, a bad storm would come up. One such occasion the sky became dark and threatening and my wife told me to quit fishing and head for home. At this time we had a pontoon boat and it was somewhat slow.

Nevertheless, we started back and the storm soon overtook us. The wind was blowing something fierce and the thunder and lightning was frightening! We turned in to a small marina and tied the boat to a piling.

The boat had a top but the wind was blowing the rain straight across us and we got soaking wet! Lightning seemed to be striking all around us and there was a tall metal pole near the boat!

It was over pretty quick and two boys who had pulled their boat in the same marina, came over to inquire if we were all right. I thanked them for their concern and told them we were o. k., just a little nervous!

After that we were more cautious when we were fishing or just cruising the lake! We found that it would be better to err on the better side of caution than the other!

102

The lake house was located at Flowery Branch, Ga., just off Jim Crow road! How either got their name I suppose I will never know, and that's probably more information than I really need!

It was a three-bedroom house that we moved fifty miles to a vacant lot on Lake Lanier, a large body of water with more than five hundred miles of shoreline.

There was a community deep well for water and in the summer on occasions the water would become scarce and dry up. One day a neighbor on the nearby hill came to our house and asked if the water was still running at our location.

My wife told her that it was and if she needed water, she was welcome to get some. The lady seemed delighted and carried a bucket full back to her house.

A few days later we were in a neighborhood store and the owner told us that there had been considerable excitement on the hill in our area a few days before! He then told us the story of a police raid made on a house up on the hill!

It turned out that the house was being used to store about two tractor-trailer loads of stolen appliances and household goods. It was the very house occupied by our visitor who wanted to get some water a few days prior!

We had remembered seeing her sitting on the porch, rocking a baby and putting up appearances of a normal family living in the house!

However, when the place was raided, the police found that the thieves using the place were police officers from a neighboring county. They were arrested and the merchandise was confiscated!

We often wondered if the lady was really in need of water that day, or if she was "casing" our lake house to see if there was anything of value that was available!

We never did get to really know our neighbor on the hill and that probably was a "good thing."

There were a lot of good neighbors around us, however, but not nearly as memorable and infamous!

Camper Rocking, Sheet Metal Flying And People Holding On

In the 90's my wife and I decided to take our camper to Flagler Beach, Fla., for a short respite from the daily grind. It was in the early Spring of the year and we had a spot for the camper that was almost at the water's edge. The weather was wonderful and the beach was busy.

About the second night, there came up a storm that we would remember the rest of our lives! It was about midnight when the worst of it arrived at the beach and a ferocious wind accompanied by lightning and thunder encompassed the area. We had visions of the camper being blown into the Atlantic ocean.

Across from the campground was a mobile home village and we could hear aluminum siding and other debris flying through the air and slamming into anything that was in the path of the wind. Many mobile homes were losing their carports and anything that was loose.

As the storm worsened, I heard some activity in the camper and looked up to see my wife moving rather fast. I asked, "what are you doing?" She replied in a positive manner, "I am going to the concrete building where the restrooms are. I think we'll be safer there."

By this time the rain was coming down in sheets and the wind was blowing so hard you could not see your hand in front of your face! But we made our way to the building and heard several voices inside. One man said, "come on in, we are all in the ladies toilet."

Indeed they were and some people were using the stalls out of necessity caused by the scary storm. Others were listening to a portable radio trying to get information on the weather.

Finally the stormy conditions lessened and the campers returned to their portable homes. The next day was almost as scary when we surveyed the damage, with all the stuff laying around where it didn't belong. Just to the back of our camper lay a huge sign that could have fallen on the vehicle but just missed it.

As we were assessing the damage and getting our things back in order, we received a telephone call. It was our neighbor back home. He said, "you need to come home because we have just had a snowstorm and a large tree has fallen on the power line to your house!"

We knew the implications of this! It meant that with no power in the house everything in the refrigerator and freezer would be ruined, along with other dangers from the downed power line. It turned out that we couldn't return for about three days since the snow made it nearly impossible to get there.

Tornadoes and storms seem to have been a part of our lives constantly while growing up and the years since.

On a business trip to Chicago one summer my wife and I took our two daughters along. We were all enjoying the scenery between Georgia and Illinois and the traffic was not bad as we drove along.

In the summer it seems that the states of Indiana and Illinois are plagued with several tornadoes each year.

As we came within a two hour's drive to our destination the weather became ominous looking! Dark clouds began rolling by and the wind was growing. Soon the rain came and thunder and lightning followed!

My wife was driving and the storm became so bad she could not see the road ahead! We came to a driveway and she turned in, stopped and we braced for the storm! The car began to rock violently with the high winds and we seemed to be in great danger!

The storm subsided, leaving the entire family well shaken! I got out of the car and looked around to see where we were because when my wife drove in you couldn't see beyond the windshield, hardly!

I was alarmed to find that we had parked directly under a huge oak tree and that we could have been crushed by the tree or some of it's limbs if had been blown down!

However, we were thankful we had weathered what we later learned was a tornado, and that it had done a lot of damage in the area!

After completing our business in Chicago, we decided to take the long route home and travel a couple of days down the famous Route 66! The first night we stopped at a motel that looked pretty good from the outside. It wasn't bad on the inside, as we looked around.

I walked to the office to pay for the night's lodging and returned to the room. I found my wife and the two daughters standing on the beds making a lot of noise! They were hollering and pointing to a couple of small mice in the corner, that were probably more afraid of us!

The mice made a beeline for the hole around some pipes where they had entered the room and I called the manager for some remedy to the situation.

The manager said the motel was full and he did not have another room to move us to, but that he would stuff something in the hole to make sure the rats couldn't return! Needless to say, we spent a restless night and was happy for daybreak to come and we could resume our trip!

Since I traveled just about every week, seeing my customers all over the Southeast, I ran into a lot of bad weather. One such trip on my way to Mobile, Ala., the skies were very overcast.

It began to rain and I could see in front of me a tremendous cloud! It seemed to be traveling across the expressway which I was driving on. I slowed the car and noticed an 18-wheeler truck in the median, where the wind must have parked it just minutes before! No one seemed to be hurt, so I continued driving! On both sides of the road trees were laying all over the ground!

Turning on the radio to a local station, I heard a voice warning the county residents of the tornado that was in progress at that time!

I drove on toward my destination and soon saw no damage at all. I must have arrived at that point on the highway just minutes after the tornado did and I was very happy that I was not there at the same time!

Another time I brought the family to Florida and stationed them in a nice motel in St. Petersburg, while I called on customers in the southern part of the state. I was returning to the city by way of the Skyway bridge on the southside of town and it had been raining for some time.

Suddenly, as I got to the very top of the bridge, the wind became very strong! I was having a real hard time staying on the bridge! I suppose the rails would have prevented me from going over, but it was un-nerving, to say the least! I wasn't sure if it was a tornado or not, but my wife back at the motel said that it was!

We had a similar experience crossing the Mississippi River at Memphis, Tennessee in a motor home one time! The family was going out west on vacation and it was stormy weather. As we crossed the river, it was all I could do to keep the vehicle on the bridge and not being dunked in the water! We were happy to reach the other side of the bridge, where we stopped and gathered our wits!

Fish Tales–Some True, Some Not True And Some In Between!

Several years ago my brother and his wife invited my wife and I on a fishing trip off the shore near Panacea, Florida. We were going out in the flats and a few miles in the Gulf in a twenty- foot boat owned by a family member. Had we been able to see a day or two into the future, this trip would never occurred!

Nevertheless, our trip began early one morning and we were all full of excitement and anticipation! That is except my brother and he was the only smart one in the crowd. He decided not to go!

The water was fairly calm in the flats close to shore, but as we left land the boat began to rock with three or four foot swells! In fact we weren't very far out when my wife was struck with that dreaded rough sea malady--sea sickness! For her the entire trip was miserable.

We tried fishing close in to land but didn't seem to have much luck. About all that we caught were "grunts" and we preferred flounder, grouper, reds and other good eating fish! So the boat headed further out away from shore and soon we were past the last channel marker, which was seventeen miles!

The fishing was good and we were hauling them in every time we dropped the line. This continued most of the day until it was getting late. One of the ladies felt a big tug on her line and began to pull in a big one! As it came close to the boat we could see that it was a small shark! Someone wanted to pull it into the boat but most of us knew this was a real bad move, so the line was cut and he swam away.

The daylight was waning so we headed back to land. A few miles back the boat motor sputtered a time or two and finally quit! We were about fifteen miles from land and we were getting alarmed! We did have a ship to shore radio but we didn't want to use it for rescue purposes!

The boat operator soon discovered that one gas tank had been used and that all that was necessary was to flip a switch for the other to flow! Thank goodness! We resumed our trip.

However, we had covered another mile when the boat stopped again, but the motor was still running! The boat had come upon a sand bar and the water was only a foot deep! We were in trouble again!

We didn't know that the tide was in when we began our trip that morning and the sand bar, which we discovered later was about a mile wide, was well covered with water. Now the tide was out and the bar was barely covered!

So, we took turns getting out of the boat and pushing it about a mile until the sand bar had been passed over. By this time it was getting almost dark and we began our fourteen mile trip back to the dock.

The rest of the trip went without incident and we had a large catch of fish to clean when we arrived on shore. But, as they say, "all's well, that ends well." Despite the set backs along the way, the trip ended well and most of us had a good time! The brother was beginning to get worried, though, with us being late returning.

More Fish Stories

Our family loved to fish and it was only natural, I guess, that after we bought a seventy-five acre tract of land in North Georgia that we had to have a fishing pond! The land was located on a mountain top and a nice stream running through it.

So we contracted with a man to build a thirteen-acre lake and the earthen dam was built thirty two feet high. It needed to be this high because the lake area was located between two hills in a valley.

The lake soon filled and was stocked with bass and catfish and in a couple of years we had a very good fishing pond. Many days and nights were spent there living the "good life" fishing, relaxing and just getting away from the crowds and telephones!

Then one day a tragedy occurred at another lake in the northern part of the state. It had been an unusually heavy rainy season and a deep lake dam had broken and several persons were drowned as the water rushed down stream.

The government began to regulate all dams in the state over twenty-five feet high in the hope of heading off further dam-breaching incidents.

One day we received word that a state dam inspector had looked over our dam and declared it unsafe without a lot of cement reinforcing. What he was proposing to be done was more than the entire lake was worth. So we did the only thing that was acceptable to the inspector, emptied the lake!

We later learned that the dam was in pretty good shape and there were no people below it to be in danger, but the inspector had fallen in the process of examining it and had broken his leg! This had evidently put him in a bad frame of mind and he must have taken out his venom out on the lake owners!

Adventure On The High Seas

My wife and I boarded a cruise ship in 1982 headed for several islands in the Caribbean Sea, leaving from San Juan, Puerto Rico. This was to be a two week journey with many stops and half way around visiting Caracas, Venezuela.

Caracas was a prelude as to what was to come later, since the inhabitants seemed to be in a state of unrest, with poverty evident everywhere. The tin and mud shacks we saw entering the city did nothing to raise our image of the city.

So, to get to the point of this story, after leaving Caracas the ship moved on to the island of Grenada, where we spent a memorable day! The natives were at the dock with their steel drums to entertain us.

The tour guide suggested we walk around the port city and see the market square, where the residents were offering vegetables, fruits, spices, handicrafts and local souvenirs. The heart of the city was only about two or three blocks and would not ordinarily take long to walk but the dirt and rock streets made it a slow go!

After this the tour guide said there were only two places to go sightseeing on the island.

These were the new airport and a waterfall in the center of the island, where a local diver would leap from the top!

Little did we know the airport would be a huge focal point the following year, since that was the time the U.S. invaded the island to rid it from the Cuban threat. We didn't understand the unrest on the island and the tour guides did not warn us not to stray far.

Nevertheless, we chose to take a taxi to the waterfall and see that instead of the airport.

The old vehicle was on its last leg (wheel) and we wondered if it would get us there and back! The narrow dirt road passed through banana plantations and that was the extent of sights along the way.

After about ten miles of wild riding we arrived at the waterfall. There were about twenty natives standing around with large machetes hacking on banana trees or anything available to hack on! We began to get nervous!

When we got out of the cab a midget appeared with a guitar and began to sing. He asked us if he could sing a song about us. We agreed and he began to compose some sort of tune with words about two tourists visiting the waterfall.

He led the way to the waterfall singing and playing his guitar all the way. Thankfully, it was only a short distance! There our attention was directed to the top of a fifty-foot ledge and a local diver jumped off and landed in a pool below.

This was the top attraction on the island, we asked ourselves? When it was over the midget informed us that we had to tip the diver, and we did so modestly. This did not impress the midget and he promptly asked for a tip for himself, since he had composed and sang a song to us as we walked to the waterfall!

I told him that he could split the tip that I had given him with the diver, and he began to show his displeasure!

We could see that we needed to leave this place as fast as possible, because the natives were getting restless. They began to hack at the banana trees faster and faster with their long knives!

My wife and I made it back to the waiting taxi without assistance from the midget and jumped in the vehicle with orders to move out fast! That he did, in a cloud of dust down the dirt road.

We arrived back at the cruise ship, nervous from our adventure and happy to get back in one piece!

Before we left to go to the waterfall, we did not know that we two were the only ones to choose that trip. The remainder of the cruise tourists took the trip to see the airport!

The cruise continued after all were aboard again, but this island was the most memorable of the trip!

The Perils of Being
A Traveling Salesman

Every once in a while a person has to reassess his progress in life and change his goals accordingly. So it was with me in the late 1950's, when I decided to go in business for myself as a manufacturer's representative. I had decided to sell lamps and lighting to dealers in the southeastern part of the States.

In order to do this, it was necessary to attend various shows held by the manufacturers around the country, to show off the products and make sales for upcoming seasons. Shows are held in High point, North Carolina, New York, New York, Chicago, Illinois, San Francisco, California and other cities.

One factory owner asked me to come to the Chicago market the first week in January, and for a Georgia boy who is used to milder weather, this was a scary thing! It was in the vicinity of zero degrees! My business was one week old and I was having to take a plane! I had never flown before!

Nevertheless, I headed to Chicago and about half way there the pilot came on the intercom to inform the passengers that the Chicago O'Hare Airport was closed because of a snowstorm.

We were informed that our flight would land at Saint Louis, Mo., and we would have to make other arrangements to continue the trip. Would you believe that I took a Greyhound bus from there and rode all night, arriving in Chicago the next morning?

I had previously made a reservation at the Palmer House Hotel for the night that I spent riding the bus. By the way, about half of this trip I had to stand since the bus was overloaded with passengers!

So, when I arrived at my hotel, I was informed that I did not have a room! I had not called the hotel and told them I was being delayed. I was getting somewhat irritated with the entire trip by this time!

Trying to find a solution to my predicament I went to our factory showroom and told my story to some of the salesmen gathered for the show. A salesman from Tennessee told me that he had a room with two beds and that I was welcome to use one of them. I couldn't believe my good luck!

I moved my luggage into his room and after going out to eat we decided it was bedtime, because we had to be at the show early the next morning. I settled in my bed hoping for a good restful night.

Within seconds my roommate began to snore and it got louder and louder! I pulled my pillow over my head but this did not help! I didn't have any cotton but I stuffed some toilet paper in my ears. Nothing would drown out the rasping, gasping, choking, grinding and sawing noises! I had never heard anything like it!

I lay there all night, wide awake and sleepless, wishing that I had found some other remedy for my problems.

The morning finally came and the salesman awoke rested and ready for the day's work. I told him what had happened during the night and he said he was sorry, that he had forgotten to tell me that his wife said he snored.

Well, I got on the phone and began to call hotels around the city, hoping to find another place to stay. I found a room at another hotel and thanked the salesman for his hospitality. He could see that by this time I was about to drop from the lack of sleep and rest and told me he did not blame me for going.

It was cold outside and you couldn't hardly stay on the streets but a few minutes or your ears would freeze and fall off! I had never been so miserable in my life!

Somehow I made it through the week, with a little sleep, and learned a little more about the business I was commencing. One thing I learned was never to go to Chicago in January!

So I returned home with a wealth of information, but most of it unusable in the advancement of my new business. In time I did overcome my slow start and the manufacturer's representative business was good to me and my family. In fact, my wife and I worked at it until our retirement about seventeen years ago.

For twenty eight years my wife and I owned and operated a lamp and lighting showroom for wholesalers in the Atlanta

Merchandise Mart. Only dealers were allowed in the mart for shopping. Sometimes celebrities were escorted through the building as a courtesy visit.

Lots of work was involved in getting the showroom ready for markets held four times each year. As we were placing lamps to be displayed one day, a young man working for us let out a yell that could be heard all around!

We ran over to check on his well-being and he exclaimed, "I just got a jolting shock from one of the lamps!" Now, in my many years in the showroom I had never received an electrical shock, so l played the incident down.

He insisted that a particular lamp was defective and asked me to check it out. I plugged the lamp into a socket and found that it was! It gave me a sizable jolt, convincing me without any doubt! Later I found there was a short circuit in the lamp and fixed it. I was hoping the factory would never ship lamps like this to the dealers!

However, a dealer did come into the showroom one time and related how a customer had switched a lamp on in his store and the result was a flash of fire across the floor about fifteen feet, as it followed the cord! It left a burned mark on the floor where the cord lay!

Fortunately no one was injured and the dealer was very understanding in this instance! We offered to make amends, but he told us to "chalk it up to experience!"

One day during a show one of my major factory owners sat down in a chair to rest a little, since it was pretty tiresome standing up waiting on customers. As he sat, there was a loud commotion coming from his direction!

Running over to check on the situation, I found my rather large and well-fed boss sitting flat on the floor where the chair had given way and deposited him! He wasn't injured, only his pride! He had, however, attracted a sizable group of people, who were gawking at him on the floor! He was somewhat embarrassed!

This was only mildly embarrassing when compared to what happened in a similar showroom in another city, however. We always had soft drinks for customers in our showroom, but this one served mixed drinks in the back and it attracted some shady characters.

One day a lady went to the back room to get a soft drink and as she bent over the drink machine, a customer who was somewhat inebriated grabbed her in a place he should not have! After jumping about three feet into the air, the lady flattened the drunk and ran from the room!

The Coffee Pot that Brewed More than Coffee

It was a beautiful fall day in south Georgia and there was a change of weather in the air. The leaves were dropping from the trees and it was obvious that cooler weather was on the way. As a salesman on the road I thought the fact that cooler weather coming would enhance my sales of a new coffee pot that the factory was promoting. People drink more coffee in cool weather, I thought.

So the first dealer I called on that day was a hardware store and it looked like they could use the coffee pot as a leader to get customers into the store since it was relatively cheap.

I grabbed my sample, entered the store and engaged the owner in my sales pitch. He thought that my idea and product looked promising, but he had some reservations. The dealer said that the electric pot, which was only a hot water heater, would likely give a shock to anyone stirring the water while it was heating.

"This product is U L approved and my sales manager assured me that it is perfectly safe," I told the buyer. To this he replied that he would buy the coffee pot if I would fill it with water, plug it into the socket and test the safety part by sticking my finger in the water.

Since the factory man told me that the pot was safe I thought this was a sure thing to get a large order, so I told him I would be happy to test the product.

115

So, I filled the pot with water and plugged it into the electric outlet and stuck a finger in the water. The resulting jolt sent me flying into a display of pots and pans and I was somewhat dazed!

When the dealer saw that I wasn't hurt he almost died with laughter! He said that he noticed that I had my other hand on a metal water cooler but too late to warn me. Somehow the grounding of the metal water cooler helped to deliver a good electrical shock to me.

To my amazement the dealer then gave me an order for the coffee pots, saying that my confidence in the product and convincing sales pitch was enough for him!

I learned later that the electric appliance was perfectly safe if the directions on the box were followed. I found also that it is always best to read them!

After the rules and directions were learned this product became a best seller for the company. The learning process, however, was somewhat shocking!

A Traveling Salesman Story that was About a "Drive-In"

There are many traveling salesmen stories circulating around the country but many of them are not necessarily true. This one is and would have been highly amusing but for the gravity of the situation.

As I was traveling through Alabama for my job selling lamps to dealers in the state I arrived in the city of Huntsville and checked into a motel for the night. Another salesman, who was a good friend of mine, was checking in also.

We decided to go to a nearby cafeteria to eat after we checked in and we proceeded to do so as soon as we got settled into our separate rooms. The salesman (I'll call him Arthur) decided that his car was standing too far away from the curb and it needed to be parked closer to the door. We were going to the cafeteria in my car.

I waited by the door to my motel room as Arthur, who was in his eighties and still working, sat in his car and began to move his auto. Something told me to move further away from the door to his room and I obeyed.

In a flash Arthur shot past me and drove into his motel room! Over the curb, through the glass and brick front and stopped about halfway into his room!

I will never forget that picture. Arthur was sitting stiff-armed and hands on the steering wheel in the car and the car was inside the room. He looked dazed and he muttered some kind of "cuss" word and said loudly, "Well, anybody could have done that!"

After I found out that he was not hurt (nothing but his pride) Arthur got out of his car into the motel room and we assessed the damage. His car was close to being totaled and the room was uninhabitable that night! A morbid sense of humor at the situation overcame both of us at that time and we had a good belly laugh!

We did finally get to the cafeteria and neither had much of an appetite. Arthur had to move his things to another room and a tow vehicle had to remove his car to a better parking place. He blamed the accident on the fact that his foot slipped off the brake and onto the gas pedal. I think that soon after that incident Arthur made a decision to limit his driving and finally retired.

Salesman Was All Choked Up

Many years ago while traveling as a salesman I found myself in Savannah, Ga. at the end of the day. Most salesmen stayed at certain motels while in town and if we wished to have dinner together we could check to see who happened to be there at that time.

It was such an occasion that day and I found several salesmen were staying at the same motel. So five of us decided to go to a real good seafood restaurant that night to eat and talk about the day's activities.

Things were going well. We were talking, laughing and eating our chosen food and enjoying our favorite stories.

Then all of a sudden, the person sitting next to me began gasping, choking and fighting at the air. He was clutching his throat and turning blue and leaning over in his chair. He began to fall out of the chair!

The salesman sitting on the other side recognized what was happening and grabbed him before he fell. He picked the man up from behind and began to perform the Heimlich maneuver. He had watched this being done on television just a few days before!

The choking man began to respond and forced out a big wad of food that had lodged in his throat. It was simply amazing! He paused a few minutes, thanked his rescuer and resumed eating again! He was o.k., but I think he slowed his eating after that.

This was the first time that I had witnessed a choking incident and the maneuver that was used to save the poor man was new to just about everybody. But thankfully, this observant man took the lesson to heart when he saw it on television, not knowing how soon he would be tested.

Salesman Loses His Pants!

Savannah, Ga. is a quaint city and many tourists flock there on vacations, business and other reasons. Many of us traveling salesmen loved to visit the town because of the good sales orders we received from dealers and the excellent restaurants there.

One such trip several salesmen checked into our favorite motel for the night and after having dinner together we settled in our individual rooms. Sleep was hard to come by that particular night for me, since the noise of the city was loud.

Nevertheless, the next morning the group got together for breakfast, and one salesman appeared to have on a pair of pants much too large for him. Before we could phrase our obvious questions, he began to relate his tale of horror!

During the night he was awakened by movement in his room. In the dim light he could make out someone going through his pants pockets! He was really alarmed!

Turning on the bedside lamp, he jumped out of bed intending to defend himself and property. The intruder bolted out the door, taking the salesman's pants with him! This turned out to be much more disastrous than it seemed. These were the only pair of pants the salesman had brought with him and they were "missing in action!"

He had several dealers to call on that day and he had no pants! Calling another salesman down the hall, he related his story and resulting plight! He was offered the loan of a pair and he gratefully accepted! However the victim of the burglary was much smaller and the trousers folded loosely around his frame.

We expressed our sympathy and as soon as it was safe to get away with it, we all broke out in riotous laughter at the sad- looking man in the very baggy pants! They never caught the burglar, but the salesman always brought along more than one pair of pants after that!

While in the same city that day, I called on a dealer and was given an order for lamps. He was in a good mood and evidently decided to have a little fun at my expense. He told me he and his employees had captured a rare animal and it was in a cage in a back storeroom.

It was one of only six captured in the world and was unusually fierce and dangerous, he said. It was called a "roustabout" and he wanted my opinion as to whether he should keep it back there in the cage.

I agreed to look the situation over, pleased that he wanted my opinion, and the man led the way to the back of the store where the animal was. In a dark corner of a cage, I could make out a fuzzy-looking object, but it wasn't moving.

Warning that I should approach quietly, he said the animal was high-strung and might break out and attack me! I was told to stand in a certain spot and the light would be turned on. He pushed a button and the fierce "roustabout" came flying out of the cage within six inches of my head!

I must have jumped six feet, trying to get away from the animal! It fell at my feet and I could see that it was not alive at all! It was a furry object made to look like an animal!

Realizing that I had been taken on a practical joke, I nervously tried to laugh with the others! I did my best to convince them the joke didn't work and didn't scare me. Little did they know! I really thought for a minute that varmint was going to chew me up and spit me out!

Savannah, Georgia is a very interesting and beautiful city on the southeastern coast and is normally full of tourists at any time of the year. Recently I read that the city is trying to develop a park on a site that has a considerable historic past.

On that spot the city fathers say a bloody Revolutionary battle occurred in 1779 and they are using radar equipment to find possible artifacts, trenches and earthen fortifications. British troops fought to drive back French soldiers and Colonial militiamen, who were trying to reclaim the city. Many deaths and injuries happened there.

Some ninety years later, during the war between the states, a building in the same general area was used as a hospital for Confederate soldiers. The building used at that time is still standing and is a furniture store now, according to the owner.

As I was calling on the furniture dealer one day, he invited me to come back to the store about midnight. He said that often he could hear the injured soldiers moaning and groaning up on the fourth floor of the building from the first floor where he was working!

He stated that he would go up to the top floor, which he used for storage, to investigate the loud noises and they would cease as soon as he entered from the elevator!

I didn't necessarily want to hear the agonizing noises he described, though, so l turned him down on his invitation!

After I finished my work in Savannah I traveled up the highway to Statesboro, Ga. and settled in a comfortable motel. About two o'clock in the morning I was awakened by a waterfall in my room!

I turned on the light and was astounded to see water flooding from the ceiling soaking all of my belongings! "Did one of the ghosts from Savannah follow me to this motel," I wondered?

I called the office and the manager hurried to my room. He surmised that a pipe had burst from the cold weather in the room above mine! When the surprises were calmed down, the manager gave me another room and offered to dry clean my clothes. They had not been damaged, however, and I settled on the dry room!

But I never found out if a stray ghost from that building down the road was irritated when I refused to come back at midnight to hear the groans and followed me to get revenge! However, on all visits to the dealer following that incident I kept a wary eye out for any unusual shadows or eerie happenings there!

Convention Trip to San Diego, California

While working in the home furnishing industry, especially lighting and lamps, it was only normal that I joined several associations that were involved with the profession. One in particular was made up of the manufacturers' representatives in the state and affiliated with the national group.

It was in 1973 that I became president of this state group and we were required to attend annual conventions in various parts of the country. One such convention was held in San Diego, California and my wife and I attended, along with several delegates.

After touring the city and completing the business of the association, we were rewarded with a trip over the border into Mexico! Our one-day trip was to Tijuana, Mexico and it took two large buses to carry the group.

We toured the city by bus and then began a walking tour in the center of the small tourist town. Everywhere we went were Mexican musicians serenading us! That night we ate at a large restaurant and were treated to all of the local delicacies along with local drinks.

Each table was adorned with many small bottles of tequila placed there for anyone to take with them after the meal. Most of the bottles disappeared as the crowd left the restaurant!

The two buses were filled and the trip back to San Diego was begun. Soon we were at the border and guards looked the first bus over and told the driver to proceed across. It was then our turn and the guards ordered everyone off to be searched. We did not know it but some of the people on the bus ahead decided to play a prank and told the guards to search us for possible drugs!

One person was loaded with the aforementioned bottles of tequila and did not know if they were legal or not! As we were filing off the bus he gingerly moved past a guard when he was busy searching another!

Having not found any drugs we were allowed to cross the border. The person that was loaded with the bottles never found out if they were legal or not! He didn't seem to want to find out at that time!

My Most Embarrassing Moment: Or No Place To Hide!

Have you ever been a victim of circumstance and bring untold embarrassment upon yourself or others? It happened to me soon after marriage when my wife was told she had to have a minor surgical procedure. It would be necessary for her to be put to sleep to undergo this. Note that it is usually a "minor" deal if it is happening to someone else, but if it is to be done on yourself, it is "major"!

Nevertheless, she was admitted to the hospital and was to undergo the ordeal the next day. She spent a restless night and so did I! I loved her very much and I sympathized with her on what she was about to endure.

Soon it was time to be carried from her room and into the operating room. I followed her as far down the hall as the medical staff would permit and wished her good luck!

It seemed to be an eternity before I received any word about the surgery. I imagined many things that could go wrong, and worried and worried!

At last, the doctor came into the waiting room and I was told that everything went well. My wife was fine and that she was still "woozy" from the medication and as soon as she recovered from the anesthetic would be returned to the same floor, but to another private room.

A nurse approached and told me my wife was on her way up in the elevator and I could see her within minutes. I was highly excited!

I stood by the elevator with anticipation, wondering how she would look! Soon the elevator door opened and the attendants rolled her out on a stretcher and her face was partly covered with the sheet that covered her body.

They rolled her down the hall to the room and I followed close behind. I noticed a couple of strange people tagging along and I supposed them to be hospital employees.

In the room the medical personnel lifted her off the cart and placed her on the bed and promptly left, after I thanked them. I saw the two people standing close to the bed observing my wife and I walked around them and looked down into my wife's face.

It wasn't my wife! It was some other woman and there I was getting close and personal while the two real relatives looked at me and wondering who I was and what I was doing there!

The truth of the matter grabbed me! I had invaded the privacy of a total stranger! I wished at that time I could have disappeared right into the floor! How embarrassing!

I mumbled some apologies, not knowing what I was saying and retreated out the door. The two ladies in the room still looked at me as if I was there to commit a crime.

Back in the hallway I saw another cart being wheeled from the elevator. I was in a state of shock and could only stand there. As it passed by I got a glimpse of the face looking up. It was my wife this time!

She was deposited in the room and I was left alone with her. There were no strangers standing around giving me suspicious looks!

Later I related the story as it had unfolded to my wife and she almost broke the stitches that the doctor had warned her about, saying that she was not to laugh much!

Embarrassing, absolutely! Never had an experience like it before or after!

My wife told of an embarrassing event happening in her home when her siblings were little. Some of them, that is. She was one of ten children and the second youngest in her family. One of her sisters was about nineteen years older and was just beginning to start courting.

A young suitor was visiting the girl for the first time and the sister wanted to make a good impression, because she was kind of "sweet on him." However, the old house was full of kids and family and they were having a hard time finding a little privacy.

The pair finally settled on an old settee, which was in a room used both as a "sitting room" and a bedroom. In one corner of the room was a bed with a feather mattress.

The couple began to talk intently and the young man was thinking of trying to hold her hand. Unknown to both of them a younger brother had hid under the bed and was staring at a bed pan under the bed.

When the pair began to get a bit closer together, they heard a noise behind them. They looked toward the bed and saw the kid scrambling out from under it. "Pee pot, pee pot," he yelled, and ran from the room! Evidently the odor of the utensil was more than he could stand!

The girl was mortified and the visitor was speechless! She began to chase the brother, intending to beat him up, but he outran her. I suppose little brothers are likely to do things like that.

Not long after that, the family had their local preacher over for Sunday dinner. It was customary for the adults to eat first and the children later.

The cooking was finished, the table was set and the group sat down and began to eat. Outside on a large rock, across from the kitchen, were all of the kids watching the activities inside.

One of the boys said, "look at the preacher, he's getting another chicken breast!" A few minutes later another brother muttered, "he's got the pulley bone this time."

Finally the kids were getting so hungry they couldn't stand it any longer. One of them yelled loud enough for the preacher to hear, "there ain't gonna be nothing left for us!"

It's not clear if the kids had their turn or if there was any chicken left. If so, it could have been like it was at our house. We ate the dark meat, legs, thighs, etc., because that was usually what was left! I was almost grown before I knew fried chicken came in white meat also!

Camping Became A Family Obsession

In the seventies the country was besieged with an oil shortage and gasoline prices began to climb higher and higher. Many of my fellow traveling salesmen bought some of the early diesel automobiles, but I couldn't bring myself to do this because they were very noisy and smelly.

However, the higher priced gasoline brought on poor sales of motor homes and campers, and dealers began to unload their inventory at unheard of prices. I loved camping but never had a real camper.

The temptation became too much and my wife and I bought a new motor home, believing that gas prices would go down soon. It was a beauty, completely contained, and even had a generator to power the appliances in the absence of electrical hookups. There was one problem though. It could not pass the gas stations as we drove along. It seemed to be thirsty all of the time!

Nevertheless, our family consisting of my wife and I and two daughters, took off on a trip out west that first summer, after the kids got out of school. We drove from Atlanta, Ga. to Hot Springs, Ark. and parked in a nice campground for the night. We were really enjoying the motor home!

After we had gone to bed a fierce thunderstorm arrived and lightning popped all around us. The thunder was deafening and the wind began to shake the motor home! This went on for a good hour and finally it was gone. The next day we considered the night's disturbance as a christening of sorts for the new vehicle!

From there we traveled to San Antonio, Texas, stopping at many gas stations as we went! Several of these I asked the attendants to check the oil in the motor but none could find the dipstick in the large motor.

Finally, we filled up the gas tank in Texas and I again asked that the oil be checked and was told the same thing. They could not find the dipstick! A local boy standing nearby said he knew where it was and proceeded to show us. It was well hidden at the bottom of the motor.

The service station attendant checked the oil and he could not find any! We had driven half-way across the United States in a new motor home and the oil was used up! Hoping for the best, we had the motor filled with oil again. There must have been a tad of oil left in it because it kept the motor from blowing.

After spending the night there we headed toward Albuquerque, N.M. The countryside was flat and as far as we could see were short scrubby bushes. The wind picked up and large rolls of tumbleweed began to cross the road in front of us.

The motor home would not go faster than thirty miles an hour, even when I would floorboard the accelerator. I thought, the motor must have been damaged while driving without oil!

We pulled into a gas station in Albuquerque, after an all day slow-moving trip, and related our thoughts to the attendant. He said nonchalantly, "you had head-winds blowing against you about thirty miles an hour." That meant, if we were traveling only thirty miles an hour, without the wind blowing against us, we would have been going sixty miles an hour! It made sense and I felt a lot better about the motor home.

Along the way we enjoyed many new sights because we had never traveled that far from home before. We saw the Grand Canyon, Brice Canyon, and finally made it to the Teton Mountains. This brought on another memorable experience that is dealt with elsewhere in this book.

The kids, who were in their teens at this stage of their lives, didn't seem too impressed with the trip even though they were exposed to many exciting sights and views. As we traveled along the roads they usually were laying in their bunks reading a book.

I said to them one day, "I bet you two are the only ones to travel across the United States flat on your backs, instead of sitting up and looking at the countryside!"

However, they were taking in more knowledge than I realized because they still remember much about the trip some thirty years later!

The trip back home was not as exciting as going out west because we were getting used to seeing things we hadn't witnessed before. We were getting tired of being away from home! Besides, we had just about given out of money!

Camping With Relatives Is An Eye-Opening Experience

Dan and Betty were the brother and sister-in-law of my wife, and they were frequent camping buddies of ours. They had their camper and we had ours. We have always believed that no camper or house is big enough for two families! Sooner or later joint ownership will cause problems!

Many memories were made camping with these two. Dan was a "jack of all trades," and a handy man to have around. He could fix just about anything, even if it took a little "rigging."

One trip with them, found us close to Monterey, California, in a campground atop a mountain, overlooking a race track for cars. We had a pretty good vantage point for the races. Several of the drivers were camping there also.

Dan decided that his Ford truck, that pulled his camper, wasn't running like it should, and he took this time to work on it. Soon he had parts laying all over the ground beside the camper! One of the racers, camped nearby, told him that he would never have undertaken that job. He told him, "you'll never get that motor back together again, and get it running!"

After about three days of stepping around the motor parts, we were beginning to think the same thing. But soon the motor was back together, after putting in some valves and rods, and other items.

He cranked the vehicle and it sounded like a freight train! I thought, "man, if we have to listen to that another two thousand miles, we'll all go crazy!" Dan said, "I know what the problem is, it's the timing chain."

I didn't know a motor had one, but thank goodness he did! After fiddling with it a few minutes he started the motor again and it "purred like a kitten." We couldn't believe our ears!

The truck ran perfectly for the remainder of the trip and our fears of having a vehicle that sounded like a "rattletrap" to listen to were resolved!

Prior to getting to California, we stopped at a campground in Arizona. Betty had made some vegetable soup and invited us over to eat. It was delicious and we slept late the next morning.

As I went out the door of the camper, there sat Dan working intently on some object at a picnic table. Going over after my curiosity had been aroused, I inquired as to what he was doing?

"I'm fixing Betty's teeth," he said. I thought he was kidding, until I could see that he had a set of "uppers" and a tube of glue nearby. But there he sat with the teeth in one hand and a loose one that he was trying to cement between them!

"I didn't know that you were a dentist too, with all of your other abilities," I kidded! He replied that it was a case of necessity. His wife had bit down on something at breakfast and the tooth had come out. I had just learned a few things, along with the fact that it is possible to make a temporary tooth repair, and another was that I didn't know that she had a set of false teeth!

She was a little embarrassed by all of this, so I didn't mention the incident again!

With the same pair we camped again at Ocean Springs, Miss. several years before they began to build all of the gambling casinos at Biloxi, nearby. With nothing to while the time away, we agreed to fish in a small lake on the property.

We got our poles and began to fish and were getting a lot of nibbles, but couldn't catch any. Suddenly Dan caught a three pound bass and was pulling him in! As he pulled the fish through the shallow water, that was filled with tall grass, the fish spit out the hook!

He was threshing about in the water, and looked as if he was going to get away! Dan was determined, however, and he grabbed a discarded two-by-four, laying nearby, and began to use it in a raking manner. He was successful in knocking it closer, where he grabbed the fish and brought it to the lake's edge.

The scene had been a comical one and I told him, "That's the first time I ever saw anybody catch a fish with a two-by-four!" We found another ability that Dan had!

A few years later we planned a camping trip to Branson, Mo. This was the last one, since he passed away a few years after that, when he was beset with Alzheimer's.

We were camped alongside the river that flows through the city and it rained several inches that week. The river rose and began to flood the area. The manager told all of us that we had to move out because the sewage facilities could no longer be used.

Dan refused to move because it was raining and he didn't want to drive in the rain. So we left and they planned to meet us in a city, about one hundred miles away, the next day.

The next day Dan got his camper ready and they left the campground. He stopped at a service station and inquired as to which road to take from Branson. The lady said, "Go to the top of the hill and turn right."

At the top of the hill he turned left and encircled the city, arriving back at the same station. Dan again inquired about directions and the lady told him, "I am going to tell you one more time, and I don't want you to come back!" She repeated the directions and it sunk in this time and he made the right turn at the top of the hill!

Later that day he met us at the appointed place. He passed the entrance to the campground and had to back up. As he backed and turned sharply, a corner of the camper caught the back window of the truck and broke it out! He finally arrived, set up his camper and settled in for the night! We spent the next day repairing the window of his truck, so that he and Betty wouldn't be exposed to the elements as they headed home.

Back To The Trip Out West And Into Canada

The trip over Mt. Laguna in southern California with a 34-foot camper was tedious. We were driving on Interstate 8 and noticed signs along the way, telling eighteen-wheelers to use another route over the mountain to San Diego.

Pretty soon we saw large wooden troughs by the side of the road, filled with water and a sign saying they were for the use of vehicles that needed water for cooling purposes. The mountain grade became steeper and steeper, and my van was "huffing and puffing" doing all it could, pulling the heavy load!

After stopping a couple of times for the engine to cool, we finally made it to the top! This was the steepest grade we had ever attempted with a camper and could see the reason for the signs below!

We spent a couple nights near San Diego and toured the city, the zoo and other sights. Getting back on the road again, we drove the coastal highway (California No. 1) toward Los Angeles.

A few miles on the road and my brother-in-law Dan, who was following in his camper, came on the CB and told me there was smoke coming from the back of our camper!

We pulled off the road to investigate and found an outside tire burning and emitting a terrible odor and lots of smoke! After putting out the fire, we replaced the tire with a spare and everything seemed ready to go again!

I looked back down the highway about half a mile and saw a crowd of people putting out a grass fire alongside the road. We reasoned that the burning tire had lost a few chunks as it rolled along, and set the grass on fire.

The grass fire was soon extinguished and we moved on. Since then, I noticed the state of California has passed some legislation to hold tourists liable for damages resulting from accidental fires of this sort!

We had previously visited Los Angeles and San Francisco, so we drove through these cities pretty much without stopping, except for gas. We did stop to see the Hearst Castle and further up the coast we spent the night near Carmel. There we were interested in seeing Clint Eastwood's Hog's Breath Saloon. We didn't partake, only looked, hoping to see the famous movie star! The place was crowded with tourists, but no star appeared.

On up the coast we traveled through Klamath and into the California redwood area. The No. 1 highway is a perilous drive in places, especially where landslides occur! At places, the road was one-lane and traffic was stopped to let cars go both ways. Pulling a camper, where the road dropped sharply to the Atlantic Ocean, was unnerving!

We marveled at the huge redwood trees and finally came to the "drive-through" tree. This tree had been cut out and a road passed through it. Of course, it wasn't large enough for the camper but later we camped nearby and came back with the van, and drove it through the tree! I have pictures to prove it!

Leaving California, we soon found ourselves going through Oregon and Washington. We were stopped at the Canadian border and asked if we had firearms, drugs and how long we intended to stay, and the purpose of our visit.

We passed the verbal test and no physical inspection was made. We must have looked honest even though we probably looked like the "Clampetts" on "Beverly Hillbillies," with two vehicles pulling large campers!

Vancouver is a large and beautiful city and is a magnet for tourists. Camping near the city, we spent a week in the area. We crossed over the large swinging bridge that is a popular attraction there. Loading the van on a ferry, we crossed the Strait of Georgia to Victoria Island.

The city of Victoria is unique, with its quaint old homes and Indian totem-poles. Along the Island, the main road passes through dense forests of redwood and cypress trees, many as large as the ones in the Big Sur Area.

From there, we took a mountainous route to Prince George and on to an Indian Reservation, where we camped beside a swift-running cold river. That night we noticed several campers coming from the north and stopping there for the night. Some were covered with a chalk-like mud so much that you could hardly see the windows!

They had taken the land route to Alaska and were returning. Some of the roads were gravel and it had been raining, covering the campers with a coat of Alaskan mud, that must have taken a week to wash off!

Dan and his wife were leaving us the next morning to take that same route overland. We had decided to drive over to Prince Rupert, on the coast, and take a ferry up the inland passage to Alaska, for a few days.

The camper was parked and we boarded the ferry, getting a nice cabin with twin beds. It was a large vessel and we understood that the waterway had some narrow passages that it had to maneuver through.

Going through Chatham Strait we visited Ketchikan, Alaska and on up the Clarence Strait to Wrangell, and Petersburg. Then on to Juneau, the state capitol. These cities are exciting places to visit, since they are different from anything in the lower states and have a lot of history in the building of each.

Each city we were allowed to get off the boat and walk around the business districts. I had heard that you might see bears just about any place on the trip and I was really making an effort to find one.

Suddenly, I spotted one and I began to point it out to my wife. She kept looking at the area that I was pointing, but she couldn't see it! I began to get irritated because she couldn't spot the bear!

Finally, she saw it. She said, "that is a dog you are looking at!" I looked again, and I could see that she was right. It was a large black dog! I was so disappointed and embarrassed and it was a big "let-down."

After that I quit looking for bears and was convinced I needed my eyes examined. I did this when I returned home and found that I had cataracts! I must have missed many of the sights on that trip.

Our trip took us on up the passageway to Haines and Skagway. We saw glaciers and mountains and many marvelous sights. One spot the mountains closed in on each side of the boat until you could almost reach out and touch the trees.

We were told that the ferry boats sometimes would have to catch the tide just right to get through this narrow place. If the tide was out, there wouldn't be enough water to float the ship.

As we returned, my wife and I were inducted into the Order of The Alaskan Walrus, an exclusive membership reserved for only the passengers on this ferry! We received a membership card, which we have today.

Back in Prince Rupert, we secured our camper and made ready to continue our trip across Canada.

Surely it was a Lifesaving Situation!

Camping in Canada was an experience of a lifetime, especially in the rocky Mountain areas of Jasper, Banff and Lake Louise, a few hundred miles north of the states of Montana and Washington in the U. S. It is just a short way from Calgary.

That is a very popular destination for tourists since the scenery is spectacular and the wildlife is plentiful. The campground was full when we arrived at Banff and we had to settle for a temporary parking space out in the "boondocks."

We were told if we would go to the office real early the next morning and stand in line with others, that we would likely get a regular space for the camper as people checked out.

I set my clock and woke up before daybreak and crawled out of bed. I dressed and made my way to the door of the camper. As I was getting into my van, I heard a growling noise and some rustling behind the trailer. Turning on the car lights, I was astonished to see a large bear, who had been prowling around the camper!

He stood there a moment and bolted for the nearby woods. It was eye-opening to see how fast such a large animal could move! He rose to his full height at a pine tree and looked the situation over. I was sure the bear was ten feet tall! Well, maybe six or seven. Anyway, I think he might have been more scared than I was, since I was inside my van.

But the important thing was that I had just saved my wife's life! She was sleeping inside the trailer and was in extreme danger! I'm convinced that bear would have created all sorts of havoc right at that very camper had I not been so brave as to scare him away! There probably were other lives nearby that I saved also.

At any rate, I went on about my business of getting a good camping spot, feeling good about my early-morning exploit, and anxious to tell the camp managers how brave I was.

The manager did give me a good camping spot for the week and promised to send someone out to capture the bear and move him, or her, to another location. I did ask for a camping space without bears!

Back To The Lower Forty-Eight

Yellowstone National Park, in the upper northwest corner of Wyoming is a marvel to see, and even more of an adventure if you are lucky enough to camp there!

We pulled into the park campground, along with our camping buddies, and settled down to new adventures. Again we were told that many bears roamed the area and to be aware of our surroundings at all times.

Moose, buffaloes and elk roamed about at will throughout the park, seemingly unimpressed by our presence.

The next day after arriving was the beginning season for fishing in Lake Yellowstone, which was nearby the camping area. We loved fishing and were delighted to grab a pole and try our luck!

We began to catch cutthroats, a species of trout, on just about any kind of bait that was permissible. The lake edges were filled with people fishing and everyone was having a great time!

We didn't know there was a limit on how many fish one person could catch in a day, so we got carried away and exceeded ours, since we were having so much fun! As we carried the fish back to the camper, we read a sign which told the limit. We had just about doubled that!

Too late to do anything about it then, we thought, so we stopped in a wooded area and began to clean the fish. One person watched for bears, which we had been warned about, and another fanned away the mosquitoes, which were huge, and the other two cleaned the fish.

The fish were delicious and maybe our conscious should have bothered us a little, but somehow it didn't!

We left Yellowstone and drove toward Colorado, where we camped in Estes Park, in the northern part of the state. Previously, our daughter had been attending a conference of the Campus Crusade For Christ, which was held there.

The event was covered in newspapers around the country, since a tremendous flood occurred at that time and several people were swept down the canyon, losing their lives!

Our daughter was in an area that the flood waters did not reach and she escaped without any problems.

We enjoyed our stop there and decided to return home. The trip had taken about a month and we were getting homesick!

"They" Say A Person Is A Part Of Everyone That He Meets!

That bothered me the first time I heard that saying, because throughout the years there have been some undesirable characters

I have met and I certainly hoped none of their qualities stuck on me! However, it is said that every person has some good qualities and it was my hope that the good ones stuck if some had to!

During my years of growing up on the farm I met many persons of exceptional character, most of whom were poor. It seemed that poverty sometimes is a character builder because it caused you to work harder and strive to do better. It puts you into the shoes of other people and causes concern for their well-being. It wasn't a requisite that you must be impoverished because we knew a lot of people who were well to do and of good character.

Poverty also begets honesty, because you have no chance of "keeping up with the Jones's" and you don't create a desire to have their property. Besides, if you do take something that doesn't belong to you, generally you are taught this is wrong! In church we were told that you might get by with doing something wrong here on earth, but your judgment would come at death in the hereafter.

Dreams are an integral part of every child's growing up, and so it was with me. Sometimes I would lay on a sack of cotton out in the fields, when I should have been working of course, looking up at the fleecy clouds and imagining that I was floating along with them. I could see into the future and plan my entire life!

Many of these plans did work out, but most didn't. I just knew that I wanted my life to count for something and that hard work was required to bring this about.

In the years that followed my graduation from college my determination to succeed began to be tested! I met many influential people and I tried hard to let a little of their success rub off on me!

My first job as a news reporter for a small county paper afforded many opportunities. The owner was a state legislator, who taught me some of the "ins and outs" of politics. While there I worked a second job with a radio station as a news announcer.

The sports announcer was Al Ciraldo, who later became the famous announcer for the Georgia Tech football team. He was well-known for his description of a kickoff when he exclaimed "toe meets leather."

One weekend the boss of the radio station came to me and said he was faced with a dilemma. The local football team was playing that night and Al could not announce the game due to a prior commitment. He asked me if I would be the announcer.

Well, I didn't hardly know a football from a basketball, but I told him that I would do my best! This was in the middle of the afternoon on game day and I worried from then on about the gigantic task confronting me! I got off in a quiet corner and asked for help.

I said, "Lord you know that I'm not trained to do this job, but I believe You and I can do it." I felt a little better after that, but still apprehensive! Would you believe that shortly after that the boss came over to me and said, "Al just got out of his other assignment and he will be able to announce the game after all."

What a load was lifted from me at that point! But since then I have thought the situation over and concluded that I had a "brush with greatness" because I could have done such a good job that I might have been the famous Tech announcer instead of Al! But, I wouldn't have wanted to stand in the way of his progress! Besides, that probably would have been a difficult job for me since I graduated from the main rival school and my partiality might have shown!

A couple of years later, I moved on to another job with International News Service as their state capitol reporter. In the meantime, a fellow by the name of Anderson took my old job. He was like me in a way, he was unknown to most people. But later he turned out to be "Whispering" Bill Anderson, the famous country singer from Decatur, Ga.

This brought on more analyzing thoughts about that situation. If I had just worked at the job a little harder I might have learned how to sing and play a guitar, and maybe could have gotten to be a famous country singer! Again, I had missed a great opportunity!

It was about this time that a book came out titled "No Time For Sergeants." The writer was Mac Hyman from Cordele, Ga.

That name sounded familiar, so I did a little research and found that I had gone to grammar school with his sister! He was a couple of years older than me and probably went to school with one of my siblings.

The book and movie made Mac famous and he grew up in the same area that I did. I thought, it could have just as easily been me that wrote a famous book. After all, I was raised under the same circumstances as he was. But then, I bet he never had to pick cotton or pull corn and probably had more time to think! Somewhere along the line, though, opportunity and greatness had passed me by again!

In my new job, however, it was my duty to make the rounds of the offices in the state capitol. I interviewed many congressmen and senators and found the work very interesting! One day I was in the governor's office for an interview and I heard a voice say, "okay, Jim, I'll send you two dozen tomorrow."

The person on the phone turned around and it was the governor. He had just sold twenty four hams to a customer and I assumed he was using time he should have been governing the state! I wondered how many such transactions went on each day!

The newspaper business was an exciting occupation because I met many famous people, including movie stars and beauty queens. One of the movie stars was Helen Hayes, who appeared in a play at the Ansley Hotel Theater. I interviewed Miss America, Yolanda Betbeze from Alabama, during an appearance at Davison's Department Store in the fifties.

I became friends with Lester Maddox, governor of Georgia, when he became a customer of mine in the furniture business. I reminded him that he had earlier run me out of his Pickrick restaurant when I had attempted to collect a bill from a worker there. He had told me that the worker could not pay his bills during working hours. I guess I should have been grateful that he didn't bring out his famous "pick-ax handle" to use on me!

Another famous person comes to mind who was writing articles in many papers sometime later and he was Lewis Grizzard, from Moreland, Ga. I never personally knew him but I did know his mother, who went to the same college I did. He was very good at writing funny and interesting columns and giving speeches all over the country. I have often wished I could write funny stuff like that! But wishing "don't make it so."

Later in the business world my wife and I operated a lighting showroom at the Atlanta Merchandise Mart. This lasted for about thirty years and many famous people came into our business. The mart would hold two furniture markets and four gift shows each year and the dealers and wholesale customers would number into the thousands. The mart would admit only dealers to buy for their stores at the shows and was never open to the general public.

In between shows sometimes dignitaries would be escorted to certain businesses. One day at our showroom I looked up from my work to see a sinewy and well- built young man, who turned out to be Muhammad Ali, the heavy weight boxing champ of the world! He was very pleasant and seemed intrigued by our display of about five thousand lamps of varied styles and sizes.

Another time Deborah Norville, the well known television personality came into the showroom. Truett Cathey, founder of Chic Fil A Corporation, came several times. We had many buyers for large corporations to come through.

One time we had a representative for the Shah of Iran, who bought a large quantity of ginger jar lamps to transport to his country. They were shipped out of the port at Mobile, Alabama and were to be moved inland to a new city built in Iran. The city was built in a circular arrangement, with the most important people living closer inside the circle. Outside many circles would house ordinary citizens. The city was in a desert somewhere in Iran.

Wendy Bagwell, the famous gospel singer from Georgia who also owned a furniture store, was a frequent visitor. He was the writer of the well known song about rattlesnake handling in churches, with the line about "where would you like a door," when he was told that the church did not have a back door! He was telling about attending a church, when the congregation began handling rattlesnakes and the preacher attempted to hand him one. He was looking for a fast route out of the building!

Sometimes your "brush with greatness" takes peculiar turns and you have very little control over it. This was the case with me a few years ago.

A friend of mine told us that her son was a movie star in Hollywood and that he was trying out for a part in the movie Deliverance. He had requested that she record some voices of southerners in order that he might copy the accents and stand a better chance of getting the part.

My wife and I were flattered when we were asked to record a segment of the story, because she must have thought our southern accents were just perfect for the situation.

We made the recording and it was sent to the movie star, with great expectations! A few weeks later we inquired as to the status of the project. We were told that the star did not get the main part in the movie, but that he had been chosen for a lesser part.

The lead part went to Burt Reynolds, but the other character was an important one also!

We were "tickled pink" with this information! Our voices must have been the clincher for the movie star to get the part! The movie went on to be a winner and much publicized all over the country.

But, do you know, we never heard from the movie star. Not one word of thanks did we receive! We like to believe, however, that we played a huge part in helping the star get his important job. Our imagined fame, though, will be humbly borne without fanfare!

Our work as a home furnishings sales representative required my wife and I to attend the shows twice each year in High Point, N.C. Salesmen, manufacturers and buyers would gather from all over the country and it was always a diverse group.

One especially obnoxious sales rep from a northern state approached my wife and asked her what kind of accent she had, evidently trying to degrade her southern drawl.

She quickly replied, "I don't have one, what is yours?" He made some sort of retort, using a few expletives and she told him he needed his mouth washed out with soap!

He walked away, looking for someone else to torment.

Neighbors Can Be a Blessing or Sometimes Pests

Generally speaking, our family has always been blessed with good neighbors, but there have been a few that could have stood improvement!

There is an old adage that "to have a good neighbor you have to be one." But, I believe there are exceptions to the rule and no matter how good a neighbor you are, you can't get along with some people.

Early in our marriage we bought a new home on a one- acre lot. It was a beautiful place and we loved it. However, as we moved in, the neighbors' kids sat on a ridge outside and watched every item that was brought into the house.

Later, the children seemed to roam the neighborhood at will and generally make pests of themselves. One teenager had access to the family car and enjoyed racing it around the outside of their house!

We thought it would improve our lot to put a nice fence between us and the neighbor. This angered him, since it left only ten feet of land from his house, and the boy couldn't race around the house anymore with the car!

While we were shopping one day, the neighbor came into our yard and cut down a nice weeping willow tree. He said he had planted it and we were not going to enjoy it! Later in the day the man and his son shot pistols at a backyard target, presumably to intimidate us.

I was beginning to get the idea they did not like the fence, even though I was within my rights to fence in my own property! They never spoke again and moved out of the area!

The couple that moved into the house turned out to be the nicest neighbors we have ever had and we became very good friends.

Another place we lived, the neighbor didn't seem to like Southern Baptists. They didn't indicate they were interested in knowing us at all. One day the woman asked me to get my garage door remote and see if it would open their door. I thought this was somewhat odd but I complied. It only opened our door.

She said she did not know what to do, that she had a problem! Their garage door would fly open at various times without anyone touching the remote! At night sometimes the door would open and scare them.

Several days later I noticed a serviceman checking the garage next door. He discovered that the door opener apparatus was located beneath the kitchen floor, and the vibration from walking over the floor would cause the opener to activate the door. That explained why the door flew open at odd times!

All this time the neighbor thought we were sitting home enjoying manipulating their garage door, trying to make them think there were ghosts in theirs!

We never received an apology, but I was somewhat amused and flattered that they might have thought I was capable of this!

Down the street from this neighbor was another who liked chickens. He had about two dozen or more, despite the county having ordinances against them.

Every morning the roosters would begin their crowing before daybreak and awaken the entire neighborhood, regardless if they wanted to be awake at that time! The chickens would cover the street and work over all flower beds and gardens they could get into. They were a general nuisance and ran too fast to catch!

Finally, the man was forced to move elsewhere since it was reported that his rent had accumulated to the point of no return and no attempts at changing that situation was made.

But the chickens were left behind and we still had a problem. The county animal control workers were called and the chickens eventually disappeared!

At the other end of the spectrum another neighbor would pick up the local newspaper from our box and bring it to our door every morning when he was in town. It didn't matter what kind of weather it was, he just enjoyed doing a good deed and expected nothing in return. Neighbors like that are really appreciated!

Occasionally, a piece of property in an area catches the eye of a developer, and regardless what the residents want, try to encroach on the piece and quiet of the area.

Such was the case on our quiet street recently, when a business across the street bought the corner property on ours. The owner petitioned the county to expand his business across a busy intersection to our street.

A bunch of neighbors fought this action before the county commission and won, preventing him from extending his business to our peaceful street. If granted, the move could have increased an already existing traffic problem on a busy highway. The road had already been the scene of numerous accidents.

Camping With Grady And Genelle

My brother Grady was the one with the middle name of "Adese," as I have reported previously. In the service he would get confused when the sergeant yelled "at ease," thinking the roll was being called. His wife was named Genelle.

We often camped with them, because they were a fun couple to take a trip with and it was always interesting!

Grady loved to smoke and would take a snort occasionally for medicinal purposes. Quite often he would keep busy at this while Genelle and my wife and I set up the campers. One such trip, Grady had gone to the office to pay the camping fee and the two women and I finished situating the vehicles.

I drove to the office to pay my fee and I heard Grady tell the park manager, "well, I guess my wife has just about gotten the camper set up, I can go back now." I paid my fee and said to myself, that's about par for the course!

We loved to fish everywhere we camped, and one spot near Brunswick, Ga. was a favorite. As usual, Grady decided to sit and smoke while we fished. Not having much luck we agreed to cease the fishing and return to our van.

There we overheard a conversation Grady was having with another person parked nearby. He was telling the man about his family and just about everything that came to his mind. Grady never met a stranger. He could talk and talk, anywhere, any time!

Genelle got a little irritated and admonished him about talking too freely to a stranger. "He doesn't know anything about you and you don't know him." Grady replied, "well, he didn't know much about an hour ago, but he knows quite a bit now!"

Every-once-in-while we would get "freebie" offers in the mail for free camping, just to introduce a new park. We received one from Panama City, Fla. one day and the four of us drove south.

Arriving in Florida, we were anticipating a great time. The next day it began to rain and continued through the night. We all went to bed, listening to the pitter patter on the roof. About midnight, I felt something wet on the covers over my feet. Getting up, I could see that a leak had developed around a skylight over the bed!

So I improvised, and placed a big aluminum baking pan underneath the leak. We both tried to sleep, but it was difficult, and we finally did doze off.

Later in the night, we were awakened with an unwanted shower inside the camper! The pan that I had placed under the skylight had filled with water and become overbalanced, dropping its entire load on us and the bed! This turned out to be a miserable night for us!

We looked at our camping buddies and someone was up with a flashlight trying to stop leaks. My bother's camper was a popup with canvas sidings and they too were getting soaked!

The rain finally stopped and we attempted to dry out. Everything was a mess, however. After getting everything under control, we gave up on that trip, and returned home.

A later trip to Panama City, my wife and I decided to play bingo at the park office with the other campers. The grand prize was a frozen turkey and my wife won the prize. It was a large turkey and the camper refrigerator was not big enough to hold it.

So, the park manager kept the turkey in his freezer until we left, when we placed the bird in an icebox keeping it cold until we arrived home.

Looking For Adventure In Eastern Canada

The call of the wild beckoned to us again one summer, as my wife and I left in our camper headed to Eastern Canada, by way of the eastern coast of the U.S.

After spending our first night at Williamsburg, Va., and touring the historical city, we resumed the trip up the coast and across the Chesapeake Bay on Highway 13. Our first mistake was made about halfway across the bay, when we spotted a rest stop and tourist area.

We followed the directions of the one-way arrows and soon came to the end of the driveway. There was a place for a car to turn around, but not for a van pulling a large camper!

We couldn't back the vehicles because the tourists had followed and jammed the road behind us. We couldn't go forward because the road had ended and the water was all around! Horns began to blow behind us! People got out of the cars and started yelling at us to move out of the way!

A state patrolman arrived and we tried to explain why we were there and he could see we needed help. He made a few cars back out from behind us, giving a little room to maneuver, but not enough.

Finally, I removed the sway bars and unhitched the camper. That gave me more room to move to a better angle for turning. After attaching the camper to the van again, it barely gave us leeway, but enough to get out of our predicament.

The patrolman stopped traffic on the busy highway above the small island rest stop, in order to let us merge. Back on the road we wondered why the road signs to the area did not warn against large vehicles entering.

We made it through and bypassed some of the large cities on up the coast, namely Philadelphia, New York City and Boston. We were anxious to get to the state of Maine! We had heard about Maine lobsters most of our adult lives but were not fortunate enough to get our hands on many.

As we drove along the coastal highway in Maine, we saw large signs saying, "Lobster Pound." Being new to us we decided to investigate and found that they were selling live lobsters and steaming them on the spot! They were selling them by the pound and the price was $3.95! You couldn't buy a hamburger for that!

During the next couple of weeks we ate thirty two lobsters together! That's sixteen each! We were in "hog heaven," or that is "lobster heaven!"

It was hard to leave Maine but we were on a mission seeking new adventures. Besides, we had eaten enough lobsters to call it "quits" for a while!

Crossing the Canadian border above Bar Harbor, Maine, we came into the Province of New Brunswick. We camped around Amherst in a beautiful wooded area. Not far from the camp was a public fishing dock, about a mile away, and we love fishing!

Making our way to the park where the dock was, we began to wet our poles. We fished for fifteen minutes, without any luck, when a large cloud began to cover the sky. Thunder and lightning began to crack around us!

I remarked to my wife, that we had better move to a safer place, and she agreed saying, "I'm trying to get my line loose from something that it is hung on at the bottom."

She kept working with the line and the weather was really getting to be threatening! She exclaimed, "there is a great big fish on my line!" I looked, and sure enough, the fish was a whopper!

Finally, she pulled it onto the dock and it appeared to be in the vicinity of ten pounds! What a fish! Neither of us knew what kind of fish she had caught.

We carried it to a nearby store and asked a young man if he knew what kind of fish it was. He said, yes, that the big fish was a trash fish and that nobody would eat a fish like that. He offered to take the fish and dispose of it for us.

His story sounded a little fishy to us, so we checked it out. Asking another person nearby, we found that it was a cod fish and that it was a delicious fish to eat! We surmised that the young man wanted the fish himself and he made up the story, thinking he had some "sucker" tourists who would believe him. We ended up putting the fish back in the ocean.

Looking at the map the next day, it didn't look like it was very far away to Nova Scotia and the city of Halifax. I told my wife, that a lot of people had told me "to go to Halifax," but that I was doubtful if they had that place in mind!

So we went to Halifax and enjoyed that beautiful city and down to Peggy's Cove, a few kilometers south. Next we parked our camper and drove the Cabot Trail on the upper end of Nova Scotia, going on to Sydney. A few miles away was Fort Louisbourg, a national historic fortress.

All through this area was fantastic scenery, beautiful fields of yellow wildflowers, mountains and lots of water! Many quaint exhibits were prevalent along the roads. One country gift shop had a large display of stuffed dummies surrounding the business and on a hillside. There must have been over one hundred man-sized dummies standing in various positions. Some women, men and children.

Driving west to Amherst, we moved a few more miles to Cape Tormentine, located on a point of the Northumberland Strait. This is a place where a ferry will take you to Prince Edward Island, another destination on our sight-seeing journey.

The line of vehicles waiting to board the ferry to cross the water to the Island was over half a mile long. We decided to camp for the night at a nearby campground, hoping the line would be shorter the next day.

Getting in line was much better the next morning, and soon we loaded our van and camper, along with many others. The trip took about two hours and we were camped on the Island later in the afternoon.

We found a lobster pound near Charlottetown and brought our catch back to the camper for cooking and another delicious meal! The next day we visited the cottage of Anne of Green Gables, and other points of interest on the Island.

We had been away from home more than a month and we were a little weary, so we headed south, working our way back to Georgia.

Along the way we enjoyed the scenery and stopped several places to see waterfalls, parks and the like.

Driving through Vermont, we were wary of animals along the roads, since there were signs warning "deer crossing" ahead. We remembered on a previous trip, when it was almost dark, driving on an interstate, a deer ran across in front of my automobile! The car was traveling at the speed limit of seventy miles an hour, and the deer just squeezed by. That was one scary feeling!

We finally arrived back at our destination, however, without any mishaps.

Traveling With Kids in Canada was Almost an Arresting Event!

One summer while the kids were out of school, we took a trip into Canada, going to the Province of Quebec. We toured the city of Quebec and our two girls were thrilled at what they saw and heard. Particularly with what they heard, because everyone was speaking French, and we didn't know the French language.

This was the first time they had been out of the U.S. and everything was unfamiliar to them. They were under the impression that everyone spoke English and the country was similar to ours.

After seeing that city, we moved on to Montreal, and were surprised again to find they too speak French. The World's Fair was held there just prior to our visit and we learned many of the exhibits were still open to the public.

Finding where the World's Fair site was, we drove downtown to see the displays. They were setup by participating countries and still being maintained. Across the way we spied a building that was a little different and we made a beeline for it.

It had a long stairway leading up to an entrance. So we proceeded to climb the stairs until we heard a commanding voice, "arreste, arreste!" Looking in the direction of the sound, we spotted two policemen moving toward us rather rapidly.

I told the kids, "It looks like we are going to be arrested. Let's go down the stairway and see what they want!"

On the ground again, the policeman began to speak in broken English, and told us we were going up to the exit and the entrance was on the other side of the building. We also learned that "arreste" means "stop" in English.

We weren't going to be arrested after all! So, that was a great relief, and we continued on with our sight-seeing, grateful that we were not going to the "slammer!"

A few years later, my wife and I were camping near the city of Montreal, and thought we would revisit some of the same places we had seen previously. As we walked on a downtown street, we came to some kind of statuary on the corner.

Coming closer, we were approached by a reporter from a local television station, who was interviewing people on the street as they passed by. He explained that we were "on the air" and he wanted to ask what we thought about the exhibit standing before us.

I looked the apparatus over and could see that it was a bunch of automobile tailpipes welded together with several mufflers and other parts. The reporter, with the camera crew grinding away, asked where we were from and was told we were from Georgia on vacation.

He said the exhibit had just been finished and placed on the street corner that week and he was trying to find out if the public liked what they saw. He wanted to know what I really thought about the structure.

I asked him, "do you really want to know what I think about it?" "Yes, I really would. Tell me if you like it or not," he stated.

So, I decided he wanted my objective opinion and I told him it looked like something that ought to be in a junkyard. I continued, that you could see the same items in just about any automobile graveyard and I failed to see any "art" in the large stack.

That didn't seem to be the answer he was looking for and our interview was terminated in short order. I asked when the interview was going to be aired and was told it would be on the six o'clock news on that station.

We left the city shortly after and returned to our camper on the edge of town, thinking that we would never see that interview on television. But, just to satisfy our curiosity, we turned on the station at six o'clock and watched.

Soon, we were looking at ourselves on the screen! That didn't look like me, I thought, that person looked old, wrinkled and ugly! But we couldn't deny it! I heard that part about the junkyard and I told my wife, "I shouldn't have made that remark in a strange country."

When the news program was over, I told my wife, "tomorrow, we better find us a campground in another city!" "These people may not like remarks like that from 'ugly Americans' like us!" My wife reminded me that she had not said anything! But I think she got the drift of the conversation.

We decided to err on the safe side, though, and hooked up the camper and headed for greener pastures elsewhere!

Segregation Was Everywhere In The South During The 1930's

Blacks and whites had separate facilities in all public places, when I was a child. They had separate entrances for restaurants and their own rooms to eat in. Drinking fountains were marked "white" or "colored." Blacks were directed to the back of all buses.

This was the way that it was and nobody seemed to make any moves to change it until around the middle of the century.

One of my assignments in 1951 as a reporter, was to cover a convention being held in Atlanta by the NAACP. We were directed by the group to only report from official news releases, and some strategy sessions we were not allowed to attend. I presumed the leaders were planning their marches, etc. and didn't want to make them public then.

Black persons have made great strides for equality since that time, but there is still much to be done.

Growing up during the Great Depression, the average southerner must have had more pressing problems at that time. On a farm as a white, we didn't seem to be affected as much as some others. Blacks and whites worked side by side, receiving equal pay for work done, such as payment by the pound for cotton picked.

Later, when times got better and people could think of something other than their next meal, their thoughts turned to other things.

Flying back from Frankfurt, Germany in 1999, my wife and I were seated next to a black couple in the inside middle seats of the plane. They lived in Chicago and were returning home. After exchanging pleasantries, the wife asked where we were from, and I told her we lived in Atlanta.

She asked, "are you a member of the Ku Klux Klan?" I was surprised by her question, but answered, "no I am not." She asked again, "have you ever been a member?" I told her "no," again.

This didn't seem to satisfy her, so she queried again, "do you know any klansmen or have any friends who are?"

By this time I was getting a little irritated at the questions, but told her, "no, I do not know any nor have I ever been affiliated with them in any way!"

She replied that she thought everyone in the south was connected to the Klan! I told her that her information sources weren't reliable and she ought to visit the south and find out for herself! With that she leaned back in her seat and went to sleep.

On a rare Sunday that our family wasn't driving the two mules and wagon to our church some five miles away, some of the neighbor's kids and I would go to a black church not far from our home.

We were always welcome but we sat at the back of the church, mostly to leave quietly in case the service was not very lively. I say this, because, most of the time there would be a lot of clapping, shouting, singing! But sometimes a different preacher would be in charge and the service would move slowly.

Also, at times the activity would get exciting and we didn't know what was coming next! One particular Sunday, the minister was really getting into the sermon and the small congregation begin to shout and talk in "tongues!"

A short totally bald deacon was sitting on the first row, shouting and getting louder by the minute! Behind him was an elderly woman, who was swaying and singing with the music!

She began waving her hands and arms in the air, and soon she was right over the bald man! She began to pound the bald head in front of her as if she were driving a stake in the ground! Someone behind her realized what she was doing and pulled her off the head before much damage was done!

Being young kids, this was a little frightening to us, so we jumped out of the window that we were sitting next to and beat a hasty departure! That was another reason we sat in the back, next to an escape route!

Another time, a group of us boys decided to go to a tent meeting in the city. A traveling evangelist was the preacher and everybody was welcome. The crowd began to sing and the preacher announced that they would have a "five dollar march."

He told everyone to form a line and march around the tent until the pulpit was reached, waving their five dollar bill, and drop it in a hat. The music began and just about everyone began to march around with the money waving in the air!

We thought this was a good time to make our exit, so we got up and began to move out. The music stopped! The preacher boomed out, "hey, you boys don't have to leave just because you don't have five dollars!"

Everyone turned around and looked at us and we were very embarrassed! The preacher was right, none of us had five dollars!

But the worst part for us was that everyone there knew it now! We couldn't stay after that!

Once in a while the family would make a trip to the nearby town on Saturday, to buy groceries and do other chores. Sometimes we had crates of eggs to either sell or trade for items we needed. Other days we would bring chickens to sell.

Most of the activity would be concentrated on two or three streets and in the middle of all this was a street car diner. The area was always crowded inside and outside the diner, with those fortunate enough to be able to eat, and the others outside gathering around to just smell the food!

Hamburgers were being sold at fifteen cents and hot dogs were a dime. Soft drinks were a nickel. Mr. Smith, the owner could often be heard hollering out, "Get 'em while they are hot!"

I rarely had enough money to buy anything, but I loved to stand outside and enjoy the aroma wafting from the diner! It really made my taste buds tingle!

One Saturday I was standing outside and there was a loud commotion coming from down the street. It appeared to be a black woman, screaming and running for her life! Following close behind was a black man with a large butcher knife! She seemed to be heading for the diner, but I suppose she was running just to get away from her attacker! He caught her about ten feet from where I stood and they began to fight! The man stabbed her many times, until she didn't move anymore. Blood was everywhere, and everyone stood around as if they were frozen in their tracks! The attacker fled back in the direction that he had come from, leaving the woman lifeless on the ground.

I never found out if the man was caught and punished or not, but I know one thing, I was scared out of my wits! The diner lost its fascination for me after that. I couldn't pass the restaurant without thinking of the poor woman's demise that day.

At this time I was about eight years old and the memory of that day lingers still! I began to be afraid of black people, because I had never seen anything like this!

Sometimes, I would be present in a group of white people who were talking at will about various subjects. One would say something like, "you better watch out when you are in the woods. There are a lot of turpentine Negroes out there." Most often the "n" word was used.

They would be referring to the workers gathering the turpentine from pine trees in the woods. The tree would be slashed about three feet off the ground with a large knife or machete, and a tin cup would be placed beneath to catch the liquid.

Most of the workers were black, since it was not a job that anybody would do unless circumstances forced them to. The mule-drawn wagons would wind in and around the woods with large sticky barrels on them and the workers would navigate the area with a large bucket, emptying cups in the container.

Snakes and animals were a constant danger to the workers. Wild dogs and rabid animals were encountered at times. The turpentine workers would accumulate their product on their clothes and would be an unsavory sight in the woods!

There were stills in several towns of the south, where turpentine would be transported from the woods, and processed into products to be sold in stores. This process of refining the gummy liquid was similar to a "moonshine" still, but was a legal enterprise. There are two such stills remaining in Georgia.

Some of the resulting products are spirits of turpentine, resin, tar and creosote. Spirits of turpentine is a good paint thinner and brush cleaner.

One Saturday I was standing in a grocery store with my dad and a black man entered the store muttering to himself and stumbling around. He looked every bit of a turpentine worker, who hadn't washed in a week. If he had taken his clothes off and stood them in a corner, they would stand upright without help! The gummy turpentine had petrified his shirt and pants.

The store owner, believing that the man was drunk, asked him to leave the business. He wouldn't leave and the owner called the local police.

They came and the man, who was under the influence of some sort of spirits, put up little resistance. A policeman hit him on the head with his "billy" club a couple of times and two of them drug him out of the store.

I supposed he was locked up and slept off his inebriation. I'm sure he had a good-sized "goose-egg" on his head the next day!

Some would argue that too much force was used to subdue the man. That's possible and very probable, but being a small child at that time my opinion was not sought. In the "olden" days children were supposed to be "seen and not heard."

Even as a child, though, I was picking up much information to be mulled over in my later years. When you are a child you think as a child, but when you grow to adulthood you should be able to separate truth from lies and right from wrong.

It takes much time and a lot of hard work to make ingrained habits go away, especially if they are bad ones! Some of the habits associated with "the good old days" are better left behind.

Common Sense Was A Family Necessity

Everyone knows what common sense is but not everybody is blessed with an abundant portion of it. There are some geniuses who have trouble keeping their own shoelaces tied!

My parents did not have much schooling, as in book learning, but both were rich in just plain common sense, and they endeavored to teach their children much of this. With this type of knowledge a person can be a success in life in many pursuits.

It seems to me that you have to possess a dose of each of common sense and intelligence to make everything work well. If you lack one, then in some areas of your life there will be a struggle for balance.

So it was for us living on a farm in abject poverty during the Great Depression. We had to use our common sense to keep something to eat on the table. In fact, we had to invent ways to keep a roof over our heads at times!

Common sense will keep you out of trouble sometimes! For instance, if you are confronted by a huge bully, and you are a small person, you want to talk your way out of trouble, if possible! Also, common sense might tell you to start moving your feet real fast to put you out of his range!

My dad used to tell about a person he knew in the past, saying that the man seemed to go around talking to himself all the time. Everybody in the town thought the man was "a little "teched," or off in the head!

One day he asked the man why he went around talking to himself His answer was surprising! "When I talk to someone, I want to talk to a smart person," he said. "I also like to hear a smart person talk," he added.

That made sense, but I wondered how anyone would be able to learn anything! If you only talk to yourself, you already know what you know! You need to "pick another person's brain" to add knowledge!

This man might have been a smart person, but he may have been in short supply of common sense!

But by using a little common sense when it is called for is a "good thing!" There were two farmers hunting in the woods and one was named Billy Bob. The other was called Quincy.

A bunch of birds flew over them and Billy Bob said "M R Ducks." Quincy said, "M R Not."

"O S A R." replied Billy Bob, "C M Wangs."

"L I B. M R Ducks," Quincy agreed.

Now for someone who is not a southerner it might be hard to interpret this example of common sense, but it is plain and simple. One man said to the other, "see them ducks." "Them are not," the other said. "Oh, yes they are," the first man said, "See them wings." "Well I'll be, them are ducks," the other agreed.

My parents taught me some other important things, like "If you see a hog running around with a stick in his mouth, you can watch out, because it's going to be cold weather soon." I never checked this out, for sure, but I assumed when winter came, that a hog must have grabbed a stick and started moving around with it somewhere in the area!

A person in the community denied that he was the culprit when a farmer missed a few of his watermelons. In fact, he denied it before he was ever accosted and my dad said, "The hit dog always hollers."

I was having trouble figuring this one out, because it was pretty plain if you hit a dog with a stick, he is going to holler-- or bite you!

It was explained to me that the old saying was that the guilty party is usually the first to deny it, or that the one that denies it the loudest is the most guilty.

Then one day, one of my sisters was complaining to Mom about her looks, as she was growing up. Mom assured her that "beauty is only skin deep, and that beauty is as beauty does." She told her that true beauty is in your heart and that she would be beautiful if she acted beautiful.

I was pretty skinny as a kid and kind of sensitive about the fact. One day as a snooty cousin was visiting us, she told my mother, "Aunt Cleo, Son (talking about me) sure looks puny in a T-shirt!" The remark "hit me where it hurt," and I remember it today!

About fifty years later I saw her again and she said, "Son, you finally made a man out of yourself!" Being irritated again by this female cousin, I was tempted in say, "well, it's a shame you never made a woman out of yourself!" But I didn't!

Growing up in the south could be both complicated and simple! Common sense is a "good thing," if you can separate the "nonsense" from the "sense." That way it generally makes "good sense!"

Quite often we were subjected to quotes, quaint sayings and myths in our everyday conversations. After all picking cotton can be somewhat boring at times, leaving one's mind to wander!

When things were not going right, a member of the family would pipe up with "Every dog has his day," or "Lie down with the dogs and get up with the fleas."

Another would say, "you can lead a mule to water but you can't make him drink," changing the animal from the usual "horse."

"A fool and his money are soon parted," didn't have much meaning to us because we never had much, if any. But some people must have had some at one time, else that old saying wouldn't have been coined.

After we ran out of known quotes, we made up a few of our own. It's easy to see why these are not quite as famous!

My dad would often kid someone about paying a debt with his saying, "I had rather die owing a debt than to intentionally beat them out of it." Concerning the stock market activities, he would say, "A good stock to buy is always a healthy milk cow."

When we finally got electric power for the first time in the 1940's, someone, marveling at the bright lights, mused, "Electricity is an enlightening subject." We had no inkling of what was to come, like television, computers, etc.

Making a play off an old mathematical adage, we made up our own principle, "For every good deed done, there is an exact opposite reaction." In fact, it is believable that the bad deeds far outweigh the good ones. I know this was true when some of our mischievous cousins were concerned!

Mama warned me when I left for college, "Always wear clean underwear when you go out in public, because you never know when you might be involved in an accident and have to be exposed!" I suppose it is always better to look good, regardless of the circumstances!

We had a lot of mosquitoes around our place and a saying was soon originated for this, "A mosquito's bite is worse than its buzz." I guess this meant something like, "Sticks and stones may hurt my bones, but nary a word can harm me."

But the most memorable description of some neighboring children, whom we deemed as "brats," was "An off-spring is a crazy kid!" We knew a lot of them like this!

Common sense kind of grows on you, like a wart that comes up on your body and you can't get rid of it! I guess some just soaks into your mind through an osmosis process, and then, at other times, you have to learn through actual experience.

As an example, when I was a small kid, I read some comic books depicting a hero who could fly. I began to study the situation and it seemed feasible to me that a person might be able to fly! After all, there it was in black and white on the pages before me!

So, I climbed into the barn loft and got two bundles of hay and put them under each arm. This would give me the lift I needed to float down to the ground, about twelve feet, I reasoned.

The door was opened and I made ready for my flight. I leaped from the barn loft and fell like a rock to the ground below! I was a little stunned but no broken bones!

Like it was reported about Edison as he was developing the light bulb, and failed for the ninety ninth time. He said, "I have just found another way to not make a light bulb." I was successful in finding a sure way of not flying! Or maybe the better lesson was how to stop flying towards the ground so hard!

At any rate, I learned not to try this again, and the actual experience taught me a memorable lesson!

But this didn't stop me from experimenting with other ways of learning. One day, a neighboring friend about my age, suggested that he and I try to ride a large bull we had in a pasture nearby.

We both thought if we could rope the bull and lead him into a freshly plowed field, it would be easier on us if we happened to fall off in soft dirt.

The bull was roped, after a short struggle, with two ropes so that we could get on either side and hold him evenly between us. He was getting a little irritated with us by then!

We led the bull into the plowed field and were trying to figure out how to get on the bull in order to ride. We couldn't turn loose either rope because we wouldn't have any control over him.

It wasn't long until that problem was put on a back burner. We had a more pressing one! I heard my buddy holler, "watch out!" I turned in time to see the snorting bull leaping in my direction! The rope my buddy was holding had broken and I was left with my rope and a mad bull!

I began to run as fast as possible, with the animal close behind and gaining! Suddenly, I stumbled and fell flat between two plowed, but not planted, corn rows! The angry bull lowered his horns and looked me square in the eyes!

Then something strange happened! The animal snorted a time or two, turned away and ran off towards the other side of the field, dragging my rope!

I was thankful that I had been spared from possible injury and I had really learned a good lesson, which never had to be repeated!

My dad had to be told about our adventure, because the bull had to be returned to the pasture and the rope taken off. To say that he was not pleased would be an understatement!

There usually was little excitement on the farm, so often we had to create our own. We had a small pond behind our house and the weather had been wet and rainy. There was no boat to float around on the pond, so I decided to experiment again.

We had some large tin tubs that were used to haul water from the well for the animals. I surmised that one of those would make a perfect boat, and I would row with my hands. The tub was carried to the pond and I eased into it. Paddling with my hands, I got a few feet from the shore, when the tub lost its balance.

I tumbled into the pond as the tub tipped over and got a thorough soaking! Swimming back to the water's edge, I had found that a round tin tub with a person in it wouldn't float long without some method of balancing it!

One day as my buddy and I were hunting in the pasture and woods on the farm, we heard a rustling sound nearby! It made snorting noises and we soon recognized our bull from the previous experience. He must have been remembering this because he didn't seem to be in a friendly mood.

Now, when I say we were hunting in the woods, we were using the only weapons we had, homemade "flips" or slingshots. These don't offer a lot of protection from a raging bull!

My buddy made a beeline for a small tree on the other side of a briar patch and the fastest way to it was directly through the thorns. With the animal gaining on him, he finally made it to the tree. He was bleeding in various and sundry places, but scampered up the tree.

The tree wasn't hardly large enough to hold him and his weight bent the top towards the ground. He was swinging back and forth and as he came down the bull was giving him a boost with his horns!

I had sought shelter in another tree and was too high to be of interest to the bull. Finally, the animal tired of his sport and took off toward another part of the pasture.

Another valuable lesson had been learned and stored away for future use. This was not a fun adventure, however, and we didn't want to repeat it any time soon!

The English Language is not What It Used to Be

Evolution has become an increasingly important subject of discussion, lately, but let me set the record straight, I am a firm believer in Creation. However, when the English language is being discussed, the evolution of some words can hardly be an improvement over what we had in the 1930's.

In fact, many words and phrases that were used in the "olden days" are hard to recognize as meaning anything near that today.

Following are some words used then and the meaning we understood.

African Killer Bee: A difficult spelling bee for blacks.

Aids: Items used in school, pencils, ink, chalk, etc.

Boob: A moron

Bull: A male farm animal (not as in the stock market).

Canned: As in canning vegetables.

Chopper: False teeth.

Colored: Not white.

Company: In-laws visiting.

Cool: Chilly weather.

Cow: Female farm animal, milk cow.

Courting: Sparking, as in courting girl friend.

Crack: Hole in floor.

Dish: Something you eat from.

Dope: A soft drink, R.C. Cola, Dr. Pepper.

Family: Pa, Ma, and kids.

Fast food: Biscuit with hole punched and filled with syrup.

Gay: Happy feeling.

Goat: A grown kid (animal).

Grass: Stuff you hoe out of cotton rows.

High Fat: High-hanging beer belly.

Hitched: Married.

Hoer: One who hoes cotton.

Indoor toilet: Chamber pot under bed.

Kicked the bucket: Died

Laid: Chicken laid an egg.

Launder: Wash and scrub clothes in tin tub.

Low fat: Low-hanging beer belly.

Mad Cow: How a cow acts when milking gets too rough.

Making Out: As in making out like you have a lot of money.

Marriage: A man and woman get hitched.

Missile: A spitball thrown in class.

Money: Long green with the short life.

Mouse: A rat.

National Newspaper: The Grit. (We used to get them free.)

Newscast: Home Farm Hour On WSB in Atlanta.

Points: As in plow points, part of a plow.

Plowing New Ground: As in turning the soil in the "back forty."

Poker: As in an iron stoker for a fire.

Queer: Something unusual or odd.

Running Water: Running with a bucket of water in winter
     time from well to house.

Shine: As taking a shine to someone, liking them.

Skunk: A smelly animal, polecat.

Sniff: Smelling Ma's pie cooking.

Spam: World War II Army vittles.

Sparking: As in going out with your girlfriend

Strange: Odd or peculiar, as in one of my first cousins.

Swinger: One who is "just a swinging in the front porch swing."

Toilet Tissue: Sears Roebuck Catalog.

Trucks: As in "trucking on down the avenue."

Walking: Can't get my Model T cranked, so I'll have to walk.

This list could go on and on and if a person could come back in two hundred years the English used today might not be recognizable then! Evolution of this sort will be with us undeniably!

Even Church Restrooms Can Yield Blessings!

Eight years after retiring from the home furnishings business, we had traveled to more than three dozen foreign countries and visited all of the United States. It was time to think about where we wanted to spend the remainder of our days and we began to look at the possibilities.

The state of Georgia had been home to both of us all of our lives and we did not wish to stray far. After much soul searching and taking into account that most of our relatives lived in the state, we settled on Lake Lanier in northeast Georgia.

We began to look at lots to build our retirement home and this became a huge job, since the lake had over five hundred miles of shoreline! Lots were expensive and many were on steep hillsides and we were beginning to wonder if the right one would be found.

Two years of looking and the "pickings were slim." We had just about given up when Sunday came and we prepared to go to church as we did each week. After Sunday School my wife made a visit to one of the restrooms in the large church.

A fellow parishioner saw my wife and asked her if she had found a lot up on the lake. She replied that no, she had not, and that it was getting more difficult by the day. A voice further back in the toilet asked, "are you looking for a lake lot?"

My wife looked around and recognized the person who was speaking, and told her, "yes we sure are!"

The lady replied, "we have a lot we want to sell because we are getting to old to build on it or otherwise take care of it." She told her where it was located and the price she and her husband were asking.

We traveled the forty miles the next day to see the property and it was too good to be true! The lot was perfect! The location was near a small town and the large oaks would make a magnificent setting for a lake home! The lake was very accessible and a small dock was already in use there! We could just picture the large fish we were going to catch!

Two days later the lot was ours and not long after we built a five thousand square foot retirement home. Later, I'll tell you many reasons why not to build a large home to retire in and the mistakes that many people make!

However, my wife and I marveled at the unsuspected blessings that can be received in a church sometimes, and yes, even in the church restrooms!

Before we built the house, the previous owners had pointed out that a neighbor on one side of the lot had cemented a driveway and it had been extended nine feet over the line onto our property. We didn't consider this to be a big problem, but they had told us that this was another reason to sell, since they did not wish to argue with the neighbor.

After contacting the neighbor, we found that they were Korean and could not speak much English. The man was named Su and his wife was Hu. They seemed to be nice but I couldn't get the point across that they would have to remove the cement driveway and a portion of their deck that was on our property.

So I contacted a lawyer and asked that he write a letter explaining the situation. I told the lawyer that if it came down to seeking a legal remedy that I was not sure who to sue! It might be Su, or it might be Hu, but as soon as I found out who, I would tell him who to sue!

But this never came about because Su and Hu did the right thing and agreed to undo what they had done! I was real happy because we didn't have to sue Su or Hu! In fact, we didn't even have to go to the trouble of finding out who to sue in this case!

A few days prior to this, the contractor we hired to build our house dug a deep hole on the property in order to bury stumps, trees, etc. This has since been declared illegal and banned on most properties.

This was a deep hole! You couldn't hardly see the bottom and I wondered how the bulldozer was going to get out, but it did.

The next morning I looked at the hole and a person was standing on the other side peering down into it. I walked over and he appeared to be Chinese! I thought, "now, this hole is deep, but could it be this deep!" "Did they dig all the way to China and one of the inhabitants came up out of the hole?"

I got my answer soon, however, because it was my new neighbor Su! He had just gotten up and was satisfying his curiosity about the large hole!

Shortly after this the contractor began to build our house and we probably became his worst nightmare! My wife and I took two lawn chairs and placed them on the driveway in an advantageous position and watched the proceedings. Every time we saw a crooked two-by-four being carried inside we vetoed that action! This went on for about six months, until the house was finished.

Finally, we ended up with a house of about 5,000 square feet, much too large for two old persons! But it was well-built, because we did our jobs as "straw bosses."

Humor has always been a large part of our marriage and I remind my wife quite often that she must have a real keen sense of humor. After all, she married me and continues even now!

It must have been true love because I think she married me for my money! However, when she found that I had to charge my wedding suit and my job as a newspaper reporter only paid $32.50 a week, she still stuck to her decision! I doubt if it was much of a surprise, though!

One day as both of us were working in the back yard, doing a little spring cleaning, my wife was using some hedge clippers on an overgrown bush and I was getting my vegetable garden ready to plant. Suddenly, I heard a loud cry, "I've fallen and I can't get up!"

Somewhat alarmed, I rushed to the spot where she was working! There was my wife, standing in a deep hole with one leg outside on the ground and the other hanging in a stump hole!

After finding that she was not hurt, I helped her out of the hole and we both had a good laugh at the ridiculous position she had found herself in!

Later, I told a good friend of mine about the mishap. He was a church deacon and I had thought he had forgotten that I told him, until we invited him to come to see us and he replied to my wife, "no I guess not. Your husband might push me in that stump hole!"

My wife got her chance to laugh at me a few weeks later. It was a Sunday morning and she was not feeling well. She didn't feel like going to church with me, as was the custom each week.

So, I dressed in a hurry and in semi-darkness, trying not to disturb my wife and proceeded on to church. When I returned, I changed into some more comfortable clothes. As I removed my pants, I noticed they had elastic all around the top!

I asked my wife if she had a black pair of pants with elastic all around? She said, "yes, why?" "Are these your pants," I asked?

She confirmed my suspicions! I had worn her pants to church and I must have been the laughing stock of the congregation! "Maybe, by some miracle, nobody had noticed," I hoped!

My wife seeing the humor of the situation, began to feel better after a good laugh! I told her my old age was getting to me and that I must be getting a little senile. I said, "but, if you ever see me putting on your panties, you can just have me committed!"

It was a common joke between us, as we often drove by an "old folks home" on the way to the grocery store, that we needed to stop and inquire about their prices, especially if one of us was feeling puny!

When our children were small, we were improving a lake house we owned and my wife and I had built a sun deck around the back. It was about eight feet from the ground and we had not yet built steps. I had placed a large board there to walk down.

My wife and children were somewhat afraid to walk the plank and I kidded them about their fear. So, I thought this would be a good time to teach them something about being fearless!

I told them to watch my example and they would learn. The journey down began well, until about half way. Suddenly, my feet went out from under me and I landed on my backside, bouncing on down to the ground!

Brushing myself off amidst the laughter, I told them they had learned one more way of not getting down the plank! I haven't lived that example down to this day!

The kids were not surprised much at my attempts to give them a "rounded" education, as these learning experiences might come at any time.

When they were small, I built a 10 by 10 utility shed behind the house, to put garden tools and other yard equipment in. The first night after it was built, the kids wanted to take their sleeping bags and spend the night out there.

They settled down for the night and I thought it would be a good time to teach them about wild animals that might be around. I began to howl and groan and make what I knew must be scary sounds.

All of a sudden, the door opened and I just knew they would spring out and run for the house! Much to my disappointment the oldest said disgustedly, "aw daddy, quit making those noises so we can sleep!"

My ego was deflated! I returned to the house feeling that my lesson was a failure!

While the children, Elaine and Carol, were still in grammar school, their mother was in the hospital for a short stay. During the time she was away, I was the chief cook and "bottle washer."

So I decided to impress the children with my cooking expertise. We all loved banana pudding, and making one didn't seem too complicated to me. After all, I had watched my wife cook one many times.

I fixed all the ingredients, bananas, vanilla wafers and made up a sauce to pour over them. I mixed up a topping and beat it up in the mixer, and placed it on top of the pudding. Reading the instructions on the cooking time, I placed it in the oven for cooking.

Soon it was ready to serve, after the kids had eaten some other easy to prepare dish, and I proudly placed the pudding on the table. One of the kids dipped a spoon in and tried to get some, and it wouldn't budge out of the container! It seemed to have shrunk half its size and settled into a hard solid mass!

After cutting chunks out with a knife and serving a portion to each child, they bravely tried to eat the pudding! It wasn't an easy task, but they tried, just to humor me!

Finally, I told them to forget it, and they happily did! I had seemingly invented a new way to make shoe leather! Feeling sorry for them, we went out to eat, so they could get the nourishment they badly needed. After that I confined my cooking to warming things and boiling water!

Both of the kids took piano lessons, and when the time came for their recital, we invited their favorite aunt and uncle to attend. The proud parents, aunt and uncle and a few neighbors gathered to watch. Our daughters performed well and we were very pleased.

Several other kids played their pieces, and it came time for a little boy about six years of age. I say little, but he must have weighed seventy five pounds, cute as he could be, but hefty!

He began to pound the piano keys and was doing well until stage fright caught up with him! He froze, and sat there trembling! Suddenly, he exclaimed, "Aw shoot!," quit playing, hopped off the stool and left the room! We felt real sorry for him, but the way he quit the project was real humorous!

Our daughters learned to play very well, and the oldest went on to major in music at the University of Georgia. She learned to play several instruments and sing.

While working with the Campus Crusade For Christ, she toured the country with the Crossroads group, often singing solos.

Part IV.

Exciting Trips Abroad

After our retirement in 1986, we had plenty of time to devote to traveling to many foreign lands around the world. We were educated and astonished at the many sights we had only read about.

Hopefully, this section of the book is entertaining somewhat, since I have tried not to make it sound and read like a canned travelogue pitch!

European Tour of Nine Countries

Extended bus tours are for the young, my wife and l found out in 1975! The physical challenge of getting up before daybreak, checking out of the hotel and getting on a bus to the next city, was a bit taxing for middle-aged people!

We began our tour, with my sister and her husband, in London, England. This particular trip we did not have much time to see the city, but did take three days to check out some of the sights.

Taking the city subway, we had trouble getting all four of us on the train. As we stood on the platform, the train arrived and all jumped aboard except my sister. Evidently she must have thought she had plenty of time to board, and the doors began to close! She made a leap for the door and we pulled her in!

We might never have seen her again if she hadn't made it, because we had never been to London before and none of us knew where we were going.

This was soon forgotten as we stopped at Buckingham Palace and watched the changing of the guard. This forty-five minute ceremony at eleven-thirty each day in the summer is a colorful activity, and watched by many tourists and locals as well.

We toured the Tower of London, where the crown jewels are displayed. Big Ben, the famous Tower clock, was ticking away the time, and we heard the chimes. Later we visited Trafalgar Square, and the memorial erected to the defeat of Napoleon in 1801.

Piccadilly Circus was another attraction nearby. Being the equivalent of Times Square in New York City, it is also an entertainment and shopping center.

Another day we took a sight-seeing bus and toured the city, visiting other attractions that were not covered before. We had a little adjusting to do when it came to conversing with the English people. They couldn't understand our southern drawl and we couldn't quite get their phrases!

However, we did visit a large department store and I was subjected to the first unisex toilet I had ever experienced! Finding the "wash closet" was not difficult, but as I was using the facility, a female cleaning employee came in and began to tidy up the place! Soon, some female customers came in, and I was beginning to think I had gone into the women's toilet! As I left, though, I noticed it was for both sexes.

Leaving London, we climbed aboard a large ferry boat and crossed the English Channel. As we passed the white cliffs of Dover, the boat captain called our attention to them.

We arrived at Ostend, Belgium and began our tour by motor coach. The first city to visit was Brussels. As we drove around the city, the tour director pointed out the main attractions. Soon, we came to an accident on the road and our bus had to detour.

We drove down some narrow streets, until we came to a vehicle parked too far in the street to allow the large bus to get by. Stopping the bus, the driver told the riders we could amuse ourselves by looking in the show windows along the street, while he searched for the driver of the automobile. He told us, "this part of the city is the Red Light District!"

A first glance told us he knew what he was talking about, since the windows were decorated with scantily-clad women! Some of the men on the bus were hoping the car driver would not be found right away. But alas, he was!

With the wives anxious to leave the area, we proceeded to The Netherlands and spent the night in Amsterdam. We were informed this city had an even larger district devoted to prostitution, but the women ruled, and a wide berth was given to that area!

We continued our journey as we drove close to Dusseldorf, Germany and along the Rhine River. There were many old castles nearby, as we entered the Black Forest area.

We found the German people to be somewhat distant and the differences in the languages could have been the reason. We couldn't engage many in conversations because no one could understand what was being said.

Stopping at rest areas along the way was interesting. Crowds of people seemed to continue their own direction without much thought to anyone in the way. German women were the worst at this, and many would jostle you out of their way.

I'm ashamed to admit, at one such stop, I was determined to hold my ground, when a huge German woman barreled her way through a group of tourists. She was making a beeline for me as I stood still. I crouched a little and braced myself for the hit I knew was coming. She barged into me and bounced off, since I was ready for the crash! As she moved around me I was given a look that could have killed, and she mumbled something in German. Probably a good thing I didn't understand what she said!

Around the city of Stuttgart, we made an overnight stop in the country at a large hotel. It was a very old five-story building and seemed to be located in the "boon docks." Chickens and other farm animals were running all around the big yard!

Everyone on the tour had to handle their own luggage. My bag weighed sixty two pounds and my wife's seventy two! My sister and her husband were the first to take the elevator, going to the fifth floor, where both of our rooms were.

That was the first and last trip the elevator made that night! It had broken and everyone after that had to lug their bags to the rooms, with most of them on the upper floors! So we struggled up five flights of steps with the heavy bags! Needless to say, we were happy to reach our room, and looked forward to a good night's rest.

That was not to be, however, with seemingly everything against us!

Inside the room, the furniture looked as old as the building! There was an old metal shower in one corner of the room, a sink standing beside it, and no further toilet facilities. We had a choice of the chamber pot beneath the bed or a trip down the hall to a community toilet!

After getting ready for bed, we discovered we had to figure out a method of getting into it! The bedding covers seemed to be sewn together, and to get inside you needed to slide into the opening, similar to a sleeping bag.

It was a cold night and we enjoyed the heavy covers for a while. But soon we became too warm and couldn't stand it. We never got it right the remainder of the night. We were either too hot or too cold!

Finally, with little sleep, we were aroused by the roosters crowing and the other animals joined in! We thought, "and for all of this good stuff we're getting, we are paying our hard-earned cash! They ought to be paying us!"

We should have been thankful for our blessings, however, because the elevator was running and we were served a good breakfast.

Boarding the tour bus again, we continued into Austria and soon found ourselves in the Austrian Alps. The scenery was beautiful and later we entered Italy. We had traveled about a hundred miles into the country, when the driver suddenly stopped the bus.

The driver must have known something we didn't, because he instructed everyone to act natural and show our passports if asked.

The bus door was opened and several men, armed with rifles and other firearms, boarded the vehicle. They seemed to be military people, but we never were informed. They asked some for passports and passed by others. One lady was somewhat frightened, because her passport was in her luggage, but she was never asked to show it, thankfully!

Whatever the men were looking for was only known to them, but the bus load of people must have passed "muster," since we were allowed to continue our journey.

Later we arrived in Venice, Italy and marveled at the city that was almost a part of the Adriatic Sea. Almost everything was floating or surrounded by water. Many of the canals between the buildings were filled with boats and gondolas and laughing singing people were everywhere!

We took a water tour through the city on one of the many gondolas, a Venetian boat with one oar, and as we moved through the area the boatman serenaded us. We missed many sights due to the lack of time.

However, as we arrived at the Piazza of San Marco we were impressed with the ancient buildings, the tourists and the multitudes of pigeons congregating everywhere, begging for handouts. Little kids and grownups alike were tossing crumbs to the birds and the pigeons seem to have no fear of humans. Maybe your life was not in danger, but your wardrobe was! As the birds flew around in the air, the danger of being bombed was almost a certainty!

Continuing our trip, we came into the capital city of Rome. Taking the usual city tour, we visited cathedrals, fountains, quaint shops and many ancient Roman structures. Most of the attractions had English-speaking guides, otherwise we could have only looked and imagined what was being said.

One night we were taken to see the fountains and this event turned out to be quite memorable for a couple of elderly ladies along for the walking tour. The Tivoli fountains were located in a park with paths winding around and between them. The area to walk in was somewhat rocky and "tricky" for younger folks, much less senior people.

The tour is always scheduled at night, with abundant lighting in the right places to bring out the beauty of the cascading water of several fountains, but the lighting along the pathways was somewhat dim.

My wife and I were walking along enchanted by the beautiful sights, when we heard a commotion behind us! The light was not sufficient to make out what was happening. But we heard some screaming!

Rushing back to the area where the screams were coming from, we saw two elderly women threshing about in one of the pools! The pool was not over two feet deep but the ladies were scrambling about letting everyone know that they didn't want to be there!

One had stumbled on a rock and fell into the pool grabbing at the other woman and pulling her in behind her! They were unhurt, except being soaked, and embarrassed that they had brought so much attention to themselves. Instead of looking at the local attraction, they became one that night!

Later, we visited the famous Trevi Fountain, which was the subject of the song and movie, "Three Coins In A Fountain." We even tossed in a few coins and made wishes!

We made a stop at Piazza Navona, where we saw the Fountain of Four Rivers. Close by was the Pantheon, Roman ruins dating back to about 200 AD. We saw the famous Colosseum, where many gladiators forfeited their lives.

The Vatican was a must-see attraction and the Sistine Chapel was flooded with tourists. We saw where Mussolini made his long-winded speeches.

Going south after leaving Rome, we proceeded down the famous Autostrada del Sole to Sorrento, where we spent the night near the Bay of Naples. We toured Naples and saw the childhood home of Sophia Loren, the actress.

The Isle of Capri was an unforgettable experience, with the only way to get to the highest point being a chair lift. Rose- tinted rocks and emerald coves abound. It is a unique attraction!

Mount Vesuvius looms over the Bay of Naples and the ancient city of Pompeii was a stop for our group. The City was buried by a volcanic eruption about 79 AD. Much of it has been excavated and we gained considerable insight as to how the people lived at that time.

Moving north we came to Florence, visiting the Straw Market with their basketry souvenirs and making a side-trip to The Leaning Tower of Pisa. At the time of our trip the Tower was stable at 14 feet off center. Climbing to the very top is a dizzying experience and you feel as if the tower is going to tumble over anytime!

There were many cathedrals, art structures and historical sights, including the famous stature of David.

Boarding the bus again we drove north along the Italian Riviera to Genoa, the leading seaport of the country. This is the place where many famous people set sail; such as Christopher Columbus.

Soon we arrived in Nice, France, where we made a trip into the Principality of Monaco, and it's capital Monte Carlo. We found out the entire country was only 400 acres! Driving up the steep incline to the palace, we looked for Princess Grace and her husband, but they were nowhere to be seen. Some time after our trip Princess Grace died in an automobile accident.

The city of Nice is a mecca for sun-worshipers and a seaport town for the wealthy. Our hotel was outstanding and probably the best facility we stayed in on the entire trip.

The trip continued north to Grenoble, France, an Alpine sports area and one of the Olympic Games sites. We proceeded along the peaks of the French Alps and into Switzerland and on to Geneva. Before long we were in Berne, the Swiss Confederation capital, and we drove on to Paris.

This city is one that tourists can forget about time, because you could spend months and never see all the things you would like to.

We drove by the Eiffel Tower, with many fountains in the area, and down the Champs Elysees to the Arc de Triomphe.

We saw the Latin Quarter, Napoleon's Tomb. Later that night we were taken to the nightclub area, where we saw the Paris Folies Bergere. This was was somewhat enlightening, because we were introduced to many types of dancing we didn't know existed!

After spending the night in Paris, the next morning we made a side trip to Versailles, the fabulous palace of Louis XIV and Marie Antoinette. Built in the Seventeenth Century, it has been the center of French Royalty and houses many art objects by the great artists.

From there we moved on to Ostend, Belgium and ended our tour with the ferry back to London, and a flight back to Atlanta. It had been an exciting, but tiring trip, having covered seven countries in such a short time.

Hugh, my sister's husband, had contracted a cold at the beginning of the trip and passed it along to all on the bus. It was a rule of the tour that bus riders would rotate their seating each day, and as we rotated his cold germs did also!

In Paris, my wife Nancy developed a sore throat and she went to a pharmacy to get something for it. The clerk could only speak French and she could speak nothing but English, so she had to resort to hand motions to show where she ached!

She grabbed her throat and stuck out her tongue and moaned a couple of times! I was beginning to think he was going to put her in a hospital, thinking she was in dire distress!

But he finally understood and sold her a box of throat lozenges, just what she needed!

The four of us returned with many new stories and memories from a trip that introduced us to many foreign customs and attractions!

My Return Trip To Hawaii, Revisiting old Army Haunts

After retiring in 1986, my wife and I began to travel considerably, either by car and camper or by plane and boat. So we decided to take a trip to the Hawaiian Islands and revisit some of the places where I was stationed in the army, during World II.

After a turbulent flight over the Pacific Ocean from Los Angeles, we arrived in Honolulu. Young ladies with hula skirts and leis greeted us at the airport, and both of us were given leis of flowers accompanied with a kiss on the cheek.

I didn't remember such a greeting in 1945, when I embarked from our good ship, the U.S.S. Drew, with all of my comrades and our equipment. In fact, there was only military personnel in view.

We took a cab to our hotel on Waikiki Beach and after getting settled in our room, we took a walk on the beach. A lot more romantic than I remembered, and more beautiful, as we looked over toward Diamond Head! How could it have been, since my wife was not with me! In fact, I wasn't even married at that time!

Wanting my wife to see more of the Island of Oahu, I rented a small car and we drove around Honolulu. I looked for the old U. S. O. building, where I worked part time, as I served in the 15th Base Post Office, during my service tenure.

It was nowhere to be found, and it evidently had been replaced with a more modern building. In fact everything had been changed. During the war it was the Territory of Hawaii, now it was a state.

There were tourists everywhere and large buildings all over the city. It was hard to find any resemblance to the wartime Hawaii!

We took a tour of Pearl Harbor, very close to where I was stationed at Ft. Shafter, and saw the monument of the Arizona, one of the ships that was sunk during the famed Japanese attack, Dec. 7th, 1941.

I remembered how one of my uncles, who was in the Navy and on one of those ships, was killed that day! It was four years later that I was assigned there.

Driving around the Island of Oahu, we marveled at the beautiful flowers, palm trees and colorful birds. We toured the Polynesian village, a popular tourist attraction, and attended a luau, with all of its good stuff to eat. There was a presentation of hula girls, dancing with their grass skirts and colorful leis. We had to get up and dance the hula, after a few instructions! It provided a lot of laughs for the tourists!

Later in the week, we noticed an exhibit in the hotel, offering a free dinner and show at one of the more prestigious nightclubs. All we had to do was attend an hour program showing the advantages of buying real estate there.

Not realizing that was a good way to ruin a good vacation, we agreed to do this. The hour spent on this was really boring! But, for our time we were given two free tickets to the dinner and show.

The function was terrific, and about halfway of the show, a waitress came by and asked what we wanted to drink. We told her that we did not drink and that we didn't want anything.

The waitress insisted that we buy a drink, because that was required for free admission. I assured her we were not told about this and we would pass on the drink.

She left and soon we were accosted by a burly gentleman, who told us we would have to leave if we didn't purchase a drink. At that, we decided it was time to go and we did so, with the man following us every step of the way! For a time, it looked as if we were going to be hauled off to jail, for not spending our money there!

That left a bitter taste in our mouth, realizing that the race for the tourist dollar was now in full bloom in Honolulu, a big change from the war era!

Another day we agreed to go to Hawaii, the "Big Island," and see the volcanoes. We went to the airport and took a local Hawaiian Airlines plane. It would also take us on an air tour of other islands.

After we had been in the air about fifteen minutes, the pilot came on the intercom and said that it was necessary that he turn the plane around and return to the airport. The plane's emergency light had come on, indicating an electrical malfunction!

It became so quiet you could hear a pin drop! Just two weeks prior to our trip a plane had crashed on one of the islands, killing several people!

Everyone was in a nervous state as the pilot turned the plane back towards the airport! Few words were said and everyone buckled their seatbelts and waited!

The landing was made without any problems and we were allowed to deplane until the trouble was located. It was, and the plane resumed the trip, without some of its original passengers.

Soon we landed in Hilo, on the "Big Island," and began our bus tour of the volcanoes, and other attractions. First, we saw Mauna Loa, an active volcano, and Mauna Kea, a quiescent or sleeping volcano. About sixteen miles away was the largest active volcano in the world, Kilauea.

As we approached Kilauea, the bus driver advised us to roll up the windows, because the yellow sulphur dust floating in the air would cover everything. We were allowed to get off the bus and look into the large bowl-shaped hole. The yellow dust covered everything around the area. And the smell of sulphur was overwhelming!

We were shown a short movie of eruptions that had occurred and the paths of hot lava flowing to the sea. At the bottom of some of these old paths were beaches of black volcanic lava-rock, where the hot liquid fell into the water.

I was reminded of my tenure with the army at Oahu, when I was allowed a two-week vacation, and a group of us went to Hilo. We rode horses around the rim of the volcano and even took a trail down into the volcano. I wouldn't want to repeat that now!

After our side trip we returned to Honolulu, without incident, and resumed our vacation there. The weather was wonderful, staying around eighty degrees. This is a year round temperature and it rains often.

The main crops are pineapples and sugar cane, which results in much of the sugar exported to the mainland (as the natives referred to the states when it was a territory.)

We ate so much pineapple when I was in the service, that I was determined to never touch it when I got back home! We had pineapple for breakfast, lunch and dinner!

But would you know, I grew to like the taste of pineapple so well, it became a habit and I guess I couldn't quit! I still like a pineapple sandwich today!.

Despite the few blips we encountered on the trip, my wife and I enjoyed a great vacation. I was somewhat disappointed with the fact that the sleepy islands that I knew back in the 1940's had grown to be such a tourist mecca, with all of its hotels, motels and everything else representing commercialism.

Alaska Tour of Large Cities, Mt. McKinley, and Eskimo Village

A tour of Alaska, for someone who has never been to the most northern state, has to be a highlight of a lifetime. It is one-fifth the size of the entire country and filled with unbeliev- able sights of beautiful scenery, wildlife, glaciers, fishing and just about anything else a vacationer would desire!

In the year 2000, my wife and I made a two-week visit to the state and it ended too soon for us. It began the first week of August and the trip was fantastic! The weather was late summer, and being from the state of Georgia, we prefer that to winter, with its snow and freezing conditions.

Being one of the few times that we flew first class, our trip non-stop from Atlanta to Anchorage, was very nice! Before this, we didn't know how the "other half" lived, but we sampled it and it was wonderful! We had sufficient leg-room, snacks along the way, good meals and all of the trimmings!

A lady flew the same airline the other day, and she asked me, "did you know that you have to buy your meals on that airline now?" I told her, "no I didn't, and I'm glad we didn't wait until now for our trip!"

We arrived in Anchorage, the largest city in Alaska, and located our hotel for one night, since we would be leaving for Fairbanks the next day, where our tour began. My luggage was on the same flight but my wife's did not make it for some reason.

We departed on another airline for Fairbanks the next morning, with a promise from the airline, that her luggage would follow her. Along the way, the plane captain pointed out Mt. McKinley, and we were thrilled to see the famous tourist attraction from the air!

Settling into our hotel for a couple of days, we checked with the airline about the status of Nancy's luggage. We were told that it had not been found yet, but they were still tracking it.

She was getting desperate about this time and somewhat angry! Relating her predicament, the spokesman for the airline gave her a small allowance to buy some underwear! We had to travel by cab to a shopping center to look for unmentionables!

So far, this trip appeared to be "snakebit" and we were hoping things were going to get better!

Fairbanks is located in the central portion of Alaska, one hundred and fifteen miles south of the Artic Circle, and 1, 533 from Seattle, Washington. The region is somewhat flat as compared to other parts of the state.

The city is at the northern end of the Alaska railroad, with the southern end at Seward. In between these two cities lies some of the most amazing and beautiful scenery in the world!

On our first morning we boarded the Stern Wheeler Discovery to cruise the Chena and Tanana rivers, seeing many small and large animals along the way. Many cabins and native houses dot the banks of the waterways.

There were dogs and sleds, and we saw demonstrations of these on the cruise. We met and talked to several winners of the Iditarod dog-sled race, which is held annually. The grueling race covers more than a thousand miles over a two- week period.

In the afternoon we took a side trip to North Pole, Alaska, and toured Santa Claus's House. We had been told that Mr. Claus was in the house everyday to greet tourists, but when we got there, a sign informed us that he was out to lunch! Our bad luck seemed to continue. I had traveled thousands of miles with my list for Santa to fill for Christmas, and he was not there!

The day was filled with activities, however, with a trip that evening to a tourist attraction for a salmon bake and a musical revue. This seemed to be a popular event, with funseekers everywhere.

Back at our hotel that night, we again inquired about the lost luggage. We were told that it had been located where our trip began and was being placed on a plane to meet us.

The following night, about three a.m., a bellboy knocked on the door. "I have your luggage," he said. There it was, sitting on the floor, with clothes hanging out one side. The zipper had been ripped half off!

We had been asleep, but this awakened us totally and we checked the bag to see if anything was missing. It was hard to remember what had been packed, so we decided to tackle the problem after the trip was over.

Before leaving Fairbanks, we had a chance to see the Trans-Alaska Pipeline, built in the 1970's for the purpose of transporting oil. It begins at Prudhoe Bay and ends at the Marine Terminal at Prince William Sound, near Valdez.

Extending nearly 650 miles over mountains, glaciers, rivers and some of it underground the pipe is four feet in diameter, with eleven pump stations along the way. It is a world-class marvel and cost $8 Billion to build. It is owned by seven pipeline companies. Each native Alaskan citizen of the state is paid annual royalties from the oil.

Much of the pipeline is constructed five feet off the ground to enable animals to cross beneath it. Along the route there are many grizzlies, caribou, moose and reindeer, and they can pass under the pipe easily.

Leaving Fairbanks, we boarded the McKinley Explorer Domed Rail to Denali National Park, a distance of about one hundred and twenty one miles and lasts about four hours. The cars have clear domes over them and we could see the beautiful mountains, glaciers and wildlife along the way.

The tour guide offered a prize for the first person to spot a bald eagle during the trip. Soon after the announcement was made, my wife pointed out one in a tree as we rode leisurely along. She won the prize! She always has had good eyesight and I have never been able to hide much from her!

Arriving at the park, we checked into our lodging at McKinley Village, situated at the park entrance. This is a jumping off place for many of the rafting tours in Alaska. In fact, just before our trip, a group of people from our previous Baptist church, took a disastrous raft trip from here. Two of our friends drowned in a whirlpool, when they fell from their raft and were pulled to the bottom of the river.

Remembering this, we decided to find other things to do and see!

The following morning was the highlight of the trip. The Denali National Park is one of the most visited parks in the country and Mt. McKinley is the prime attraction. We climbed into a guided tour bus and began our wildlife trip that sometimes take visitors as far as ninety miles into the mountain.

The road is paved about fifteen miles and after that mostly dirt. The first miles were exciting with many animals in their natural habitat, but as we had completed about half of the trip, we came upon a sight that was amazing! The tour guide told everyone, that in his eighteen years of doing that work, he had never seen what we witnessed that day!

In a dry river bed alongside the road we saw a large grizzly bear and two cubs, sitting on a moose and devouring as much of the animal as they could! A pack of wolves was circling the bears, trying to get their portion of the moose!

The wolves had killed the moose and the bears ran them away and helped themselves. Now, the wolves were jumping at the bears, but staying at a safe enough distance to avoid the long-armed swipes from the large mama grizzly.

The wolves finally aggravated the bears enough to make them leave for quieter places, but not until they had gorged themselves on fresh moose. As soon as the moose was available to the wolves, there was howling and grabbing like you have probably never heard before!

Several tour buses had arrived by this time and the bridge above where the action occurred, was filled with tourists taking pictures and disregarding the danger they might be subjected to!

As we watched the action, from a safe distance, the excitement became too much for one man on the bus. Either the melee that was occurring or a kidney problem, urged the man to ask the driver what he could do about his problem! There were no toilet facilities on the bus or in the area, so the driver instructed him to go behind the bus.

A bigger problem, that loomed at that time, was a large grizzly that was nearby and another not far behind this one! The tour guide told the man to watch the bears and if either one started toward him, to run for the door!

The tourist decided his immediate problem was serious enough to attempt his mission, which he did, and safely returned to the bus. I'm not sure that was bravery or urgency!

Traveling further into the park, where public traffic was not allowed, we saw a total of eighteen grizzlies that day. Moose and caribou would walk across in front of our bus, paying us little attention. Dall sheep could be seen on the highest craggy cliffs, and many other wild animals were there for all to see.

At the end of the road, we could still see adventuresome backpackers plodding along, with their camping equipment! It would almost take an act of congress to convince me to camp anywhere in that area!

The trip lasted the better part of the day, and it was awesome! We returned to the hotel tired but mesmerized from all of the wild animals that we had seen up real close! Any trip to Alaska should include the Denali National Park.

After two days exploring the wonders of Mt. McKinley and the surrounding area, we resumed our journey south by tour bus. The trip was some two hundred miles through fantastic scenery along the Alaska Mountain Range.

We passed the spectacular Turnagain Arm, where the incoming water from the sea turns and flows back from where it came from. Much of the land we passed that day is somewhat unstable, with the freezing cold of the winters causing a permafrost, and the normal heat of the summer melting it. This causes a sinking sludge, damaging many buildings foundations.

Arriving at our destination, Alyeska Resort, Alyeska, we settled into our luxurious room at this world class lodging facility. An equally famous restaurant sits at the top of a mountain, a cable car ride away, leaving from the hotel.

The next day we drove to Seward, Alaska, where we boarded our cruise boat for a full day of sightseeing in the Kenai Fjords National Park. Cruising through Resurrection Bay, we passed Cheval Island and on to Holgate Glacier.

There, the boat captain shut off all engines and told us to listen to the sounds of the glacier, as it moved toward the sea. It was awesome, as great chunks of ice would break off and fall into the sea!

On some of the rocky islands, near the water, sea lions lay in the sunshine, some weighing up to a ton. Females were smaller, with some weighing up to 650 lbs. Sea otters, seals, humpback whales, Orcas (killer whales), and many birds were viewed as we cruised.

Too soon, the day was over and we returned to our hotel at Alyeska. The next morning we departed for Anchorage, where we added a couple more days as an option to our trip.

This time we were headed by plane to the Artic Circle and the Eskimo village of Kotzebue. As we approached Alaska's largest Eskimo village, we wondered where the plane was going to land. We could see a short and narrow strip leading right up to the sea, but our plane was fairly large.

The landing was made without incident, however, and we were met at the airport by a group of Eskimos, with their traditional rubbing of the noses. I was a little hesitant, since my nose-rubber was a heavy-set male!

After a lunch of salmon and other local dishes, we toured the small village of cabins, huts and small buildings, I was a little disappointed in not seeing the entire village made up of tents and igloos!

We were taken on a short trip to see the tundra, which is the very unstable ground that the village was built upon. It is boggy and wet, and you wonder how any building could stand on it. But we were assured that, even though the ground shifts, allowances are made to keep the buildings stable.

My wife and I were inducted into the Artic Circle Club and our tour guide, who did the inducting, turned out to be a former Miss Alaska. I mused to myself, "why couldn't she have met me at the airport, to rub noses instead of the rough- looking man!" Since my wife was standing nearby, I didn't muse out loud!

We enjoyed an Inupiat Eskimo culture slide presentation and saw demonstrations of traditional dancing and blanket tossing. As we toured the village along the sea, there were many pole frameworks full of salmon, drying in the sun. These were high enough that the animals couldn't get them.

Later in the day, we boarded our flight to Nome, a famous gold rush town, only accessible by plane, boat or dogsled. This is the end of the famous Iditarod annual race, starting in Anchorage. Again we saw dogsled demonstrations and panned for gold. Our one night stay there was in the Gold Rush Hotel, a somewhat rustic place to stay.

Returning to Anchorage, we spent our final night there, resting up for our trip back to Georgia. Back home in Atlanta, we had "a bone to pick" with our airline, since we had to hold my wife's luggage together with safety pins the entire trip. The zipper could not be repaired after the airline semi-destroyed it!

Around the World in Thirty Days, With Side Trips

In 1999, my wife and I were approaching our 49th wedding anniversary, and we made a decision to celebrate our 50th a year early. After all we were not getting any younger and for what we had in mind, we would need all of the physical stamina we could manage.

A trip around the world always appealed to us, but we didn't know if that was possible, considering the cost, time involved and other details.

Elaine, one of our daughters, lived at that time in Singapore with her family and visiting them would require flying half the distance. They were there as missionaries for the Campus Crusade For Christ, but have returned to their headquarters in Orlando, Fla. for the present.

Working out the details with a travel consultant, we set out to "spend our fortune," and not to "seek our fortune," as an old saying goes!

Our itinerary would take us to Singapore, by way of Tokyo, New Zealand, Australia, Thailand, Greece, Turkey, Spain and Germany. From Frankfort we flew back to the United States. The entire trip encompassed over 40,000 miles.

It takes about twenty-five hours for the flight from Atlanta to Singapore, and that much time on a plane is somewhat tiring. But the excitement of the trip kept our adrenalin going and we made it in good shape.

We secured a hotel room to make it more convenient for ourselves and our daughter, since they had a small apartment, and there was five of them. Besides, this enabled us to sleep as late as we wished. After all, old folks need their rest!

Singapore is a large ultra-modern city and would take longer than the one week that we had to do justice to sight- seeing. It is predominately Asian, but just about any nationality can be seen on the streets.

After reuniting with our relatives, they set about showing us the city. Almost everything can be accessed by the rapid transit system, and we made use of it.

From Mount Faber we took a cable car across the Singapore Bay to the Island of Sentosa, a beautiful resort with a blend of sun and sea. The flora and fauna, along with the manicured gardens are something to see!

The many museums and exhibits are linked by a small train that circles the park every few minutes.

One of the most memorable events of the trip occurred on this island as we finished a tour of a ship museum. As we exited from the building, I could see a group of monkeys sitting around the area. I had seen them in other areas moving around at will, and I supposed they were somewhat tame.

Outside the museum door, in a flash, we had monkeys all over our backs, jumping around and looking for food! A couple of the grandchildren had backpacks and the monkeys zeroed in on those. They reached into the packs searching for candy bars or anything to eat!

Thinking that we were under attack, I began to jump around kicking and beating the monkeys off! They retreated, all except one large one, who was the leader of the pack. He stood his ground! We slowly backed away and fortunately they didn't follow.

Later, we learned that the monkeys were generally not as aggressive, but we didn't want to tempt them anymore. This was a first for my wife and I! We had never been attacked by a band of monkeys before!

After spending some quality time with our daughter, son-in-law and grandchildren, we visited and toured the city- country of Singapore a little more, and said goodbye, reluctantly.

We flew to Auckland, New Zealand for a four-day whirlwind tour of the Northern Island by bus. The city of Auckland is modern and beautiful with its colorful flowers and is known as the "City of Sails." This is the home of America's Cup, sailing event.

Beginning the tour of the North Island, we boarded a bus for Waikato Valley, center of the richest farming districts in the world. At Waitomo, we took a boat through a group of caves, called Glow Worm Grotto. Inside the caves, we could see millions of glow worms on the ceilings, lighting our way!

That evening, in the city of Rotorua, we were treated to a performance of traditional Maori songs and dances at a local theatre. The entire city is set aside for the Maori natives, as a tourist attraction.

The next morning we toured an area of boiling mud pools and steaming underground rivers. The area is filled with volcanic pools and geysers. Later we saw a demonstration of sheep-mustering, with sheep dogs, and shearing.

Since the time of our trip was in October, the weather was very nice, this being their spring. We found that New Zealand's seasons are the opposite of the Northern Hemisphere.

Our next stop was Sydney, Australia, the cultural center of the continent, with its famed Sydney Opera House, opened in 1973. This is a delightful, varied and interesting large city to visit.

After settling in our hotel, we toured the city by land and water over the next two days. We took a short tour of the Opera House and listened in on a concert in progress. A visit to a Koala Park was interesting.

The ten-acre park included many animals in addition to Koalas. There were kangaroos, dingoes (native dogs), wombats, birds of all kinds, emus, wallabies, Tasmanian devils, crocodiles and reptiles. Some of these could be viewed up close.

A couple of days later, we flew to Cairns, Australia, where we toured Port Douglas. Next day we took a Quicksilver boat to the Great Barrier Reef, off the coast of Australia. There, at the visitor's platform, we saw many types of large and small fish, from an underwater tunnel. The reefs below the area were spectacular in color and formation.

Snorkeling was offered on our trip, but we decided to pass on this. We could watch, though, as others snorkeled and fish larger than the people would pass near them, including sharks!

Our viewing platform was about sixty miles out from Port Douglas and we were told there are over 2,900 individual reefs in the network. Our catamaran traveled about thirty-five miles an hour, taking us about two hours each way.

There was a feeding time for the fish, and it was interesting to watch the smaller wrasse fish cleaning the teeth of the larger fish, that came to the area for food and dental cleaning!

Leaving the area, we flew back to Sydney to prepare for our longer flight the next day, to Athens, Greece, with a short stopover in Bangkok, Thailand.

Spending a large amount of our vacation on planes and getting to airports, we finally arrived in Athens, Greece. From the air it appeared to be a very large city, with many colorful buildings.

We speak no amount of the Greek language and had never seen a Drachma, the local currency. At that time, we were told a U. S. Dollar equaled about three hundred Drachmas. It was all "Greek" to us!

This particular flight had been unusually rough on my wife's luggage and the bag was pretty much totaled. After complaining to the airline, a representative showed up at our hotel with several bags, offering a replacement. Nancy chose a nice bag and was pleased with the service she received.

The first three days in Athens were devoted to touring the city, both the ancient portion and the modern sections. We drove by Constitution Square, the House of Parliament, Memorial to the Unknown Soldier and the Greek Orthodox Cathedral.

We learned we could conduct our own walking tour of the downtown area, by catching a bus from our hotel and telling the driver to let us off at McDonald's Hamburgers. Yes, the same McDonald's as in the U. S! We couldn't get away from them! They are located as close to the center of the city as they could get.

The tour bus dropped us off at the Acropolis, which is a large hill and the site of much ancient history. It was a difficult climb up the stone steps to the top of the hill where the Parthenon stands. Further around is the Temple of Athena Nike. Most of the buildings are ruins, centuries old, but some restoring has been done.

It was explained to us that the Turks destroyed much of the architecture centuries ago during an invasion. Prior to this, the Greeks claim that many of the marble sculptures were looted in 1801 by Lord Elgin, of Great Britain, and have been on display in the British Museum ever since.

After seeing many tourist attractions in the city, we embarked from Piraeus on a four-day cruise of islands in the Aegean Sea.

Our ship was a large one, named World Renaissance. Our cabin was nice and comfortable.

Mykonos was the first of these islands and we enjoyed a leisurely stroll around the narrow winding cobble-stoned streets, many with shops and stores tempting the passing tourists. Windmills dot the landscape as you look out at the nearby hills.

The next stop was in Kusadasi, Turkey, where there are many carpet businesses and you can watch it being made. You are given sales presentations on fine floor coverings and urged to send one home.

Boarding a bus, we rode up the Mountain of Doves to see Mary's House. This is a stone structure where the mother of Jesus lived her last days, according to historians. The building was prepared originally by John, the Apostle.

Leaving the area, we drove down the mountain to the biblical city of Ephesus. This is one of the largest excavations of ancient cities of the world. The entrance of the city is the Magnesian Gate. We walked by Hadrian's Temple, Odeon (concert hall), the steamheated Baths of Scolastika and The Great Theater, where Paul preached to crowds up to 24,000. We walked down Arcadian Way, where Mark Anthony and Cleopatra rode in processions.

Going back to our cruise ship, we continued on to the Isle of Patmos. We visited the Monastery of St. John, built around 900 years ago, housing manuscripts, mosaic icons, vestments and jewelry, in the museum.

The bus transported us to the Grotto, where we saw the cave that the apostle John lived in during his exile. In the wall of the cave was a niche, carved out for John's head to rest as he slept. According to the Gospels, John wrote the last book of the Bible, Revelations, in this cave.

Another day we arrived at Rhodes and took a short tour of the island. Our tour bus took us to the city of Lindos, and we walked inside the ancient medieval walls and saw many old structures.

The next island was Crete, with Heraklion being the fifth largest city of Greece. The island is mountainous with museums and ancient artifacts everywhere. Many churches and monasteries dot the island.

Santorini was the last island on our trip and we had to board a smaller boat to get to land. Reason for this was the rough sea, making it dangerous for larger cruise ships to get near the docks.

We boarded the tour bus and visited the excavated city of Akrotiri, similar to the famed city of Pompeii in Italy. This city was older, however, dating back 3,500 years. The entire city currently being excavated was covered by a huge canvas structure to protect the work and workers from the elements.

Returning to the city of Fira, we toured the narrow alleys of the picturesque village. To get back to the port pier, we took a cable car, since the descent down was too steep for automobiles. The small village sat on a mountain rim above the Aegean Sea.

The cruise ended as we returned to the port of Piraeus, and even though it had been educational, adventurous and highly enjoyable, we were happy to get our feet on land again!

Spending another night in Athens, we readied ourselves for the last leg of our journey, before we returned home.

The next day we were transported to the central place to catch a cab or bus going to the airport. We had been warned to avoid the large black limousines offering rides, since they were often scam artists, charging high fees for the ride.

Not finding a cab readily, I flagged down one of the limousines and asked his price. I was given a price that seemed reasonable, and even though it was quoted in Drachmas, the driver seemed honest.

He took the long way to the airport, showing us a lot of scenery on the way. He had lived in New York City, he said.

Arriving at the airport, we soon understood why he was trying to seem friendly. I was told the fee was $65. The usual bus ride cost $15. I refused to pay that much, since he had quoted about $20. We argued and I threatened to call a nearby policeman to settle the dispute. He didn't want that, but to get rid of him I offered $50, and he took it, complaining all the while! I learned a good lesson about foreign scam artists!

There were many good memories left with us about Athens and the Aegean Sea Island Cruise. However, the scam artist and one other thing left us with a flawed impression about the city of Athens.

Dogs! There were stray dogs everywhere. As you sit in some of the sidewalk restaurants, and there are many, dogs of all descriptions wander around the tables begging for food.

Before the Olympics in Athens recently, the city officials began a campaign to pick up all of the stray dogs and keep them contained while the crowds were there. Whether they were successful or not, I have no knowledge. It had to be a huge job, since there were thousands.

Our last side trip was to Madrid, Spain, and to get there we first had to fly to Frankfurt, Germany. There we had to change planes for Spain.

At the Athens airport we checked our luggage and boarding passes and sat in the lounge area for our flight. The time for the flight to leave, came and passed. We were told the departing plane had mechanical problems and it would be delayed.

For three hours we sat and waited and finally the plane was ready. By this time we knew our connecting flight in Frankfurt would leave without us!

Arriving late at the German airport, we furiously worked to get another flight out to Madrid, where our hotel had been booked that night. We were in danger of losing our reservation there.

Finally, we made arrangements for the flight out and sat again in the lounge to wait. The wait was approaching two hours in Frankfurt, when we were escorted to a plane. We could only sit on this plane, because another was being readied for our trip!

The plane being readied had encountered problems upon landing, with a flock of birds, and the engine was damaged!

After about thirty minutes we were allowed to deplane from our resting place and catch trams to the plane that was to take us to Madrid. By the time we were settled on the final plane, we were in a foul mood, and "tired to the bone."

We arrived at the Madrid airport about five hours late, but we did have some good news. Our hotel had held our room, eliminating one worry! However, we discovered there was another problem. Our luggage had gotten lost in all of the day's activities!

Checking into the Hotel Opera, we explained to the manager the problems we had been subjected to that day, and that our luggage had not followed us. The airline having assured us the luggage would soon be found, we asked the hotel management to bring it to our room when it arrived.

Tired and weary with the night half gone, we headed to bed after we showered. We had no clothes to change into, so we did the best we could under the circumstances!

With a touch of humor my wife said, "I sure hope there is not a fire in the hotel tonight, because we might have to grab a sheet!"

I told her we would be in style, since I had seen a lot of people on the street seemingly wrapped in something similar to colorful sheets!

Our luck was changing, though, and there was no fire that night. The next day the luggage arrived and we were turning over a new leaf.

That afternoon we decided to take a stroll around the area. The Madrid Opera House was directly across the street from the hotel. This seemed to be the culture center of the city. The Royal Palace is nearby and the Gran Via, with its traditional shops and fashion stores.

We spotted a Seven-Eleven store down one of the streets and entered to see if it was similar to the ones in the States. It was, and as we were walking toward the exit, we were confronted with a commotion of sorts!

Two women began to struggle with a man in the doorway, and the man began yelling, "pickpockets, thieves, help, help!" The man was holding his pocket containing his wallet, with all of his strength!

The store management rushed to his aid and the two women fled down the street. The man turned out to be an American tourist and he had just encountered two of the many wallet-snatching thieves, that we later learned were numerous in the business area.

The poor elderly man, who must have seemed to be an easy hit to the thieves, was somewhat shaken, and we felt sorry for him! As we left the area, my wife and I both secured our wallets and valuables with renewed attention.

Later that evening we dined at The Hard Rock Cafe, just down the street from our hotel.

Happy with the fact that our luggage was once again with us, we slept well that night. No fires, no burglars in the room, everything uneventful!

We took a tour of the city the next day, seeing the Mayor's Palace, the Christopher Columbus Monument, The Prado Museum, many cathedrals, gardens and other tourist attractions. It is a large and beautiful city of ancient and modern history.

We spent three days and nights in Madrid and toyed with the idea of going across the Strait of Gibraltar to Morocco, but there had been some unfavorable publicity about Americans being welcome there.

I wanted to see the Rock of Gibraltar, which we have heard about all of our lives, but there were so many places and sights to see, it was obvious we were going to miss a lot of them. We had heard of the vicious apes on the big rock, but were not inclined to see them!

It would have been nice to visit Lisbon, the capital of Portugal, but it wasn't in our plans or finances.

As we left Madrid, we had to go back to Frankfurt and catch our flight back to the United States. The return trip was made without incident, but was another long day.

Back at the Atlanta airport, we spent a large part of the day going through customs, claiming our baggage and retrieving our car, which had been stored for the entire trip.

Making it back home, after going around the world in thirty days, we were wiser, more tired than when we left, older and definitely poorer! But it was an experience to remember!

Our Trip to the Orient was
A Lifetime Experience

Excitement filled the air as my wife and I claimed our seats on the plane headed for Tokyo, Japan, some seventy two hundred miles from Atlanta, Ga. It was the early days of November, 1982, and a winter chill was already in the air.

Our plane would take us to Los Angeles and on to Tokyo, after a short layover. We had been discussing this trip for months and I had even toyed with the idea of starting an import business from the Orient upon retirement.

We planned to visit some brass factories in Taipei and Hong Kong, further researching the idea, and making up our minds if we really wanted to do this. Also, our daughter and her family lived in Manila, Philippines and we would visit them for a week.

After the long flight we arrived in Tokyo, bushed but anxious to see new horizons and explore waiting adventures! At this time the population of the city was nearing nine million people, one of the largest in the world.

So, we settled into our room at the Hotel New Otani, after a late arrival not permitting us to explore our new surroundings much. The room was luxurious and we enjoyed a good night's sleep.

The next day we signed up for a visit to Mt. Fuji and a ride on the bullet train. The mountain was partly obscured by a dense fog but the ride on the super-fast train was exhilarating! As we passed the power poles along the track, they looked like matchsticks lined up together. As the train started its acceleration the gravitational pull was tremendous with increasing speed.

We visited the city of Kamakura and saw the giant figure of Buddha, which was cast in 1252, and now a National Treasure. The face of this Buddha measures almost seven feet long. There are many Buddhist Temples throughout the country, since that is one of the dominant religions along with Shinto.

The following day we toured Tokyo, visiting Meiji Shrine Outer Garden and Asakusa Kannon Temple, with its Nakamise Shopping Arcade. Many of the items for sale were contributed by Buddhists for the upkeep of the priests. That included home-canned foods, meats, clothing and other items.

Earlier as we walked along in the restaurant district of the city, we noticed the eateries advertised their meals with a life size picture of a plate containing the food, on the window. I thought, this is a great idea for tourists who do not speak Japanese. All they have to do to order is to point to the picture!

Saying "sayonara" to Japan, we flew to Beijing, China, a place vastly different from what we experienced elsewhere in the world. Communism was very much in evidence and we were made aware of it from the beginning to the end of this part of the journey.

Tourism had not been openly welcomed many years prior to our visit, so we were screened considerably. They issued us Chinese Script for our use as money and could only spend it at the Friendship stores. We were warned not to call it "funny money" before Chinese officials.

Upon leaving China we had to exchange all money that had been issued to us, since it was not allowable to take their currency out of the country.

The hotel in Beijing was very comfortable and we had to ask for keys, since it was not their custom to lock doors. It was our custom, however, to lock the door and feel safe!

The first day there included a trip to a local zoo, where we saw all of the native animals, including the giant Panda bears. As we walked along the rocky path near the Panda area, one of the elderly women in our group fell and broke her arm.

The Chinese officials rushed her to a nearby hospital and gave her immediate treatment. She related how they had taken her into a room and x-rayed the bone. Taking the x-ray picture into the next room, the doctor read it by holding it up before the one light bulb hanging in the middle of the room.

After they placed the cast on her arm, she was in the process of being dismissed, when she realized she didn't have enough Chinese money to pay her bill. To her amazement the doctor and nurses took up enough donations to pay the bill! They ushered her out the hospital door, having made a staunch friend.

Part of the Beijing tour included the Forbidden City and Tiananmen Square. The latter has been in the news a good bit the last few years, following many protests by Chinese activists against government treatment.

The Forbidden City is an attraction on every tour. Yellow is the symbol of the royal family, resulting in that color being used throughout. Outside it is surrounded by a moat and red wall.

This was the imperial palace during the Ming and Qing dynasties and is the largest such facility in the world. Consisting of two sections, the northern and southern, the palace is now used as a museum and tourist attraction. Many artifacts and cultural objects adorn the place.

The Ming Tombs were on our tour, this being the burial mausoleums for thirteen emperors of the Ming Dynasty. All underground and decorated with marble and gold bricks, the main attraction is the gold imperial crown.

The next day we had a trip out to a commune near Beijing. Everyone in the tour was excited about seeing this, since we had only read about the Chinese peasants living in groups such as these.

As we arrived by motor coach, we began the tour at the central living area, surrounded by farm crops as far as you could see. Neat rows of cabbage and other vegetables, rice, herbs and crops dotted the landscape.

We were taken to visit one farm house, which consisted of a combination living room and dining room, and a bedroom. All around the walls were photos of relatives and Communist leaders. Outside the room was an outdoor kitchen, where the cooking was done over a stone barbecue pit. This was a kind of arbor and open to the elements and insects!

Toilet facilities were in a small building similar to our outdoor "privies," except there were no half moons on the door!

Each commune has its own Communist leader, similar to a town mayor, with authority delegated to various other members. They have a group hospital and we were given a tour of the building, with patients lying on hard uncomfortable beds.

The rooms were dirty and hot with one electric bulb hanging in the center of the room. There were no screens on the windows, no curtains or pictures on the walls.

My wife had broken a cap off one of her teeth and saved it the day before. As we passed by a dentist chair in one room I teasingly asked if she would like to get the tooth repaired there? I didn't have to wait long for her answer, which was a resounding "NO!"

The hospital didn't have many patients, probably because they made them so uncomfortable that they would have to be really sick to want to go there!

The fields were busy with workers and some women were herding pigs and other animals along the roads. Others were washing clothes in a nearby river, wringing them dry and hanging them out to dry in the sun.

Some men were driving three-wheeled motorized trucks and women were pushing or pulling two-wheeled carts. Women were carrying poles over their shoulders balancing baskets on each end, filled with farm products.

Returning back to our hotel, the day had reminded me of my childhood work on the farm, but thankfully it was under much better conditions and circumstances!

Everything around the city of Beijing is steeped in ancient history, with the many revolutions in the past and cultural changes brought by each. Chinese historians claim that "Peking Man," a primitive man in the stone ages, lived in a cave near Beijing.

The city was made the capital of the People's Republic of China in 1949, and at the time of our trip had a population of almost nine million.

Other sites visited while there were the Summer Palace, with its colorful lake and parks; the Temple of the Reclining Buddha; Temple of Heaven; and Beihai Park, with its lake and Jade Isle, having many splendid pavilions.

We could not wander at will around the city, but had to pretty much stay with the tour party. Each morning the businesses would allow all of the workers to exercise in the streets for thirty minutes or so. No traffic was allowed on the streets at this time.

At night the cars passing through the business district were not allowed to turn on their headlights, with the reasoning being it would blind the bikers. The streets were filled with people riding bicycles night and day.

During the day there were many odd-looking carts being moved through the streets, some motorized and some pulled by animals. Others were pushed by people. There were many automobiles also.

Along the streets were businesses selling food on the sidewalk. There were chickens, ducks and other animals hanging from racks, without their feathers or hair. Cabbages were everywhere. Some dried, some fresh, others of all descriptions! All stores had large piles of them outside on the cement.

At the time of this trip I was convinced that the national food was cabbage, along with rice!

On a day trip from Beijing we took a motor coach to see the Great Wall of China, probably the best-known tourist attraction of the country. While there, another tour was visiting the same area, and we were really surprised as we recognized two people in that group.

They were one of our son-in-laws parents from Denver, Colorado! They had earlier surprised us on the plane to Beijing, having planned a China tour at the same time as ours. What were the odds that we would run into them on this trip nine thousand miles from home and neither knew the other was there?

The Great Wall is an architectural structure that boggles the mind, when considering that it dates back over 2,500 years, and the untold labor, money and time involved with the gigantic project. It has long been considered one of the World's Wonders.

Reconstruction of some of the Wall has been underway for two hundred years or more, since many of the invaders from neighboring countries destroyed portions of it. Much of the wall where we walked is steep and filled with rough stones, making it difficult to stay on your feet.

Back in Beijing, this was our last day there, and it just happened to be our thirty-second wedding anniversary! We had long wanted to have a meal of "Peking Duck." This seemed to be the best opportunity we would have.

Going to one of the finest restaurants in the city, we ordered the duck, without checking the price. We didn't want to ruin the meal before it even got there!

Finally, the roasted "Peking Duck" arrived. It was nothing like the picture on the menu, which showed a large whole duck, lying on a plate, tantalizing your taste buds! Mine was about half the size, and resembled a large wharf rat, dried and wrinkled! My wife's was all cut up and pulled apart, and dry as a bone!

We couldn't eat it and left the restaurant greatly disappointed, and still hungry, but not for any kind of duck!

The next morning we left by plane for Hangchow, for more exciting adventures in this land that was so very foreign to us!

After the trip we learned that our son-in-law's parents had left Beijing about the same time and toured the ancient city of Xian, with its 6,000 life-size terra cotta soldiers. Upon leaving Xian the only plane available was a very old Russian relic.

The seats inside were dining-room types, sitting straight up, with seat belts. They were very uneasy about the trip, and as they rattled down the runway to take off, the woman said, "Ed, I guess this is it, goodbye!" But they did make it, although somewhat shaken!

Arriving in Hangchow we found that the city was noted for its picturesque scenery. The explorer, Marco Polo, described it as one of the most beautiful cities in the world. The climate is mild year round and the floral and fauna growth is somewhat colorful.

One of its most popular attractions is West Lake, with its floating gardens, waterside pavilions, and stone pagodas. We saw the Jade Spring and Botanical Garden, a "paradise" for fish.

There was a monastery and the Six Harmonies Pagoda, where we climbed the stairs to the top, giving us a good view of the area. The Flower Harbour had a viewing bridge, where thousands of colorful fish could be seen.

One of the large parks was having a chrysanthemum show and there were many visitors, both locals and tourists, moving along the paths alive with color. A young Chinese mother was showing the pretty flowers to her daughter, who appeared to be about three years of age. The child seemed very friendly and my wife asked permission to take a picture with her. After permission was granted, the picture was taken and there was a short wait until the Polaroid image came out.

The mother and child must not have seen that kind of camera before since they were amazed at the picture. My wife gave the picture to the child and that must have been the cue for everyone in the area to gather and look!

I thought she was being attacked, since she was surrounded by a large crowd, but they were only curious about the picture. Many requested photos for themselves, but she had to gracefully decline.

We moved away from the area but the mother and child followed us for another thirty minutes, curious as to who we were, I suppose!

The visit to Hangchow was educational and delightful and we wondered what the city of Shanghai would be like, since it was next on our list.

Arriving there we checked into the Jing Jiang Hotel and began to check out this large metropolitan seaport city of over eleven million. It has developed from a sleepy fishing village over the years to an important center of industry, science and technology.

There was a large Friendship store in Shanghai giving us an opportunity to shop for silk, jewelry, arts and crafts, and other Chinese products. It was rumored that the prices were higher than regular Chinese stores, but that was the only place we were allowed to shop.

We toured the Shanghai Zoo, the Yu Garden, a silk factory and watched as they produced items on old time looms, and visited the Children's Palace, where we were treated to a concert by the children.

One of the most enjoyable parts of the city's tour was a short cruise on the Yangtze River, which runs through the city and into the East China Sea. The tour guide informed us that we were not allowed to photograph any military installations on either side of the river.

He said, that Chinese police were on the ship and if they caught anyone taking that kind of picture, their camera would be confiscated! We took a lot of photos but we were careful not to invite trouble.

With our time running out on this tour, we caught a plane to Canton (Guangzhou), the last stop in China proper. Upon leaving Canton we were going to Hong Kong, but at this time it was still under British rule.

Canton is located on the southern end of China and is a city of more than six million. We checked into the Dong Fang Hotel and had luxurious accommodations, with mosquito nets over our four-poster bed, and other amenities. I wondered what these were for because I hadn't seen a mosquito since we had been in China.

Many elaborate temples, mausoleums, Buddha statues and other cultural points of interest adorn the city. It is a busy seaport located on the Pearl River which empties into the South Sea. The surrounding land is fertile delta soil and many small farms dot the area.

Touring Canton was interesting and informative along with tasting some of the world's best Chinese cuisine. We saw factories for machine-woven carpets of all descriptions, and others for seat-coverings for vehicles and furniture. Many produced drapery material and others dealt with silk products.

We were very comfortable in the luxurious hotel room we occupied in Canton and were reluctant to leave, but our schedule called for a train ride south to the exciting city of Hong Kong.

The Kowloon-Canton railroad is a good way to see some of the countryside in south China. It wanders along through rice fields, duck and chicken farms, vegetable fields and cattle grazing meadows.

Many areas were built up to make terraced farms. Further along we saw monasteries, ancient temples and tree-lined bays.

The train itself was unique, in that some coaches were reserved for tourists and others were similar to cattle cars. Tourist cars had fairly decent seats but the others had some seats and standing room areas.

As we moved slowly south we began to see why some rail cars were a bit rugged. At stops along the route many local passengers would board these with animals of many types. Some would hop aboard with chickens under their arms. Others would be leading pigs, and some would have ducks. I don't suppose any had cows because it would be a little difficult to get one of those in a rail car with people.

It seemed that this is a common occurrence, since this is a good way to get their animals and products to markets in Hong Kong.

I'm glad they kept tourists separated from the locals, because that would have been a miserable ride with a pig on my lap!

After this interesting land trip we arrived in the world-renowned city of Hong Kong and were taken by coach to the Regency Hotel, a new one just built by Chinese interests along with a prominent architect and developer in Atlanta, Ga.

This city proved to be one like no other in the world and we were excited beyond words!

Beginning our seventeenth day of the tour, we had made an appointment with the owner of a large brass factory in Hong Kong, who insisted on taking us out to eat, but we didn't accept his offer. We were there to tour his plant and possibly order products for export to the U. S. Besides, we were a little tired of Chinese food by this time.

He only spoke Chinese and conversed with us through an interpreter. At times the conversation became humorous, with much sign language. Finally, when our tour was over and we were saying goodbye, the factory owner said he was making a trip to the United States soon, and would we take him out to eat when he came? I assured him we would be glad to!

Later in the day we took a Harbor sunset cruise and visited a "floating city." We were advised not to eat in a "floating" restaurant, however, since sanitary conditions were questionable. We did eat a Chinese meal nearby, which was good, but we were longing for a good American meal, after two weeks of the same. By the way, we never did master the art of eating with chop sticks, and the waiters really gave us the evil eye when asked for forks.

Outside the restaurant could be seen boats of all descriptions, junks, ferry, pleasure and most were very colorful. We were told that some of the boat people rarely leave their junks, making them their full-time homes.

The next day we took a trip by coach of Hong Kong Island, crossing under the harbor through a tunnel to Victoria Island. Driving to the Aberdeen Fishing Village, we continued to Repulse Bay Beach. We visited the Tiger Balm Garden, a colorful attraction.

We took the scenic tram to Victoria peak, overlooking the harbor and giving us a bird's eye view of Hong Kong. Eating lunch in the Peak Restaurant was quite an experience, with the magnificent panorama from high above the city.

That afternoon was free and we wandered through many shops along the main streets. We were reminded that purchases were duty free and the pressure to buy was great. There were suits, jewelry, baskets, and electronic gadgets of all kinds.

I was tempted to buy a zoom lens for my camera, which was about half the price back home. The clerk in a camera store told me he didn't have my brand but would have it the next day. Returning the next morning, the clerk showed me the lens and I noticed it didn't have my brand name on the product.

As I pointed this out, the clerk became enraged to the point of threatening to throw me out of the store! It looked as if an international incident was about to occur!

Despite the argument, the bargain was too good a buy to pass up so I ended up purchasing the item. It turned out to be worth the price. The hassle was a little unnerving, however!

The city of Hong Kong was at that time still controlled by the British, but has since been returned to China. There probably have been many changes since our trip.

We left the exotic city to continue our itinerary and headed for Taiwan for a few days. Having scheduled another appointment with a brass factory owner, we were looking forward to seeing his products.

As we checked into the Taipei Hilton we were told that the hotel could not honor our room reservation, since the hotel was filled. However, they could put us in the honeymoon suite on the top floor at the same price.

They had no trouble convincing us to take the suite and it turned out to be luxurious! It had a living room, bedroom, couple of baths and showers and a kitchen. We could get used to living like this! We had no need for the kitchen, since we didn't plan to cook.

Our appointment arrived at the hotel and we asked him to come up. I'm sure he must have been impressed with our accommodations, and he brought us a gift, being a Chinese custom.

He took us on a short tour of the city and to his factory, which seemed to be thirty miles from our hotel. The roads were pretty bad, with potholes everywhere. We passed through many sections of the large city, that were rundown, despite the main business area being modern and impressive.

Reaching the factory, we found that for some reason the electricity had been cut off for the entire area that day. The factory workers had gone home and the building was dark. The Chinese man drove us back to the hotel, after giving us catalogs of his products, and we thanked him for his efforts.

The following day we scheduled a coach tour of the northern tip of Taiwan, which is somewhat mountainous and cooler than Taipei. The entire island bisects the Tropic of Cancer and the weather can get quite warm at times.

On the tour we found that the city of Keelung is one of the wettest in the world, with an average of 214 days of rain each year. It also is the home of a seventy four foot statue of Kuan Yin, the Chinese Goddess of Mercy.

About halfway around the tour, the driver said he would take us to a very unique restaurant for lunch if we approved. Describing the place, he stated, "this is the place the politicians and officials come for a rare delicacy!"

Continuing, he said, "the meal they serve is illegal, but the restaurant is popular so they stay in business." He then told us that the meal consisted of monkey brains! The animal is strapped in the table with his head protruding slightly. The server whacks off the top of his head and the diners begin their feast, with the monkey still kicking!

Needless to say, not one person on the bus wanted to eat at that restaurant! In fact, the driver had just about killed the appetite of everyone for any kind of meal!

Further along the route we entered Yehliu National Park, where there were many natural formations of rocks, having been sculptured by the wind and sea erosion, leaving them as marvels of nature.

Back in Taipei we toured the main attractions, the National Palace Museum with its Chinese art treasures, the National Palace, and others. Leaving the bus we walked around the city and discovered it must have been a holiday of sorts. We had been told that the streets were converted to open air restaurants for the worship of individual gods on these observances.

The streets were filled with little stands cooking, serving and people squatting on the sidewalks eating! My nose was not accustomed to the smells that came from some of the stands and I wondered what kind of meat was being cooked!

Early the next morning we caught a plane for Manila, Philippines, where our daughter and son-in-law, who were missionaries with the Campus Crusade For Christ, lived. They had lived in the country more than a dozen years.

They met us at the airport and it must have been twenty miles or more to Quezon City, where they lived. We rode through streets that were one continuous pothole, instead of having one now and then! Many streets had raw sewage running alongside and were quite smelly!

They had improved their little home there and it was very comfortable. Not very far away was a small store that was somewhat unique. To buy items the person had to stand at a counter outside and ask for the item and it would be brought to the window.

About fifteen feet from the window was a partition all across the room, being made of chicken wire. Behind this were live chickens all over the place, presumably for sale.

207

At night, vendors would travel through the neighborhood, yelling something like "bellute," the way I sold peanuts as a kid, calling out "boiled peanuts."

It was explained to me they were selling baby chickens that hadn't been hatched, still in the egg. I suppose they had been cooked, but I wasn't interested in eating one, either way!

We spent about a week there and were shown many of the sights. We saw a large graveyard, where the bodies had been stacked aboveground in vaults. Cemeteries are not my favorite places to visit.

The hot climate of Manila makes the daytime miserable wherever you are, unless it is in an air conditioned building. This was in November and the heat was unbearable.

Throughout the city the streets are crowded with people, either walking or riding the "jitneys." These are the local method of transporting people and they are spectacles to behold!

They are all crowded, with people sitting, standing and hanging from the vehicle any way they can. The accident rate must be high in the city, but they all seem to know how to hold on and not fall off. Each vehicle is painted in bright colors.

We were taken to a large church in the middle of the city, called the Church of the Black Madonna. Here we saw worshipers crawling on their knees to the altar, beginning out on the street and continuing through the long building. We thought, these people must have a great deal of commitment to crawl a distance of about one hundred and fifty feet!

One night we saw a concert with local Philippine dancers and were very impressed at their talent and the color of the occasion!

We enjoyed the week with our daughter and son-in-law, but it was soon over and so was our vacation. Returning home, we had made many wonderful new memories!

Visiting Scandinavian Countries for Three Weeks

Departing from Atlanta in May of 1985, we began a three-week tour of the Scandinavian countries and Finland, with two of our traveling relatives, Dan and Betty White. We were all excited about this trip, and the Whites were particularly happy to come along, since this was their first venture overseas.

My wife and I tried to soothe their nerves as we all got aboard the plane. After all, we had made several trips abroad and were veterans! Little did we know what we were in for on this trip, however!

The flight was uneventful until we neared Amsterdam, where we needed to change planes. The pilot began to speak on the intercom, saying that we had encountered a small problem. A strike by the airport workers had just begun at Amsterdam and our flight would be diverted to Brussels, Belgium.

No flights were being allowed in or out of Amsterdam, and the pilot advised that we would be landing within the hour at Brussels.

After landing, we found our plane was one of many that had been rerouted, and we were required to sit on the airport tarmac two hours before we were allowed to leave. Finally a bus transported us to a receiving area, where we could go through customs.

Inside the airport was one big state of confusion! People filled the place trying to find planes to other cities that had been their original destinations.

We tried for another three or four hours to find a flight to Copenhagen, where our tour was to begin the next day. The next flight would be sometime the next day or two, and they seemed very uncertain about that.

Getting desperate, we were told that we could take a train from the airport to downtown Brussels to the railway station and ride the rails north to Copenhagen, Denmark.

This seemed like a logical alternative and we proceeded out of the customs area to the train downtown. As we moved through the line, being very weary from the days aggravations, my wife's turn came to be allowed through the gate.

The customs agent asked her what she had to declare? "I declare that I am about dead and I am about to drop," she replied with a good bit of agitation! The agent, being aware of what was going on inside the airport, laughed and said, "go on by." Since the four of us were together he motioned us to pass on through.

Catching the train, we arrived downtown in about thirty minutes. There was a train going to Copenhagen that was to leave in forty-five minutes. After getting tickets and waiting for the train to arrive, we were told that there was a national holiday going on and the train might be crowded.

Being warned about the holiday didn't help at all, as we entered the door we could see that everybody in the country was already on that train! They were standing and laying on the floor everywhere!

Going through several coaches, we finally found two seats for the four of us and we knew it was going to be a long ride. It was several hundred miles to Copenhagen. But we were informed that we had to change trains in Frankfurt, Germany.

We had a little wait in Frankfurt and we went outside to get a bite to eat, with the only thing we found, being a sausage on some kind of bun. It was tough to swallow!

The train finally arrived and we hopped aboard, only to find it as busy as the other, with people almost hanging out the windows!

We finally found a purser and inquired about a sleeper car for the night. They were all filled, he said, but seeing how bedraggled we looked he would check to see if anyone would give theirs up for us.

We didn't receive much encouragement from his words, but pretty soon after that he returned and said he had a place for us! He showed us where it was and we jumped into the four empty bunks, two on either side, with one above the other.

About to doze off, we heard two young men coming in the unlocked door. They informed us that they had the top bunks and that they would be climbing over us to their beds. We didn't even know there were two more bunks up above!

It was a little unnerving, however, since both had long hair and looked every part of being "hippies!" So, we secured our money and valuables as best we could and fell asleep, being very tired.

The next morning we talked to the two and found they were from California and backpacking around Europe. They turned out to be very nice and we were a little ashamed that we had judged them so quickly!

Arriving on the coast of Germany about daybreak, we found that a ferry boat would take the entire train across the Baltic Sea to a port near Copenhagen. This was something to see! This was the largest ferry I had ever seen!

After floating for a couple of hours we made it to land, where a bus was caught to our hotel, the Hotel SAS Globetrotter. It was nice and luxurious and really looked good to us at that time.

We checked in and found that our luggage hadn't arrived, since it was on a plane, originally ticketed to Copenhagen and we didn't have it to bring on the train. Being about noon we found also that our tour had begun that morning without us, but would be back that evening.

That suited us fine, being in the need of rest on a bed that didn't move! We got into bed and didn't wake up until about time for the tour bus to come back to the hotel that afternoon.

We had missed the city tour of Copenhagen, including the Christainborg Palace, seat of the Danish Parliament, the stock exchange and other attractions. We were supposed to see The Little Mermaid on the tour we missed, but we had seen her as we came into the harbor.

They did have a trip that evening to Tivoli Gardens, the city's colorful amusement park, but we were not too enthusiastic about it, since we were weary. We did go, however, and glad that we did, because it is a beautiful place!

There were a lot of bright lights and colorful flowers every-where, with many of the flowers being tulips. There must have been some sort of festival going on since there were many people with colorful paint and unusual hair! They seemed to be celebrating something!

We ate dinner in the park and had a tasty meal. Returning to our hotel, we found our luggage had caught up with us, and we could take a shower and change clothes! We were in the need of both!

Not desiring to push our luck, we didn't ask our relatives what they thought of my wife and myself as tour guides! This must have appeared to them a poor way to begin a tour abroad for the first time!

The next day we took a coach for a short trip to Halsskov, Denmark, where we boarded a steamer across the bay to Knudshoved. There, we caught another tour bus to Odense, the birth place of Hans Christian Andersen, the father of fairy tales. We toured his home and the surrounding village.

We spent the night at Arhus and drove north the next day. At the village of Randers we saw one of the main attractions, a stork nest high on a smoke stack with a stork residing in it. Later, our coach boarded a ferry boat across the water to Gothenburg, Sweden.

Our coach took us on to Oslo, Norway and along the way seeing some beautiful scenery on this coastal route. We were booked to spend two nights at the Park Royal Hotel in Oslo. The hotel was very modern and comfortable, located in a green-forested area with beautiful gardens surrounding it.

We missed Constitution Day, a national holiday on May 17, when children march down the streets singing and dressed in native costumes. However, the city itself is quite an attraction, being encircled by hills and over-looking many lakes and forests.

Touring the city, we saw Akershus Castle, the fourteenth century fortress guarding the harbor. We visited the City Hall, National Theater, Parliament and the Royal Palace. King Olav V was the ruler at this time, and our tour didn't include an invitation inside for a social visit!

Next we stopped at Frogner Park, with its hundreds of life-sized statues of animals and people created by Norway's greatest sculptor, Gustav Vigeland. These statues leave nothing to one's imagination depicting them at all stages of life and situations!

A visitor shouldn't skip the Holmenkollen Ski Jump, which was featured during the 1952 Winter Olympics. It is a celebrated ski area, with tourists and locals milling about. The weather was somewhat warm when we were there and many local sunbathers were soaking up the sunshine semi-nude!

We visited the Viking Museum, where three large Viking ships, having been restored, were on display. They date back to 900 AD.

Leaving Oslo, the capital of Norway, we drove further north to Bergen. On the way we stopped at Kinsarvik, located at the Hardanger Fjord, another beautiful coastal city.

Bergen is a city of about a quarter million people and is surrounded by seven mountains. It is a coastal city with some industry and tourism and fishing. The Bergen Fish Market is alive with activity as the salmon and trout are brought in by the boats.

They were celebrating the International Bergen Festival as we arrived. This is a celebration with music, drama, folklore, opera and ballet. On one street we observed a band of musicians playing their instruments on a second-floor overhang above a sidewalk! They could be heard all down the street!

We toured the home of composer Edward Grieg and the twelfth-century Castle Bergenhus before leaving for the Filefjell Plateau. Our motor coach took us to Stalheim for dazzling views of the Naerodal Canyon and a tour of the Stalheim Hotel. The Germans took over the entire hotel during World War II, when they invaded this area.

We then drove down the mountain to Gudvangen.

There at sea level, we took a two-hour cruise along the blue-green Sognefjord on a fjord steamer. This was a cruise that boggles the mind, in that the greenery, mountains and Scandinavian scenery were all unbelievably beautiful!

Driving to Borgund, we saw the country's oldest Stave Church, and on to our hotel at Nystova, Norway.

Being near the Artic Circle and the Land of the Midnight Sun, we marveled at the sun still shining at eleven o'clock in the evening. Since we retired to bed around ten o'clock, in order to arise early to continue our tour, it was difficult to fall asleep! It didn't feel like nighttime and took some adjusting!

The beautiful resort town of Lillehammer was our next stop. This city was an Olympic attraction a few years after we made the trip and was somewhat taxed to find accommodations for the huge crowds. The population of city is around 20,000.

We saw a museum of Gudbrandsdal farm houses, dwellings, work shops, tools and items used centuries ago.

The small town is a popular year-round destination, with fishing, swimming and horseback riding in the summer. In winter there is skiing, with eight ski-lifts in the area and ice- skating.

Karlstad, Sweden was the next city, on the shores of Lake Vanern, with a population of 73,000. An attraction there is the Varmlands Museum with its collection of arts and crafts.

The next day we made it to Stockholm, the capital and largest city in Sweden. It is noted for the Nobel Award made annually to world leaders, named for Alfred Nobel, who invented dynamite in 1866.

Hotel Palace was our lodging in Stockholm and was very picturesque and comfortable. We toured the Town Hall with its festive blue and gold chambers. Riddarholm Church was next with its burial area for Swedish Kings and we saw the Royal Palace.

The city is located on the shores of Lake Malaren and there are many skyscrapers, shops and apartments located around it.

After a couple of days in Stockholm, we took a night ferry across the Baltic Sea to Helsinki, Finland. This was quite an exciting experience on a large and comfortable ship, with nice and roomy cabins.

At daybreak we arrived in Helsinki and began a tour north to Finland's beautiful Lake District. We toured museums along the way and took a cruise on a Silverline boat in a pristine lake near Valkeakoski.

We arrived in the city of Tampere for our lodging that night in the Hotel Rosendahl. The next morning, we visited the Naesinneula Tower where you could see miles and miles of surrounding lakes and forests.

Later in the afternoon we went to a glass factory and watched glass blowers in action. Then, the coach took us to Turku, the former capital of Finland, where we spent the night at the Hotel Marina Palace. Next morning we toured the thirteenth century Turku Castle and other local points of interest.

Completing a triangular trip, we arrived back in Helsinki to explore the Finnish capital and make ready for our return flight home.

We found that Finland was once part of Russia, but now is a beautiful forested country called Suomi by the Finns. It is the least populated of the Scandanavian countries with about five million people.

Helsinki has a half million people or more and is a popular tourist destination in the summer. In the morning we strolled through the colorful market alongside the harbor, seeing ceramics, crystal and art objects for sale.

In the afternoon we toured the city by motor coach, going to the Presidential Palace, Parliament House and Lutheran Cathedral. We saw the Olympic Stadium and Sibelius Monument.

Lodging at The Intercontinental Hotel that night, we had completed another exciting day of our vacation!

Since we were supposed to have begun this trip in Amsterdam and were diverted because of a strike, we caught a plane to that city to spend a couple of days after leaving Helsinki.

Checking into the Grand Hotel Krasnapolsky, we found that it is located in the center of Amsterdam, and across the square from the Royal Palace. We had been to the city before and taken tours, so this was a leisurely two days of killing time!

We did take a canal trip through the city on one of the many glass-topped excursion vessels seen everywhere. One day for lunch, we ate in one of the many small cafes along the sidewalks. Dogs entered and left the place at their own pleasure and pace.

I told my wife that Amsterdam reminded me of Athens, Greece, since hundreds of stray dogs roam the streets and eating establishments there.

Soon it was time to leave Europe and return home. The airport strike was over and planes were flying in and out of the city again.

The trip had been wonderful and educational. But the four of us were ready to return to the United States, the best country in the World, without a doubt!

We arrived at the Hartsfield Airport in Atlanta and proceeded to customs. Dan White, one of the four, reached in his coat pocket for his passport and came out empty! Without his passport he was in a "heap of trouble!"

Going back to the plane, he looked around the seat he had occupied and found it! It had fallen out of his pocket as he napped!

We waited for him and as we passed through the customs line they stopped him because misplacing the passport had made him extremely nervous! That made the customs agent suspicious of his baggage and he was pulled aside for a complete search of his luggage.

Finally, he was cleared through and we were allowed to proceed out of the airport. The trip had started with obstacles and finished up the same way! That was the last time we were able to convince first-time travelers abroad to let us lead the way!

Part V.

Stories That Probably Should Not Be Told

Short Subjects and Unmentionables

A salesman friend of mine relates the story of how he returned home late one night in a slightly inebriated condition. He had recently bought a hairpiece of questionable quality, and he was wearing it that night. It had moved around in a tilted position on his head, after an active night of celebrating.

In a hurry to get into bed, he threw the hairpiece over in the corner of the room. The next morning, he got up with a headache and eyes glazed over! In the dimly lit room, something caught his eye in the corner of the room. It appeared to be a large rat!

He grabbed a broom and proceeded to kill the animal! After he was sure the rat had expired, he turned it over and recognized his wig! He had killed his brand new hairpiece! This sobered him quickly, and he vowed never to take another drink!

This same friend decided to have a little fun at a furniture market in High Point, N.C., where we were camping for a show. Our campers were parked with about twenty feet between us, and the area was wooded with a lot of underbrush.

About midnight, after my wife and I had retired for the night, we were awakened by a loud screeching noise outside our trailer! It sounded like a wildcat, or some other ferocious animal!

As we ran outside to investigate the noise, we saw our friend almost doubling over with laughter! He had attached a wire to the metal on our camper and his, and was rubbing the wire with rosin or some substance. It was making the ungodly sound that alarmed us!

My wife and I returned home during a furniture show in Atlanta. It was January, and we had one of those rare snows that happens occasionally. The white stuff had covered our front lawn and driveway.

The house was sitting on a slight hill and I decided to park the car on the street, knowing the driveway was too slippery to drive on. My wife avoided the concrete and began to walk on the grass.

She got halfway up the hill and could go no further! I said, "hold on a minute and I will help you!" I made it as far as she had and, suddenly, both of us slid about fifty feet back down the hill! Several attempts were made after that before we finally reached the door.

A few days after that we received a call from a neighbor, saying, "we saw two drunks in your yard the other night, scrambling around in the snow!" "I didn't know if they were trying to break into your house or not!"

We related what had happened and all of us had a big laugh over the situation!

Not long after that Nancy, my wife, and I went for a little ride in the north Georgia mountains, and were enjoying the scenery. We became hungry and stopped at a fast food place to get a hamburger.

The place was busy and the waitress was cordial. She took our order and about ten minutes later brought our meal. Nancy started to take a bite out of hers, and the sandwich seemed very thin.

She pulled back the top piece of bread and saw mayonnaise and lettuce. There was no meat! Calling the waitress over she said, "do you not serve meat with your hamburger? She showed the meatless sandwich!

The waitress was embarrassed and returned shortly with a hamburger with beef in it!

We bought a twenty-eight-foot trailer and parked it in the driveway at the front of our house. Across the street lived a Presbyterian minister and his wife and they came over to look at the new camper.

They were admiring the inside with its new smell and looks and walked to the back of the trailer, where the bedroom was. "Oh," the minister's wife said, "I really like the bedroom, but you have twin beds!"

My wife, quickly catching on to what she meant, replied, "well, we only use one of the beds!"

Camping at Carlsbad, New Mexico for the first time in the state, we toured the Carlsbad Caverns. We loved to explore caves, especially ones with the smoothed cement walkways and lighted exhibits.

We were really fascinated with one of the entrances to the cave, were you could witness the hordes of bats coming out at dusk each evening! I suppose they returned at daybreak.

Back at our camper in the afternoon, we were enjoying a rather mild day under our camper awning, when I spied the largest spider I had ever seen! My neighboring camper said, "that's only a tarantula, it won't hurt you."

I had read about tarantulas in books, and all that I had ever heard was that they are extremely poisonous! There was no way that I was going to let that thing out of my sight!

So, I informed the man, if that huge spider came onto my rented property, he would soon be deceased.

The varmint must have heard my comment and decided to challenge me, because he made a beeline toward my camper. I was really frightened, not knowing how fast those long legs would carry him!

He looked real ominous and I gave him the benefit of the doubt, until he came within three feet of my foot! At that time I zapped him, to my neighbor's dismay.

We soon left that campground for greener pastures, not knowing if that tarantula had some buddies lurking in the bushes. Besides, the other camper kept giving me menacing looks!

Seems that animals are attracted to campers. There is a campground near St. Petersburg, Fla., that is close to the Skyway Bridge, that has raccoons everywhere. If you open the door, they will come inside and help themselves to anything edible and some things that are not!

As we camped there one time with my wife's brother and spouse, we left for a short time to fish under a bridge. We returned later with a few flounder and other fish and noticed a water fountain near our trailers. We hadn't seen that before.

Soon, we found out why! As we came nearer, we could see the fountain was coming from the relatives' water hose. A coon had chewed the water line in two and the water was making a nice fountain!

Leaving that place, we returned to a campground in north Georgia. We had brought a boat along and had been out fishing on a large lake.

As we returned to the camper, we were almost overcome by a putrid smell all around the area. After investigating, I found that a squirrel, or some animal, had gnawed into the propane gas line, spraying the stuff all about!

Lucky for us, we hadn't left the gas burner on the hot water heater going, or else there might not have been much left of the camper or animal! We soon got the situation under control, however.

――――――――

It was time for my dental examination and we had just moved to a new location. We didn't know the dentists in the area, so I picked one nearby. Going in for my examination, I was a little uneasy as I entered the door.

He led me in to an adjoining room and I sat in the dentist chair, waiting for my exam. I noticed that the room was somewhat dark, except around the chair.

Looking in my mouth, he said that I had a disease of the gums that could be serious. I forget what he called it, but he said it was similar to cancer, only it was in my gums!

I was scared to death! I might be in real danger! He gave me the name and address of a nearby dental specialist and told me to see him right away.

After making an appointment, I saw the specialist. I was told that the first dentist was right and that he could cure my problem with treatment. I asked the price of the treatment and was told some astronomical figure.

I knew that I could not afford his services, so I changed dentists. Besides, I couldn't feel any pain in my mouth. I would have to take my chances!

Almost fifty years later, I still have all of my teeth. My gums are healthy and I have no problems in my mouth! The two dentists must have had some kind of scam going.

My wife had an opinion, since she went to the same dentist with the dark examining room. She said to him, "you need to open the curtains and turn on some lights, so you can see in here!" Evidently, she was right, because he misdiagnosed me for some reason!

A friend of ours told my wife recently, that she was in a doctor's office, waiting for a physical exam. There had been no activity in her exam room for some time, when she noticed some of the lights went out.

She sat a little while longer, waiting for the doctor, and noticed more lights being turned off. Getting a little uneasy, she walked outside and found everyone had gone for the day! Her husband was sitting in the waiting room, and he stated that he had noticed people leaving the office! Needless to say, the experience irked them somewhat!

The same lady took her husband to a local optometrist and he sat in the exam room for a long time. Getting uneasy about him, she went into the room and saw him sitting as if he was in a daze!

She called his name and asked what was going on? He anxiously exclaimed, "I can't see a thing, I'm blind as a bat!"

Calling the technician, the lady told her that something was wrong with her husband's eyesight. He had suddenly gone blind!

The technician checked the situation and found she had left the patient looking through a thick glass and he could only see light, with everything blurry!

She released his head from the optical contraption and he could see again!

Previously, our friend had noticed a patient come into the same office carrying a new pair of glasses. She told the secretary, "you must have gotten my prescription mixed up with another patient, I cannot use them at all."

The optometrist checked them over and found that the bifocals had been installed upside down in the frame! She couldn't see anything close up or far away!

Our friend changed eye doctors after that experience!

My wife had a small problem as she went for a physical examination a few years ago. She was escorted to a room and told to remove her clothes and put on a paper gown.

It was cold in the room as she waited, and waited for the doctor. Finally, a nurse walked into the room and asked if the doctor had finished his exam. She told her that she had not seen the doctor at all, and had been waiting almost an hour!

The nurse checked on the doctor and found he had been doing book work all this time. It seems that no one had told him the patient was waiting, or if he had been told, he had forgotten!

Finally, going in to examine my wife, the doctor apologized She told him, if she had just known it was going to be that long, she could have taken a nap!

A friend of ours was on vacation and traveling through the city of Las Vegas. Spending the night in the city, she and some friends decided to walk around and look at the sights.

Everywhere they looked, they saw hotels and casinos with glittering lights and many fascinating buildings. They were mesmerized with all of the activity!

As they passed along the streets, they came to some sort of gambling exhibit on the sidewalk. There were slot machines and other devices for entertainment. An attendant told our friend she could pull the slot machine one time free.

She told him she did not gamble, but the man insisted that it would not be gambling, because she did not have to pay anything. So with that in mind, she pulled the handle. The machine wheels began to rotate and up came the numbers 777! These were winning numbers! She had hit the jackpot!

Bystanders, seeing what had happened, began to shout and congratulate her! This perked her interest and she asked the attendant what was the meaning of this. She asked, "did I win anything?"

The man informed her that she had won fifty dollars, and proceeded to pay her winnings!

Being and avid churchgoer and member of her local church, she didn't know whether to bring her tithe into the storehouse or not. She had heard that the minister was adamantly against a lottery in the state, so she surmised that he would also be reluctant to accept slot machine winnings!

I never found out if the tithe made it to the church or if she "took her winnings and ran!"

Several years ago, I needed a haircut and went to a local barbershop. There were several customers waiting, so I had to wait about forty-five minutes for my turn.

At that time, I sat in the barber's chair, and he began to cut my hair. I noticed him looking intently at one of my hands, resting on my leg.

Pretty soon he said, "that's a rather large wart you have on your thumb, does it give you any problems?" Surprised, I replied, "why, yes, it does get in my way often, and sometimes it gets a little irritated."

I have always been a little sensitive about warts, since I had several on both hands as I was growing up. In grammar school, when the teacher asked for answers to questions, I wouldn't raise my hand to respond. I was afraid someone would see my warts!

The barber then told me, "I can cure your wart, if you want me to." Surprised that a barber could cure warts, I laughed, and asked him how he went about the curing process.

He stated. "I just have a gift of curing warts, and all I have to do is rub the wart and in a few days it will fall off."

I thought this was rather neat, and I told him I would really appreciate it if he would rub my wart and make it go away! I extended my hand, doubtful of any miracles occurring, and the barber rubbed the wart three times and put my hand down.

"Just go about your regular daily duties and forget about the wart," he said. "In about four days it will drop off," he added.

I said to myself, "uh huh, I bet it will!"

The man finished cutting my hair and I left the barbershop, forgetting all about the incident. Four days later, I looked at the wart and it wasn't there! It had disappeared, just as the barber had told me! I couldn't believe my eyes!

A few days later, I dropped by the barbershop and showed the barber his prediction had come true. No more wart! Showing little surprise, he said he had found there was some chemical in his body that attacks warts and he was happy to pass on his gift to others!

A friend and I were talking about smoking, and why neither of us never picked up the habit. When I was a kid I tried smoking cross vine, rabbit tobacco and "stingy green" tobacco from north Alabama. All of these made me so sick, I decided it required too much effort to look "cool." So I quit before I started!

My friend said he was trying to smoke rabbit tobacco when he was a kid. He rolled up a wad and needed to light it some way. Nearby was a kerosene lamp, so he stuck the cigarette in his mouth and proceeded to hang his head over the lamp chimney.

This resulted in a quick flame, and in the excitement he grabbed the lamp chimney with one hand! It was real hot! He dropped it and stomped the tobacco flames out on the floor!

Spending most of that night with the injured hand in a bucket of water, he made a decision to end his smoking then and there! It was a habit that was too painful! There probably would be fewer smokers today if they started the way we did!

My family was attending a convention in Charleston, S.C. back in the 60's. The men had their business meetings and the women and children were taking in the sights of the charming Southern city.

Fees for the convention were already paid and we assumed that everything was covered, including meals at the hotel. At least that is what we were told.

My wife and I were a little late for one of the evening meals and we told our two daughters to go ahead and start their meals. The oldest was about nine and the other six, and they asked what should they order?

"Anything you want," I told them, "the fees have already been paid." I should have known what to expect next, when I saw both of them grinning widely!

Finally, we made it to the dining room and sat at the table with the children. Looking at their plates, we could not determine what they were eating. So I asked, "what did you order?"

The oldest had ordered Pheasant Under Glass, and the other one Southern Quail! "What," I said, astonished beyond words! I didn't know they had ever heard of such a delicacy, let alone brave enough to order it!

I couldn't complain, though, because I had told them to order their choices. But I had my doubts that those items were approved on the convention fee list.

My fears were affirmed when I was brought the bill! It was some astronomical figure for the two meals. The bill was paid, with trepidations, knowing that I probably had to work an additional two weeks to pay for it!

Now, some forty years later, we can all laugh about it but it brought a few tears at that time!

An appointment was made with the family doctor to check out a sore spot on the arch of my right foot. The doctor said that it looked like a carcinoma and to make another appointment and he would take care of it.

The visit to the doctor was made on a Friday and would be the next week that I was to see him again.

Saturday, the next day, I read an article about a deadly form of cancer called melanoma.

The article went on to say that persons having this could expect to live about five years if treated.

Having gotten confused at what the doctor told me was my problem, I began to believe that he said it was a melanoma! I was only in my fifties and I had only five more years to live!

Over the weekend was a hard time to get in touch with the doctor, so I was going to have to wait until Monday to talk to him. It worried me something fierce!

Monday came and I called the doctor early and explained my problem. I said, "did you diagnose my ailment as a melanoma?" He replied, "no, it is a carcinoma at this time, but it needs to come off."

"Thank the Lord," I told him! Then I related my fears and how they were brought about and he assured me that my problem was not a large one. He removed the spot and it never returned.

I learned at that time that misconceptions can bring on unwanted problems and that we should be more precise in learning and listening!

One day I passed a man on a dirt road and he seemed to be talking to himself. No one was near him and he seemed to be having quite a conversation!

I asked him who he was talking to and he said he was talking to a post on the side of the road. "Is it talking back to you," I asked?

"No," he replied, "but my daddy told me I would argue with a sign post, and I didn't want him to be called a liar!"

He said his daddy was a smart man and he gave him some advice that had really been useful to him. He had admonished him to "always watch what you do in a 'tater patch, 'cause them 'taters have got eyes." "Also, be careful what you say in a corn patch, 'cause there are a lot ears in there," he added.

I walked on down the road, a much wiser man!

As I was calling on a small town furniture dealer, I noticed a brand new Cadillac sitting in the parking lot. It was shiny red and really pretty!

Going inside the store, I met another salesman leaving as he had finished his visit with the owner. We exchanged greetings and I asked him if that was his beautiful new car outside in the parking lot.

"It sure is, I just bought it this weekend," he proudly said, "how do you like Cadillacs?" I told him that I loved them and that his was a beauty!

About that time the store owner walked up and asked the other salesman, "did I hear right that you have a new Cadillac outside?" "You sure did and I am really proud of it," the salesman replied.

The dealer said, "tear up that order you wrote for me. I don't buy from salesmen who drive big cars like Cadillacs!"

Laughing as he walked to the door, the salesman began to make his exit, not believing that the dealer was serious.

"I told you to tear up the order, and I meant it! I don't buy products that are marked up so high that the salesmen can drive expensive cars like that," the owner yelled!

He believed him this time and complied with the owner's order. As he left the store, I apologized for causing a scene and him losing the order.

Being a little uneasy myself, I began to get my mind on what I had gone there for, to sell lamps to the store owner. I noticed several end tables without lamps and began to show pictures of my wares.

He liked them and bought a couple dozen. I thanked him and left the store. He didn't accompany me to the door, thankfully, and I jumped into my two-week-old Cadillac and left the parking lot in a hurry!

I was certainly hoping that the dealer wasn't looking out the window and saw my new Cadillac!

In all of my forty years on the road calling on dealers, I had never run across one so opposed to a salesman driving a big automobile! He must have thought that in order to drive a car like that, the product must be marked high enough for more commissions!

Generally, I found the dealers liked to do business with salesmen who looked successful. This probably indicated that they were representing good products.

During the course of my thirty-five years as a self- employed salesman, I have been aware that many sales have been made at unconventional places. Many are made on golf courses, conventions, entertainment functions and various and sundry places.

Likewise with sales planning between factories and their sales representatives. For instance, one factory in a large northern city that I represented would make some decisions about producing a requested item at a time and place I would never imagined!

The factory owner would occasionally have a stomach disorder and he had an extension phone run to his toilet, so that he would never miss an important phone call! (This was before the day of the cell phone.)

While talking to the man on many such occasions I just assumed he was sitting at his desk in his office, and would never have known where he was if his secretary had not squealed on him!

———————————

Speaking of private places, I knew a man with a questionable sense of humor, who decided to play a trick on his wife one day, since Halloween was around the corner.

It seems that he had acquired a full-sized manikin or dummy and dressed it up to look as life-like as possible. His wife had gone shopping and would be home soon.

When the wife returned and placed all of her groceries in the appropriate spots, she made a trip to the restroom. Opening the door she was frightened out of her wits!

There on the commode sat a fully dressed man that she had never seen before! After gathering her senses, and seeing that the man was not moving, she realized that he was a dummy!

I never heard "the rest of the story," as the famous TV and radio announcer says, but I'm sure the wife looked for a little revenge after that.

My wife and I, along with a gift store owner, invented a lamp that was a fantastic seller. It was a clear ginger jar, filled with colorful seashells. We collaborated with a factory in New York to produce it with a nice empire shade.

It was so popular that the Shah of Iran bought thousands to put in houses of a new city he was building in an Iranian desert. The city was built in a circular arrangement, with the most important officials living closer to the inner circle. As the importance of the people diminished, they were place further from the center.

Evidently, the city had a power plant to light up these beautiful lamps. If not, they were still a pretty decoration!

The lamp was so popular that thieves in New York City just had to have one! It was reported that a store window of a jewelry store was smashed by a thief, and all that he took was one of our ginger jar lamps, that was displayed in the window!

Later, many variations of the lamp were sold, as we experimented with other objects inside the clear lamp. A lamp, using a peach basket for a shade, was also popular!

We had a large showroom, filled with some five thousand lamps, pictures and chandeliers in Atlanta. It was only open during markets and each Wednesday. It was the largest such facility in the southeast.

One day a lady came in and picked out ten large expensive chandeliers for her new condominium. She explained that she was getting a divorce from her dealer husband and they were going to be charged to her husband. She insisted that she wanted the best we had!

The husband must have approved because he paid the invoice and we assumed the lady was pleased with her purchase because we never heard from her again!

When I was very young, our family of seven lived in a two-room shotgun house, that wouldn't hardly meet the requirements to be called a shelter from the elements. Being poor was not uncommon in the Great Depression era.

My dad always told me, that it was not a shame to be poor, but to stay that way was!

So this house was only a stop on our journey toward better times.

But I still remember my mother getting sick at this time, and she was confined to her bed. It began to rain and rain! The roof had holes and there was not a dry place we could move the bed in order to keep her from getting soaked!

Fortunately, a week or two before she got sick, a couple of my brothers were rummaging in the trash behind a store in the local town, and found a couple of damaged umbrellas. The owner did not mind if anyone did this, since he placed goods out back for people to take if they could use them.

The umbrellas were a godsend in helping to keep my mother dry as the children took turns holding the wobbly umbrellas over the bed. The rain quit eventually and the house dried, making it usable again. My mother regained her health and everything returned to normal once more.

After a few years, things began to get better and the family had moved to a large farm with a good house to live in.

We had a lot of good neighbors, including several black families who were tenant farmers like us. One day as I played with the kids of a black family, it became time to eat the mid- day meal. The kids' mother invited me to eat with them and she said she was having fried turtle that day.

Now, I had never eaten a turtle before. I had played with them, but never thought about eating one! So I was a little leery of the offer, but I was hungry!

The lady, sensing my reluctance, said, "it tastes just like fried chicken, I bet you will like it!"

I said o.k., and she sat me down at a small table and I waded into a big chunk! It did taste like chicken! It was very tasty, and finishing that piece I asked if I could have another?

She had plenty, and I ate an excellent meal with them that day. I thanked them and returned home not feeling hungry for a good long while!

The community church for blacks was near our farm and on occasions I would go there on Sundays. One such Sunday, the preacher began to preach on buying clothes. I was too young to understand most sermons, and this one had me a little confused.

The Preacher said, "you go in to a clothing store, intending to buy a white shirt and your mind has been made up that is what you want." "But when you get inside, the clerk tries to sell you a blue shirt, and that's not right," he stated.

"The clerk has sinned and has tried to sell you something you don't want," the pastor said.

Well, I was trying to sort this out in my mind, when he began to sing his message and brought out some other gems I didn't understand. As he was singing, a big red dog came through the open doors and walked down the aisle.

"Get out of this church you big old hound," he continued singing, "before I have to knock you down!" With that he made a run at the dog and the animal took off the way he entered!

The congregation began to sing along and as they sang the song, "Holy, Holy, Holy," a large woman began to swing and sway with the music, and as she bent over, a sizable rip appeared in her dress! Someone grabbed her and covered the exposure!

By this time, I had more sermon than I had come for and I quietly sneaked out the back door.

———————————

Our two daughters were a delight to care for and to watch as they grew into beautiful young women, and to see them happily married with three children of their own.

When they were kids, I was on the road traveling a lot in sales work, so the brunt of raising them fell on my wife,

Nancy. She has been the steadying influence on our family's existence.

We loved to take trips with the kids and to show them new things and places. We vacationed together and enjoyed good family times. They never gave us many problems growing up. None that caused much concern.

We built a tree house for the kids when they were small. It was fifteen feet off the ground and built between three large trees. It was a pretty good place for them to play. But it didn't take long for them to outgrow it, though, and they began to think about other ways to entertain themselves.

That was a good thing, because not long after they had deserted the tree house, lightning struck one of the trees and damaged the building. Thankfully, they were not in it!

One night as we were sitting in our den reading the afternoon paper, our oldest daughter came running in the room. She excitedly said, "there is a man peeping in the bathroom window!"

Knowing that she was not imagining this, I jumped into action! Since the "peeping Tom" was at the back of our house, I decided to go out the front door and slip around the side and surprise him.

I forgot to get a baseball bat or any weapons, or even a flashlight! As I quietly moved around the house and toward the back, my foot hit a loose piece of drain pipe and kicked it across the cement patio. With all of the noise I made, I could also hear someone scrambling over the fence behind the house!

He had gotten entangled in the fence, but broke loose, and was gone by the time I reached the area. He had dropped a match cover under the window where he stood, and it came from a place that a young man up the street was working.

We never were able to identify him enough to have him locked up, but I really believe he got a good scare that night. Hopefully, enough that he never did it again.

One time as we vacationed in Daytona Beach, Fla., Nancy and I were having a good time with the kids playing in the ocean. The kids were small and I thought that it was my duty to teach them how to dive into the waves that were coming toward the shore.

I saw a nice big wave splashing toward the shore and I told the kids to watch me and they would learn to do this. I dove into the wave and the down pull of the water seemed to grab me and stand me on my head into the sand with great force! I saw stars of all colors as I hit the sand!

As the wave went out again I came up out of the water, not knowing if I was standing or laying! Seeing that I was all right, the family had a big laugh about my efforts to show off' I found that it was hard work to teach your kids new tricks!

Soon the kids were out of high school and going to the University of Georgia. They didn't have a car at this time and had to ride the bus home on weekends. This was humiliating for them, because most kids had their own cars.

It was especially embarrassing as the bus driver approached each little stop along the way. He would call out the names, "Between," "Split Silk," and finally coming to our daughters stop, "Pea Ridge!"

But as they were about to graduate from college we gave each a car as a graduation present. This was the beginning of a different kind of worry!

It was a joyous time to celebrate Christmas and other holidays with our children. I guess we tried to give them the things we didn't have as we were growing up. For instance, I never received a birthday or Christmas gift when I was a child.

Really, I guess it was a sort of a gift, when the children in my family put a shoe box under the bed on Christmas Eve night and the next morning there would be an apple and orange in it. Sometimes a candy cane, but nothing else! We were always too poor, and I'm sure my parents wanted to do more, but couldn't.

For birthdays, if it was a brother or sister, we all administered paddling "licks" in the amount of the birthday years. Nothing else, just a few "whaps" on your rear!

I guess this allowed my family to put more emphasis on the real meaning of Christmas and Thanksgiving, rather than get tangled up in the commercial aspects. However, my wife and I tried to do both for our kids, hoping that nothing would be left out!

My wife sometimes reminds me of my roots, with little surprises along the way. As this past Christmas, I got up out of bed and found a shoebox under the Christmas tree. It contained two apples, an orange and a couple of candy canes. It brought back old memories.

My birthday came around when we were attending a furniture show in High point, N.C. We brought our camper and she was giving me a private birthday party that evening. As the party progressed, she came out of the restroom with a cake of soap and on top of it was a candle, beaming brightly! Later, she brought out a real cake.

In another part of this book I wrote about the "ins and outs" of plowing mules. How you need to know your "gee" from your "haw" in order to control the animal.

The expression of being able to "gee-haw", as in a marriage, or just getting along with anyone, must have emerged from the farm.

Growing up on a farm, we had a neighbor that could not get along with his mules. He could be heard "cussin" his mules a half mile away, as he beat them with the line when he plowed. Evidently they went left when he wanted them to go right.

I was reminded of an episode in the Bible, where the prophet Balaam was asked by King Moab to help put a curse on the Israelites. God gave the prophet instructions as to how to proceed in this and as he was riding his donkey to have a conference with the king, the donkey balked.

Balaam beat the animal, and the donkey began to talk to him! He asked, hadn't he been faithful to him, and why was he beating him? This can be found in the Old Testament, at Numbers 22:28.

Now Balaam was astonished at the donkey having a conversation with him, and if one of our mules had said a few words to me, I probably would have been a candidate for a "crazy house," especially if I told anyone about it!

I was trying to remember some things that happened in the past, the other day, and I did remember what my stockbroker told me regarding this. He said that his wife told him that he doesn't have Alzheimer's disease yet, but that he just has "some- timer's!" That seems to be my problem.

Remembering the most unusual sale that I made while in business, it must have been one I made in a hospital. A buyer for a furniture store in another city was in a hospital near my home and she called to tell me she needed an order of lamps for her business.

She had recuperated enough from her illness to think about jobs she needed to do, so she contacted me. I was very happy to accommodate her and made the sales call as she was still in her hospital bed. I thanked her for the order and mused as I left the facility, that was a first for me!

Thinking about unusual customers that I called on, I had to give the winner's stamp to one who would not shake your hand, when entering his office. He had some kind of aversion to diseases that might be lurking on the caller's hand.

I offered to shake hands with him, while calling on him one day, and he refused. He told me, "I don't know where your hand has been before you came into the store!"

So, I left the man's store and never returned. Later, when he came into my showroom I returned the favor and wouldn't shake his hand!

The most inconsiderate store buyer has to be one who purchased goods for a large chain store. I called on him one day after making an appointment for a particular time. I waited and waited for him to appear in his office.

Finally, I asked a salesman if he had seen the man, and told him that I saw him briefly with a young lady, but he hadn't returned. He replied that he hadn't seen him, but that if I saw him going upstairs with a young lady, more than likely he would not return that day.

The salesman seemed to know something that I didn't, so I left the store a little agitated because the man did not honor his appointment.

Briefly, I was in the insurance business early in my career, and at that time I made the most dangerous call of my career. I sold an insurance policy to a young lady and I had to return later in the evening to pick up the premium from her husband.

I returned to her home after the husband got home and knocked on the door. He let me in and I told him why I was there. He searched around in his pockets and came up with a bunch of change. I counted it and informed him he needed another dollar.

At this time, I could see that he was agitated about something. He suddenly knocked all of the change off the table onto the floor and grabbed a butcher knife that was sticking upright in a corner of the table!

I took the hint and made a beeline for the door, with the drunken man in hot pursuit! I reached the porch, which was about four feet off the ground, and didn't bother with the steps!

Leaping into my car, I called out, "if you want your policy, you can pay it at the office!" I didn't stop to give directions to the office!

Needless to say, the policy was never paid, never issued and I never returned to that house! In fact, when I was in that neighborhood after that incident, I gave that residence a wide berth!

————————

When I was about eight years old, I was walking over to see a neighbor boy, at a nearby farm. As I approached the house where he lived, I heard someone screaming at the top of their lungs.

I ran toward the direction of the distressful noise, seemingly in the yard behind the house!

As I rounded the house, I could see my little friend "naked as a jay bird," in a large tin tub! His dad was dunking him in a liquid solution, and every time he would immerse him he was hollering with pain.

Finally, the dunking ceased and the boy's father explained what he was doing. He said that the boy had caught the itch at school from some of his playmates, and the liquid in the tub would cure it!

He called the cure "citicide," but I believe it was closer to suicide! I dipped a little of the solution on a raw bump that I had and I had never felt a painful burn like that! Imagine it all over your body!

The cure was successful, however, and the boy left his case of the itch in the tub! I'm not sure which was more painful for him, the cure or the disease!

From that time on, I tried to choose my playmates more carefully!

Every farmer in our part of the county had dogs of one kind or another, to keep unwanted visitors and wild animals away. Then some had hunting dogs, and some wanted a dog for a pet.

Our family had two dogs. One was named Flop and the other Sandy. About the only thing these two would do was chase rabbits.

One day, as I sat on our back porch, Sandy began circling the house barking and howling! I could see that he was foaming at the mouth and acting crazy!

About the time I made a decision to run in the house, Sandy ran up the back steps toward me! I had never seen the dog act like that, and I felt inspired to move fast!

There was nothing on the porch that would protect me from the rabid animal, that I could see! Suddenly I saw two large nails in the wall that were about six feet off the floor and I made a leap for them!

I made it, and holding onto the nails I drew my feet up as high as I could get them. The dog must have decided he had bigger problems than me and ran off in the woods! I dropped to the floor and ran in the house.

Later, we looked for Sandy, but never found him. He probably had been bitten by a rabid raccoon and died from the rabies.

On a recent trip to my hometown I visited the old home place and it was still standing, but was being used for storage. Checking the back porch wall, I saw those same two nails that had given me sanctuary that day! Brought back old memories!

When my dad was a small child, he had an accident while chopping a block of wood. He cut off the end of his right index finger, just below his finger nail.

The nail grew across the end of his finger and he used this to his advantage as his children were growing up. If we misbehaved, he would rap us on the head with that finger. It was about like getting hit on the head with a hammer!

It really served him well when we were eating and acted up at the table. He sat at the end and could reach most of us on both sides. When we were tempted to throw a biscuit at a sibling, we remembered his make-shift hammer and wisely decided against it!

He never missed that part of his finger. In fact, it served as an asset, since it kept him out of the army during World War I, being his trigger finger.

Grandchildren can be a pleasure to watch and associate with at times, but at others your patience can be tried to the limits!

Trying to entertain ours one day when they were small, my wife and I decided to introduce them to the fine art of fishing. Since we live on a large lake and have a pontoon boat that is slow, like us, it made a good place to start the process.

The kids were excited as we loaded the tackle, bait, buckets and other things we would need. We cruised to our favorite fishing spot on the lake and set about the sport of catching fish.

The smallest exclaimed she wanted to catch one of those big-mouthed bass! Another said she wanted to catch anything.

All three were girls and were starting from scratch on the learning process.

We taught them how to use a rod and reel and soon they were casting off the boat. The oldest granddaughter made a cast and we heard a blood-curdling scream! The hook had gone awry and had caught the youngest in the nose and she was yelling "bloody murder!"

After getting the hook loose, tending to the wound, and calming everyone down, we all agreed that the first fishing lesson was over for the day! The wound was not as bad as it had seemed, but the thoughts of what could have happened was frightening.

The rest of the day went well, but later when the mother arrived she had a few misgivings about leaving her daughters in our care.

One time when our children were small we were out on the lake cruising and generally enjoying the warm balmy weather. The boat motor coughed several times and finally quit.

A strong wind began to blow and it looked as if a thunderstorm was approaching. The wind blew the boat into some weeds and rough shoreline.

The oldest child said she had heard that in cases such as that someone should wave a piece of clothing and call attention to your plight. So she pulled off a thin sweater and began to wave it frantically!

Soon we were rescued and the daughter was elated that she had saved our lives!

We were fishing in the small cove behind our home and had brought along two relatives. We were catching a few small ones when Betty, the sister-in-law, began to reel in her line rather briskly.

The fish put up a terrible struggle and when she pulled it to the boat she wanted to let it go real fast! It was about three feet long and had teeth like an alligator! I knew it was a gar fish but she had never seen one and it did look scary!

We cut it loose and it wasted no time in moving out of the area. As far as I know, the fish is not edible and probably is a "trash" fish. There are a lot of them in this lake but not many are caught.

Soon after that Betty made another catch and she began to pull it out of the water. At the surface it was evident that it wasn't a fish, but a cheap rod and reel someone had probably dropped over the side of a boat.

She seemed to be the only one catching anything, but her last two catches would have been hard to digest. We were doomed that day to eat our fish out of a can!

One evening my wife and I were reading the local paper and watching TV, generally enjoying some quality time at home. Suddenly, the lights went out and we were left in total darkness.

This wasn't so bad, we thought, because we had candles and flashlights and the lights would probably come back on soon. They did come back on, but it was about two days later.

Checking with the power company, we found that a sail boat had sailed under a high voltage line in the dark that evening and the mast had pulled the line down. In the process the boat was set on fire and other damage incurred.

The man had just brought his boat from somewhere in Florida and was not familiar with our lake. He had really messed up quite a few people's lives by his carelessness. The line that was broken furnished all of the power for a large resort nearby in addition to our residential neighborhood.

When I was a small child living on a farm in South Georgia we would save our pennies until they amounted to "two bits," or if you're not from the south, that's a quarter.

You could get into the local movie house for that amount and see a good Tom Mix cowboy "shoot-em-up!" Not many times I could get up a quarter so I probably never saw more than a half-dozen shows as a child.

One day I did have a quarter and I tried to get a buddy of mine to go with me. He didn't have the admission price, but he did have something that might get him in, he thought!

He had an Octagon soap coupon in his pocket that he had been saving for a prize when he got some to go with it. The coupon looked somewhat like the ticket that was given when someone bought a theater admission.

He headed into the lobby and gave his Octagon coupon to the ticket-taker. Not waiting for the man to tear the ticket and give him the remainder, he took off into the movie! The man took off after him when he noticed what had been given him.

The boy hid under some seats and even though they searched with flashlights he was not found. But the boy couldn't enjoy the movie for fear of being caught and he could only listen from under the seats.

I paid my fee and went in and enjoyed the movie, but I was a little worried about my buddy. He told me later he had finally left his hiding place and slipped out a side entrance. His coupon had gotten him into the movie but he didn't get any enjoyment from being there!

While I am dwelling on bad influences when a child growing up, reminds me of a boy I knew that didn't seem to have a whole lot of character. This was emphasized when the county fair came to our town, as it did each fall.

The county would have exhibits of farm products sewing, etc., and award prizes for first, second and third places. The boy decided he wanted to win a prize on cotton, so he made a trip to the local cotton gin and was given a sample of cotton. It had been ginned and looked like a winner.

He carried his exhibit to the fair and when the judging was made won the grand prize! The prize was a jar of jelly and it probably made him sick thinking how he had won it!

We didn't have many rules at our house on the farm, but we knew when we were crossing the line of no return, because some actions were just plain taboo. A fast swat on our backsides kept the kids on their toes!

No alcohol of any description, except rubbing alcohol, was allowed on the premises. There was no smoking and no "cussin."

The closest we came to inebriating spirits was the cane-skimming pit, which held the pummels after sugar cane was fed through the mill. The squeezed stalks and the residue skimmed off top of cooking syrup were tossed into the pit.

In the summer time you could pass by the pit and the sour aroma permeating the air around it would make you a little dizzy if you breathed it in! You also had to dodge the yellow jackets and bees, because they loved the smell!

Evidently learning about these things was good training for me, since I never developed a habit for any of those vices.

I had an uncle who reminded me of "Pa Kettle" from the movies. He would try to get everyone to give him a lower price on an item in any kind of store. One day while in a "ten- cent" store he was trying to buy a comb that cost a dime. He offered a nickel for it and when the owner stuck to his price, walked out without buying!

He was a deep thinker though. One time while we were riding across a mountain, he asked, "how do you suppose water gets up here, since it would have to flow uphill?"

I told him that was an easy question and replied, "they haul it up here on trucks!"

"Pa Kettle" got into an argument with his brother one time. They both were employed at a factory as night janitors and he stated that "surely he was the night boss, since he had worked a few weeks longer."

The other brother said that it was plain as day that he was the boss since he was smarter!

It never was made clear if either one was declared the boss and it didn't seem to matter since they were the only people in the plant at night. There wasn't much bossing to do!

We were at a small party playing a friendly game of cards with some people and the lady of the house had just put her children to bed and joined us.

After a few minutes of the game, we were interrupted by a small child about three years of age appearing in the doorway without a stitch of clothing on her body!

She exclaimed gleefully, "look at me! Look at me!"

A young man, who was present along with his wife, began to break out into laughter. He had just had surgery that week on his stomach and had been told not do anything that might pull out his stitches! The hearty laughter was almost his undoing!

Meanwhile, the mother grabbed the child and put her back to bed after a couple of licks to get her attention! It was easy to see that the woman had been quite embarrassed!

Early in my attempt at going in business for myself, it was necessary for me to attend a furniture market in Chicago. Before the market began we had a sales meeting to acquaint ourselves with the prices and products offered.

The factory owner was a tyrant and wanted everything to be perfect for the buyers. We were told if a price was forgotten as we waited on a customer that he would administer a kick in the rear to that salesman. Every price had to be committed to memory with no identifying tags.

Being struck with fear of embarrassment I memorized the prices perfectly and never made a mistake. The local Chicago salesman did, however, and was placed in full view of everyone in the showroom in a bending position.

The boss landed a good boot at the aforementioned target and everyone except the recipient had a big laugh!

Not long after that incident I changed factories, deciding that life was too short to be bothered with that kind of nonsense!

I never was very fond of Chicago, since it was unbearably cold in January when the markets were held. Being from the deep south, I couldn't take that zero weather. Crossing the street to eat at a restaurant your ears would almost fall off!

In July, when we were there for the summer show, the weather would be hotter than it would be in Georgia. Lots of people live there and like it. I love the South!

Beginning my newspaper work in 1950 on a local county weekly publication, my duties ran the gamut from reporting to selling advertising. My title was news editor and that was my first duty, to see that the local news was covered and the text was a balance to advertising space.

One day was an exciting one from a news standpoint, as I was assigned to cover a plane crash about five miles from the newspaper office. A small two-person plane had crashed to the ground at the base of an oak tree. There was hardly anything left of the plane or the two unfortunate passengers.

I began taking pictures of the crash and it was all I could do to keep from getting sick at the tragic remains. County workers gathered all they could find of the body parts strewn around the area. One worker stated in a tone as if he was used to the job, "here's another foot," and tossed it into a tub.

My indoctrination into the reporting business was almost finished before it began with this assignment! I had a lot of trouble sleeping for two weeks after that! But the job requirements improved following that incident!

Two years later, having become bored with my job, I took another in public relations work. The business owner was well known in the city and promised much success working for him.

Starting the job on a Monday, I was placed in an office interviewing other potential employees, who were answering the same ad as I did. Wednesday morning of that week, I asked the boss some of the questions I should have asked before I started the job.

For instance, I wanted to know my salary and when payday was. I was told by the boss he had forgotten to give that information in our interview. He continued, my salary was dependent on sales of public relations contracts I secured. Payday depended on sales made also.

Not liking his answers, I made a call down the street to a newspaper office, and was told they needed a reporter. On my lunch hour I had an interview and secured a job that day!

I returned to the boss's office and gave a one-hour notice I was quitting my non-paying job. He said he didn't blame me!

I learned later his job was a come-on for a public relations training school he was selling to trainees! He evidently was looking for people who were desperate to get out of a deadend job, and somewhat foolish as I was!

Being a manufacturers' representative called for a lot of travel, especially by automobile. I covered several southern states and usually was gone from home Monday through Friday each week. I made it a point to stay in touch with my family as much as possible and called home as often as I could afford.

One week, I was traveling in north Georgia and something came up that my wife needed to talk to me about. She knew the city where I was spending that night, but not the motel Checking the motels where I usually stayed, she decided on one to call.

She made the call and was given the operator for the motel. Asking if she had a person checked in a room with my name, the operator queried, "Ma'am who is he with?"

My wife, not understanding the woman meant what company I was with, replied somewhat irritated, "He better not be with anyone!"

The call was put through to me and the operator advised she hoped I didn't have anyone else in my room! I didn't, and there was no family crisis impending! It did strike me as being a little humorous, however.

———————————

My sales presentation to dealers required me to carry a large bag filled with photos of lamps, and other products, weighing forty two pounds. At the end of a day I was usually "dragging," from carrying that much weight.

I explained to some of my dealers, the heavy bag resulted in causing my chest to fall somewhat and settled around my midriff. This caused another problem of having to buy larger pants!

That heavy bag caused me many problems through the years, because I have walked out of stores, forgetting it, and having to return for it after traveling many miles!

I must have had a subconscious desire to strike back at the heavy bag, because after leaving a dealer's place of business one day, I was called back inside the store for a minute. Before going back inside the store I set my bag down next to my auto.

After answering the dealer's question, I returned to my car and backed out of the parking space. I felt a big bump, as if I had run over something and got out to check. There lay my large bag on the cement! It was crushed and looking as if I had killed it dead! I gathered it up as well as I could, administered first aid and resumed my sales calls.

The Concluding Summary

Zero to Eighty on the Road to Paradise is just a name for this book, but it is intended to tell my story from birth to the elderly age of eighty (I'm only seventy eight now, but by the time I get this written I'm sure I'll be eighty).

Alzheimer's has not conquered me yet, but as a friend of mine states he is getting "sometimers," and I told my wife it is urgent to finish this before my onslaught begins, since my mind already wanders on occasion!

Paradise is the name of the home we occupy on Lake Lanier and my wife and I met at a place called Paradise fifty seven years ago. Our marriage has lasted fifty five years up to this point, and even though it hasn't been all Paradise along the way, it has been heavenly!

From that marriage, two daughters have evolved and two son-in-laws, and eventually six grandchildren. Now one grand-daughter has married and brought in a new husband to the family.

One thing that we are exceedingly proud of is that all thirteen members of this family are "born again" Christians, having accepted Jesus Christ as our Saviour somewhere along our life's journey!

There have been some "bumps" on the road through the years, but none we couldn't get over or around with a little perseverance and experienced wisdom, along with guidance from above.

Having started my life on a farm during the impoverished years of The Great Depression, there was nowhere to go but up! Poverty can be good if it builds motivation to do better. As I have stated in this book, "it's not a shame to be born in poor circumstances, but is more than a shame to continue living there."

I read the newspapers, books, periodicals and the Sears and Roebuck catalog, gleaning information about living conditions elsewhere, building a yearning inside me to experience some of those things myself!

School was great, not only did we learn things, but we got out of picking cotton! My siblings and I loved school.

Later, after going out on my own, I read every self-help book I could get my hands on, and enrolled in many classes such as those given by Dale Carnegie. I even wrote a manual for my own business, attempting to encourage my employees to learn more.

During the early years of starting a new business as a manufacturers' representative, the going was tough. Money was scarce and my family had to do without many things that we needed.

I traveled constantly and road expenses were tremendous. Many Fridays I would return home from a week of problems and few sales, telling my wife that I was quitting! Over the weekend she would talk me into trying again. Monday, I would hit the road for another go at it.

This went on for a year and half until the business began to make some progress. Soon, it got better and better! Persistence had paid off!

From that point we never looked back. Failure was not an option in our minds and with our daily seeking encouragement and guidance from above, success was assured.

My wife and I tried to set a good example for our two daughters as they were growing up and learning their own life lessons. Often we wondered if the efforts we made were sinking in, or if they should, understanding that we were not infallible ourselves.

Our questions were answered at the celebration dinner our daughters gave for our Fiftieth Anniversary and we were very proud of them as they spoke their thanks for their up- bringing.

Elaine, the oldest daughter who has spent twenty-five years on The Campus Crusade For Christ, along with her husband Mark, spoke and wrote in her journal for us, "I am grateful and proud to call you my parents. For all that you are and all you have done for me, I thank you Mama and Daddy!"

Carol, our youngest daughter wrote and read, "Thank you for the model of staying together in marriage through sickness or health, for richer or poorer. The sermon of your marriage sealed with that vow continues to be a standard for me. I love you both very much."

Sometimes, when I get discouraged with the everyday problems that confront me I read these journals again and find that they are a constant source of solace and pride. I was told as a child, "if you sling enough mud on a wall, some of it is bound to stick."

Likewise, if you choose good mud to sling, the results are going to be better! My wife and I have made every effort to influence our children and teach them to be good citizens of unquestionable character and a credit to their purpose in this world.

We are never satisfied with everything that we have done through the years, and many things we would change if we could. In the absence of that ability, we need to take every care to make the most of the time we have on this earth, as it has been said, "we will only pass this way once."

Being brought up as a child under meager circumstances gave me plenty of time to use my brain, not only to try to figure some ways to get out of work, but to develop an attitude that would make work and other endeavors more bearable.

As my thinking capacity increased, I developed a sense of humor so that even when I was subjected to a lot of misery, I was able to find a humorous angle to divert the pain! Humor has served me well throughout my life journey.

I realize there is a time for humor and vice versa. I'm hoping that I haven't made light of a situation when there should have been a serious concern, but I'm sure that I have been guilty at times.

When I have been made the butt of a joke, I have joined in the fun, unless it has been meant to degrade instead of being friendly "kidding."

I believe The Lord Himself, has a great sense of humor, in order to put up with the shenanigans that we find ourselves involved with at times! I once heard a preacher state that he wanted to be buried standing up! He wanted a Bible placed at the bottom of his coffin, so that people could say he stood on the Word of God!

Well, I have my own preference concerning that, I had rather be buried lying down and people could say, "he relied on the Word of God!" Besides I believe it would get tiresome standing up for an eternity!

Several years ago, I had a good friend who was very smart and good humored. One day he told me that he was going to leave me his brain when he passed away. Not long after that he died, presumably of a brain disorder.

I know that was not the way he planned it, but the thought struck me the other day, that he must be up there somewhere having a good laugh over the fact that he had used up the item he was going to leave me! That he was having the last laugh!

Realizing that some subjects should not be the objects of humorous bantering, I hope that I won't be held accountable on the grounds that I have a little difficulty in sorting out the available subjects! I plead the Fifth!

Laughter is good medicine, I'm told, and I am convinced that if people all over the world would laugh and sing more, there would be less time for making war! In fact if more people would sing as I do, it would cause more laughter!

A man told me the other day that he was going to make me a national treasure. He said, you have silver in your hair, gold in your teeth, rocks in your head and lead in both feet! I told him he was wrong, that I do not have gold in my teeth!

However, I'm not worried or concerned about not having gold teeth. My final destination is the *Real Paradise* and even the streets are paved with gold there!

Part VI.

PHOTOS

Our Last Camper and Custom Made Van

Our Peaceful Lake on Round Top Mountain

Two Beauties
Cleaning Fish,
Genelle Westbrook
and
Nancy Westbrook

Nancy at the
Market Square
on the
Island of Grenada

The Main Street
of Capital City
on Grenada

Juarez, Mexico, Looks Like The Pilot Missed The Runway

The Owner of This Volkswagen Wanted Something Different

Huge Redwood in California, You Can Drive a Van Through

Clint Eastwood's Hog's Breath Inn, Carmel, California

The Famous Swinging Bridge, Vancouver, British Columbia

**Betty White,
Nancy Westbrook
and Totem Pole at
Victoria, Vancouver**

**Skagway,
Alaska and
Its Main Drag**

Coastal Scene Near Skagway

Lake Louise, Banff National Park, British Columbia, Canada

Dan White and the Author on a Glacier Near Lake Louise

We climbed a little higher so we could watch for bears!

This bear looked hungry. We didn't want to be part of his lunch!

St. Marks Square And the Basilica

**Venice, Italy and
One Of Many Canals**

**The Leaning Tower
Of Pisa**

Assisi, Italy

Nancy Pretending to be Princess Grace at Door of Her Palace

Garden in Bern, Switzerland

Eiffel Tower in Paris, France

**Nancy, at
Versailles Palace
Near
Paris, France**

Downtown Anchorage With Its Beautiful Flowers

Santa's Reindeer Resting Until Christmas

Nancy Thinking About A Whirl Around Fairbanks

Nancy and One of Our 32 Lobsters We Ate on This Trip

Moose Standing On Road In Denali Park

Salmon Drying In The Salt Air At Eskimo Village of Kotzebue

Mt. McKinley From The Air

Louis Standing Under The Alaskan Pipeline

Nancy, Caught In Seward, Alaska

Holgate Glacier

Sea Lions Lounging On The Rocks Near Harris Peninsula

Sky Ride To Sentosa Island In Singapore

**Mountain Monument Overlooking Auckland, New Zealand,
Cows Mow Grass**

Sydney, Australia

Kangaroos In wildlife Park at Sydney

**Scuba Diving At The Great Barrier Reef, Cairns, Australia
Note The Large Fish**

Feeding The Fish At The Great Barrier Reef

The Parthenon At Acropolis In Athens, Greece

Athens, Greece From Overlook

Nancy Resting on Ruins Of Ancient City Of Ephesus

The Virgin Mary's House Near Ephesus At Kusadasi, Turkey

Greek Island Of Rhodes

Santorini Island In Aegean Sea

Louis At One Of The Many Squares In City Of Madrid, Spain

Mayor's Palace in Madrid

271

Chrysanthemum display At Buddhist Temple

Buddha Statue at Temple in Tokyo

Soldiers Marching in Tiananmen Square in Beijing

The Forbidden City in Beijing

Commune workers on way to the city

Woman Pulls Cart in Chinese Commune Near Beijing

Commune Worker Guides Pig Down Road

Chinese Woman Does Her Laundry In River,

Great Wall of China

Elephants
Guarding
Dingling
Tombs
Near
Beijing

Top Left: Nancy With Small Chinese Girl in Park,
Top Right: Seventeen Story Pagoda
Bottom: Chinese people crowd around Nancy to see Picture taken
of little girl. All photos near Hangchow

Floating
Restaurant
in
Hong Kong

Chinese Junk
in Hong Kong
harbor, many
families live
on them.

"Jitneys" in Manila, Philippines

Beautiful Sunset Over Manila Bay

Courtyard of Hans Christian Andersen's Home, Odense, Denmark

Grass Roof House Near Oslo, Norway

Life-Sized Figures in Frogner Park in Oslo

There are Hundreds Created by Gustav Vigeland

The Famous Ski Jump at Oslo, Norway

The Fish Market at Bergen, Norway

**View of
Naerodal Canyon
Near
Stalheim, Norway**

Farm With Goats on Road to Lillehammer

Business Street Scene in Downtown Stockholm, Sweden

Inside Town Hall at Stockholm

The Midnight Sun Setting on Cruise From Stockholm to Helsinki

Church Carved Out of Rock at Helsinki, Finland

Inside Rock Church at Helsinki

Dam Square and The Palace in Amsterdam, Netherlands

Church in Amsterdam Accessible From One of Many Canals

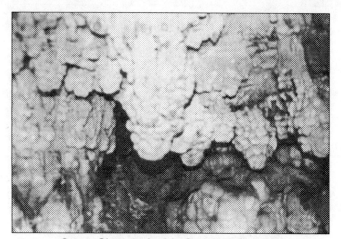
Grape Clusters Inside Carlsbad Caverns

Stalactites and Stalagmites in Carlsbad Caverns